Military Transformation and Modern Warfare

Military Transformation and Modern Warfare

A Reference Handbook

Elinor Sloan

Contemporary Military, Strategic, and Security Issues

PRAEGER SECURITY INTERNATIONAL
Westport, Connecticut • London

Library of Congress Cataloging-in-Publication Data

Sloan, Elinor C. (Elinor Camille), 1965–
     Military transformation and modern warfare : a reference handbook / Elinor Sloan.
          p.   cm. — (Contemporary military, strategic, and security issues,
          ISSN 1932–295X)
     Includes bibliographical references and index.
     ISBN 978–0–275–99405–1 (alk. paper)
     1. Armed Forces—Reorganization.   2. United States—Armed
Forces—Reorganization.   3. Military art and science—History—21st century.
4. Military doctrine.   I. Title.
     UA10.S62   2008
     355.3—dc22   2007043638

British Library Cataloguing in Publication Data is available.

Library of Congress Catalog Card Number: 2007043638
ISBN-13: 978–0–275–99405–1
ISSN: 1932–295X

First published in 2008

Praeger Security International, 88 Post Road West, Westport, CT 06881
An imprint of Greenwood Publishing Group, Inc.
www.praeger.com

Printed in the United States of America

The paper used in this book complies with the
Permanent Paper Standard issued by the National
Information Standards Organization (Z39.48–1984).

10 9 8 7 6 5 4 3 2 1

Contents

Preface

How national militaries have sought to adjust to the post–Cold War era, now some two decades old, is a dramatic story that has played out against the backdrop of an ever-changing security landscape. Security, an absence of threats to values, is not something that military force alone can guarantee. Indeed, it often has just a small role to play. But this role is in many cases an important, even deciding, one and so it matters just exactly how militaries are sized, structured, and equipped to address potential threats. Even before the end of the Cold War theorists were hypothesizing as to what would be the impact of new military technologies on the character and conduct of war. Soviet writers began to talk about a military technical revolution (MTR) in the late 1970s and 1980s, and analysts in the Pentagon picked up on and elaborated these ideas in their 1990s discussions of a revolution in military affairs (RMA), which added the doctrinal and organizational dimensions. By the turn of the century the new terminology was "transformation," which started off similar in meaning to the RMA, but then gradually accumulated a wider basket of issues to the point that, within a few years, it had become what one analyst has called "a generic buzzword for ill-focused change."

The purpose of this book is to establish the parameters of "military transformation," to assess the manner in which certain countries are transforming their military forces, to determine the relevancy of transformation efforts to modern conflict and, in drawing out the key areas of emphasis on the part of various countries, to provide a window on the future global security environment. Chapter 1 examines the meaning of military transformation, setting out a three-part framework that forms a prism through which to analyze the transformation efforts of several countries. Chapter 2 looks at measures the United States has taken in the RMA and "transforming transformation" dimensions of military transformation, the latter of which has been driven by contemporary experiences in Iraq and Afghanistan, while Chapter 3 centers on wider understandings such as homeland defense, new thinking about deterrence, and unhindered access to space. Chapter 4 is devoted to Western allies, including Australia, Britain, Canada, France, and Germany, while Chapter 5 considers the allies as a whole in the context of NATO. Chapters 6 and 7 examine China and Russia respectively. The concluding section discusses the relevancy of the various components military transformation to modern conflict, and what the patterns of emphasis in transformation efforts may portend for future conflict.

When thinking about the military technical revolution, the revolution in military affairs, and military transformation, it is useful to conceive of a series of concentric circles, each progressively more expansive but each continuing to encompass the earlier core or cores. When I first began to analyze the changing nature of warfare as a defense analyst in Canada's Department of National Defence in the 1990s, the military technical revolution and its technological confines were already considered the old way of understanding change. My focus turned to the broader notion—in comparison to the MTR—of a revolution in military affairs. The outcome was a book called *The Revolution in Military Affairs*, published in 2002 but completed largely before the 9/11 attacks. The rapid pace of international events in subsequent years was such that I had often considered revisiting the subject. And so it was that when Praeger Publishers approached me in 2006 to write a volume on the revolution in military affairs I readily agreed. But by then it was the RMA that seemingly constituted yesterday's perspective. What follows is my attempt to "think outside the circle" about the still more expansive concept of military transformation, what it means, which elements various countries are focusing on, and what an examination of national military transformation activities may suggest about the future course of world affairs.

Elinor Sloan
Ottawa
November 6, 2007

CHAPTER 1

What Is Military Transformation?

Perspectives on what comprises military transformation are numerous and varied among members of the defense community. Explicitly or implicitly they range from narrow views on how technology has impacted warfare, to broader ideas on the need to bring together technological, doctrinal, and organizational change, to still more expansive outlooks on how military transformation can help militaries adapt to the security challenges of the post-9/11 world. Each of these perspectives, and especially the latter two, captures the essence of "transformation," which can be defined as "a marked change in character or form, usually for the better." Government documents, speeches by policymakers, and scholarly articles often discuss military transformation in terms of how contemporary and future war differ in character and form from that which the West prepared for, but never fought, during the forty years of the Cold War. And for advocates of military transformation, a transformed military is inevitably seen as being a better tool for conducting politics by other means than was the Cold War military machine.

What follows is an attempt to delineate what we mean by military transformation. The chapter begins with a discussion of the intellectual origins of military transformation, including the Military Technical Revolution (MTR) and the Revolution in Military Affairs (RMA). It then outlines the several understandings among members of the defense community as to what comprises military transformation. Finally, it puts forward a specific view of the contemporary components of military transformation, which forms the basis for the analysis in subsequent chapters.

The Military Technical Revolution

Military transformation is only the latest in a list of interrelated terminologies that have appeared over the past few decades to describe changes underway in Western militaries. The progression began with the MTR of the 1980s and early

1990s, then proceeded to the RMA in the mid and late 1990s, and finally made the rhetorical transition to military transformation around the turn of the century and especially after Donald Rumsfeld became Secretary of Defense in early 2001.

Many of the technological components of contemporary ideas about military transformation date to advances in military technologies in the United States in the late 1970s and 1980s. Throughout much of the Cold War, the United States and its western allies were dependent on America's strategic nuclear deterrent (as well as British and French nuclear weapons) to provide the balance against the Soviet Union's numerically superior conventional forces—somewhere in the order of double or triple—as compared to that of the North Atlantic Treaty Organization (NATO). This was the basis of NATO and the United States' refusal to rule out a nuclear "first strike" option and this policy remains in place despite the dramatic change, since the 1980s, in America's conventional force capabilities.

The change began with a decision on the part of Harold Brown, U.S. President Jimmy Carter's Secretary of Defense, that the West should try to "offset" the Soviet's quantitative advantage with qualitative, technological advances, since NATO could never hope to field as many soldiers as the Soviet Union. Capabilities were to be pursued in microelectronics and computers with the idea that rather than buying new and more tanks, ships, and aircraft, or seeking to increase the size of Western military forces, existing platforms and personnel could be given a significant competitive advantage over those of the Soviet Union through the application of new technology. The U.S. military conducted research and development on advanced military technologies throughout the 1980s and experimented with them in war games and simulation exercises, but it was not until the 1991 Gulf War that they were actually tested in battle. Those technologies that were especially crucial to the success of coalition forces in the Gulf War included developments in the areas of command, control and communications, intelligence and surveillance sensors, precision-guided munitions, and the suppression of enemy air defense systems.[1]

The dramatic military technological advances that the 1991 Gulf War revealed were almost as much of a surprise to the U.S. military as they were to the general public and American allies. In fact, it was America's Cold War adversary that was perhaps most attuned to the potential of U.S. military advances. In the late 1970s, Soviet military writers had begun to write about an MTR in which the application of computers, space surveillance, and long-range precision missiles would enable the West to compete on par or better against the East in conventional military capabilities. These ideas took hold and in the early 1980s the Chief of the Soviet General Staff, Nicolai Ogarkov, became convinced that the United States was in the early stages of an MTR. He advocated increasing the Soviet defense budget and buying technologically advanced equipment to enable the USSR to keep pace, but growing economic difficulties and the eventual collapse of the Soviet Union precluded such measures.

Nonetheless, the term "military technical revolution," or MTR, stuck and made its way into American defense policy circles. Andrew Marshall, Director of the Office of Net Assessment, took the events of 1991—a year that was bookended by the Gulf War and the collapse of the Soviet Union—as an opportunity to look for historical analogies as to what may be the impact of the MTR on the United States military. The search took him to the interwar period when Germany combined new technologies that had just emerged in the latter stages of World War I with new doctrinal and organizational changes to produce its revolutionary (by the definition noted below) Blitzkrieg form of warfare in World War II. Taking this historical analogy into account, as well as others from the interwar period, Marshall argued that although the military technical advances on display during the Gulf War had been sensational, the U.S. military had to go beyond the MTR and look more broadly at the accompanying doctrinal and organizational changes that would bring about an RMA.[2] Thus at this early stage the focus had moved beyond technology, at least in rhetorical terms.

The Revolution in Military Affairs

In 1993 an influential Washington think tank argued that "the Military Technical Revolution . . . refers to many aspects of military force besides technology; in fact, it is a timely combination of innovative technologies, doctrines, and military organizations, that is reshaping the way in which wars are fought."[3] Underlining this point, Marshall's office replaced the MTR terminology with that of the revolution in military affairs or RMA. He defined an RMA as "a major change in the nature of warfare brought about by the innovative application of technologies which, combined with dramatic changes in military doctrine and operational and organizational concepts, fundamentally alters the character and conduct of military operations,"[4] thus underlining that the changes underway encompassed more than military technology, regardless of whether one called it an MTR or an RMA.

The RMA was a predominate term in U.S. military and defense policy circles during the mid and late 1990s and continues to be used to a certain extent in Europe, perhaps more so than military transformation which, like the RMA terminology before it, has lagged a few years in crossing the ocean. Important documents of this time period include *The Military Technical Revolution: A Preliminary Assessment*, completed by the Office of Net Assessment in 1992, which provided the intellectual basis for the Pentagon's pursuit of the RMA; *Joint Vision 2010*, released by the Chairman of the Joint Chiefs of Staff in June 1996, which set out the operational concepts the military services should strive to achieve as they integrated new technologies (dominant maneuver, precision engagement, full dimensional protection, and focused logistics)[5]; and *Joint Vision 2020*, released in May 2000, which carried forward the ideas of *Joint Vision 2010* but also reflected a more cautionary view of the promises of technology.[6] As with the military transformation concept, there was no real consensus as to what comprised the RMA. Nonetheless, it is possible to identify those technological, doctrinal, and organizational concepts that were/are most often associated with the RMA.

RMA Technologies

Military technologies that make up the RMA center on those that were first developed as part of the offset strategy, and then made their campaign debut in the 1991 Gulf War. These categories of military capability have subsequently advanced significantly, as was made evident during the 1999 military intervention in and around Kosovo, the 2001–2002 war in Afghanistan, and the 2003 war in Iraq. They include advances in precision-guided munitions (PGMs); intelligence gathering, surveillance, and reconnaissance (ISR); and command, control, communications, computing, and intelligence processing (C4I) (the latter two are often combined as C4ISR).

Precision-guided munitions are those that are guided to their target using lasers or satellite coordinates from the Global Positioning System of satellites. Examples include America's satellite-guided *Tomahawk* cruise missile that can be launched at targets far inland from ships and aircraft carriers, or satellite-guided Joint Direct Attack Munitions dropped from strategic bombers. Standoff precision force is also increasingly being applied to land force platforms, for example precision-guided artillery shells. In the years since the 1991 Gulf War PGMs have become ever more prevalent, accurate, and capable of being launched from progressively further distances. Precision force has allowed for greater discrimination in warfare, with the objective being to cause as few civilian casualties as possible, while the standoff component has reduced friendly casualties in war.

Advanced ISR capabilities include a whole range of manned aircraft, unmanned aerial vehicles (UAVs), and satellites, all of which have as their objective increasing "battlespace awareness" or the ability to "see over the next hill" to know the location of enemy forces, as well as friendly forces to avoid friendly fire accidents. The manned Joint Surveillance and Target Attack Radar System (JSTARS) is an airborne ground surveillance system that can look through any weather to locate and track vehicles and ground movement up to 150 nautical miles away. The *Predator* is an operational UAV in terms of its flight altitude and the length of time it can fly over a mission area that has a similar bird's-eye view of the battlefield as the JSTARS, while the *Global Hawk* is a strategic unmanned aerial vehicle that flies even higher and can loiter even longer. Numerous tactical (lower altitude; shorter hover time) UAVs are also employed by various armies around the world to help them see the battlefield. Finally, satellite-based military sensing systems—often referred to as spy satellites—provide the most strategic picture of what is happening on a battlefield. In future, commercial earth imaging satellites are likely to increasingly play a role in military operations, for example in a military response to a humanitarian crisis.

Better and more detailed sensing information is of little utility unless one can act on this information and this is where it relates to advanced C4I and "battlespace control." Technologies have been developed which more rapidly process and make sense of the vast amount of information that has been gathered and then transmit it in near real time to the commander or platform that needs to act on the information. During the 2001–2002 war in Afghanistan, for example, advanced command and control technologies enabled special operations forces on the ground that had pinpointed the coordinates of Taliban to relay this information in near real time to aircraft carriers several hundreds of miles away, which then launched PGMs against those locations. Similarly, sensor information from Predator UAVs operating over Afghanistan was sent in near real time to commanders at standoff distances who then took decisions on whether or not to instruct the UAV to launch its precision-guided hellfire missiles. The objective of rapid information processing and transmission is to reduce as much as possible the time within the observe-orient-decide-act (OODA) loop, thereby giving commanders the potential to control a battle from one moment to the next. Technological advances in the years between the Gulf War and the Afghanistan conflict were such that in some scenarios the OODA loop was reduced from two or three days to less than thirty minutes.

RMA Doctrinal Changes

Throughout the 1990s a number of military doctrines were put forward as being part of the RMA. The overarching theme was a need to make the shift from the massive, heavy, armies of the Cold War that would fight "in place," that is to say that were located in Europe and would fight in Europe, to lighter, more deployable armies that would be expeditionary in that, although located in Europe or North America, they would deploy to operational theatres around the world. This need was driven by the changing nature of the international security environment. As opposed to a large threat in Europe, allies were faced with a range of smaller risks and threats that emanated from, or needed to be addressed, in many areas of the world. In the 1990s these were largely humanitarian crises. But in the post-9/11 environment the greater concern has been that strategies previously effective in warding off dangers, including deterrence and containment, are inadequate to dealing with threats from nonstate actors. The requirement, therefore, is to go "to the threat," addressing it as far away from the homeland as possible.

Rapidly deployable, or expeditionary, forces, then, was (and continues to be) a key doctrinal tenet of the RMA. It would be facilitated in part through the application of new technologies to make military platforms lighter. The United States, for example, is developing a Future Combat System of vehicles that will use new technologies to develop vehicles with the same level of protection as the 70-ton Abrams tank but at a weight of only 20 tons. America and its allies also began placing greater emphasis on wheeled vehicles, for example the Stryker mobile gun system and the light armored vehicle, which are lighter than tracked vehicles (but also provide less force protection). The use of PGMs for things like artillery also lessened the load because their greater effectiveness meant that military forces were not reliant on as much ammunition as had previously been the case. Rapid deployability would also be assisted by—indeed would be dependent on—the existence of strategic lift and especially strategic airlift.

Mobility on the battlefield was a second key doctrinal tenet of the RMA. Military operations would be characterized by highly dispersed forces facing no front line of "enemy" combatants. Soldiers would have to be able to move quickly to respond to rapidly changing situations. Mobility on the battlefield would be facilitated by the use of medium- or heavy-lift helicopters and, in some cases, combat helicopters, as well as the lighter ground force platforms noted earlier because these could move more quickly around the battlefield than Cold War tanks.

The RMA also included the air force doctrinal concepts of precision force and standoff force projection. This would be accomplished through a combination of PGMs, strategic bombers, UAVs, as well as naval vessels and aircraft that can launch precision munitions. Stealth or low-observable technology in military platforms is also important for achieving standoff force projection. At the same time, the combination of precision weapons and UAVs foresaw the emergence of a new air force doctrine of unmanned combat.

One of the most important doctrinal tenets of the RMA was the emphasis on increased jointness, or the ability of the navy, army, and air force (and Marine Corps in the U.S. case) to operate together. The RMA foresaw a seamless battlefield in which all three (or four) military services would contribute to the achievement of a military objective. Thus, ground forces may pinpoint a target and relay coordinates to an air force Predator UAV, which in turn may relay the information to carrier-based aircraft to launch precision munitions to strike the target.

Part of the challenge here was to overcome technological barriers that were preventing different systems from operating together. In the mid-1990s Admiral William Owens of the U.S. Navy noted that each of the military services was striving to increase their capacity to use military force with greater precision, less risk, and more effectiveness. But they were hampered in this regard by the existence of three "stovepipes" of military technologies: sensors or ISR, C4I, and PGMs that were developed independently and were not interoperable on the battlefield. The requirement, he argued, was for the creation of a "system of systems" in which those that provided for battlespace awareness, battlespace control, and precision force used more compatible software and hardware, thereby increasing their ability to work together.[7]

The RMA as enunciated during the 1990s contained an important shift in naval doctrine from blue water, open ocean warfare to littoral combat and the projection of naval power from sea onto land. This, again, was facilitated by the application of precision force technology and is a reflection of an overarching doctrinal change among navies and air forces in which their primary mission has become to support the activity of friendly ground forces and target adversary ground forces, as opposed to battling other navies or air forces. Thus, for example, U.S. fighter aircraft today are far more likely to conduct close air support for friendly ground forces than air-to-air combat against an enemy air force.

During this period the U.S. Navy also pursued an important doctrinal shift from "platform centric" to "network centric" warfare. The original idea behind network centric warfare was to place a greater emphasis on the ability of naval platforms to work together and communicate with one another, rather than on the individual characteristics of specific platforms. Under the network centric warfare concept the Navy sought to use compatible technology to network large numbers of disparate and dispersed sensors, shooters, and deciders that were previously unable to "talk" to one another. In the period since 9/11 the concept of network centric warfare has also become central to land and air force doctrine.

RMA Organizational Changes

RMA organizational changes centered on the creation of smaller units (but not necessarily smaller overall force size) made up of more highly qualified, trained, and educated soldiers, sailors, and airmen. Forces were to be divided up into more mobile and agile units that could be tailored and brought together for specific kinds of missions. Personnel would need to be as high-tech savvy as the equipment they were working with, and they needed to be able to be deployed beyond a nation's borders. Because conscript armies could not do so, a central organizational change associated with the RMA was a shift from conscript to all-volunteer or professional armies.

Military Transformation

In the late 1990s members of the U.S. defense community began to speak less of an RMA and more about military transformation, or simply "transformation." In fact, as early as 1993, Andrew Marshall had talked about the RMA as being about a "process of transformation,"[8] and the May 1997 Quadrennial Defense Review included a section on "transforming U.S. forces for the future." But it was a late 1997 report by the bipartisan, congressionally mandated National Defense Panel, entitled *Transforming Defense: National Security in the 21st Century*, which most definitely began the move away from the earlier RMA rhetoric to the new transformation terminology. George W. Bush's speech to The Citadel in September 1999 referred to both a "revolution in the technology of war" and "the transformation of our military," while the Quadrennial Defense Review of 2001 discussed an "ongoing revolution in military affairs" and the "transformation of the U.S. Armed Forces." The Quadrennial Defense Review of 2006 makes no reference to the RMA, but speaks of "transformation" on more than two dozen occasions.

The name change is important. It reflected in part an attempt to dampen the expectations and apprehensions that accompany the word "revolution." "The ambiguity of the word *transformation* is almost certainly one of the reasons it replaced the earlier phrase, *revolution in military affairs*," the Acting Director of the Pentagon's Office of Force Transformation argued in 2006, "RMA connoted rapid, radical, and uncontrolled change—an uncomfortable notion for many military professionals."[9]

Perhaps more importantly, the new name also reflected a desire to more accurately capture the nature of the developments underway. Revolutionary change, by definition, "renders obsolete or irrelevant one or more core competencies of a dominant player."[10] If, for example, standoff precision airpower (a new core competency) can effectively target tanks, then it can be argued that massed tank warfare (a previous core competency) has been rendered obsolete. Or, if a non-state actor engaged in Fourth Generation Warfare (see later) can use superior political will to force the withdrawal of a state's conventional military force, then that force will have been rendered obsolete, at least in some scenarios.

But the notion of revolutionary change indicates a definitive end-state; a point at which the change has been accomplished. Military transformation, by contrast, captures the idea of ongoing change. The Quadrennial Defense Review of 2001 was perhaps the first official U.S. policy document to state that "transformation is not an end point." Since that time, the idea of transformation as a continuing process rather than a destination or event has become a mantra in Western defense policy thinking. "Change management in the 1990s was leading us to an end-state," notes a high-ranking official at NATO's Allied Command Transformation, "Today, transformation sees no end-state—just a constant spiral to greater capabilities."[11] The Pentagon has accordingly developed a slightly less demanding criterion to judge whether or not something is transformational: whether the change allows for "accomplishing military missions that were previously unimaginable or impossible except at prohibitive risk and cost."[12]

At the same time, transformation is more than modernization. Modernization is in the realm of evolutionary change and it involves incremental upgrades through which an organization tries to improve its ability to do what it is already doing. Transformation, by contrast, contains within it the idea of a discontinuous increase in capability along the lines of, but less ambitious than, the "discontinuous leap" in military effectiveness previously associated with revolutions in military affairs.[13] "Transformation is not about doing the same things better," notes the same NATO official, "it is about doing better things."[14] Thus while modernization improves the ability to execute missions under existing standards, transforming military capabilities redefines the standards themselves. A good example was the transformation of the U.S. Army's ability to fight at night using night-vision devices. This forced other armies to meet a new standard of success of being able to fight at night as though it were daylight.

Transformation in "How We Fight": The RMA

One understanding of military transformation sees it as conceptually similar to, if not interchangeable with, the RMA, including all of the RMA's technological, doctrinal, and organizational components. For this understanding, explicitly or implicitly, the only thing that has changed is the name. Some scholars and policymakers explicitly equate the RMA with military transformation. Others give descriptions of military transformation which echo earlier RMA discussions in that they center on the development of expeditionary military forces with increased mobility, deployability, adaptability, and flexibility; forces that use advanced information technologies and operate jointly; forces that operate in terms of dispersed or nonlinear military operations; smaller ground force units; fewer casualties; and the use of precision force at standoff distances.

Former Secretary of Defense Donald Rumsfeld has argued that transformation includes the development of "rapidly deployable, fully integrated joint forces, capable of working with our air and sea forces to strike adversaries swiftly and with devastating effect," and that it encompasses "new ways of thinking and new ways of fighting" much as Germany's Blitzkrieg doctrine married new technology with new ways of thinking.[15] All of these ideas are consistent with those of the RMA. Similarly, the (now disbanded) U.S. Office of Force Transformation stated that transformation "includes new technologies, but goes well beyond this to include new operational concepts and organizational structures"[16] —a precise recipe for what was stated in the 1990s to be an RMA. And the former Supreme Allied Commander Europe has discussed NATO transformation in terms of the NATO Response Force, a force that has been designed in line with the RMA's technological, doctrinal, and organizational components,[17] while the NATO Secretary General has equated military transformation with "acquiring modern capabilities."[18]

Transformation in "How We Fight": Transforming Transformation

A second understanding of transformation is emerging in the wake of the ongoing insurgencies in Iraq and Afghanistan which proposes to "transform transformation"[19] or move to the "next stage of transformation"[20] to address the types of challenges faced by Western militaries in those countries. This understanding, like that of the RMA before it, centers on a narrower "how we fight" approach to transformation, but at the same time it recognizes that "transformation is not a static doctrine. It has itself been transforming since the attacks of 11 September 2001,"[21] most notably to incorporate lessons learned on the battlefields of Afghanistan and Iraq.

The changing parameters of the "how we fight" component of transformation include a number of important areas. One is an increased emphasis on special operations forces (SOFs). As one scholar has noted, "special operations forces really came of age in the Afghan war [of 2001–2002]."[22] SOFs are those that are specially trained, equipped, and organized to carry out, by generally unconventional means, missions to achieve specific military or political objectives. Once used sparingly, since 2001 they have become important components of military missions and in some cases they have carried out entire missions with minimal or no assistance from conventional land forces. Conventional land forces are now often given a certain amount of training in SOF techniques, and entire units are being created to support SOFs.[23]

The growing role of SOFs is a response to the types of threats Western militaries are facing in the contemporary security environment. The unconventional nature of the enemy in Afghanistan and Iraq, and the shadowy network of terrorists scattered in countries around the world, is forcing the United States and its allies to pursue an unconventional response. The tactics of the present enemy are such that Western militaries need combat strike forces that are trained in sabotage, guerrilla warfare, and covert operations. SOFs are thus crucial both for major conflicts and for tracking down and killing individual members of terrorist cells in "peacetime."

Other key components of transformation's changing parameters include counterinsurgency capabilities and the ability to carry out stability and reconstruction operations. Today, with coalition forces in Afghanistan and Iraq facing asymmetric threats and unconventional foes in the form of roadside bombs and suicide bombers, transformation must account for a whole new set of military challenges. Indeed, for some observers real military transformation is looming in irregular warfare—and this form of warfare is ill suited to the high-tech underpinnings of the RMA.[24] The requirement is for counterinsurgency missions, operations in urban environments, and the development of new military concepts that can help protect against and detect suicide bombers. At the same time, a greater number of "boots on the ground" is needed for nation building. Operations in Iraq and Afghanistan have revealed that successful military campaigns must be quickly followed by civil reconstruction to solidify local support.

Special operations forces and unconventional and irregular warfare are linked to the notion of Fourth Generation Warfare (4GW). This concept had its origins in a seminal 1989 article by William S. Lind and his colleagues that argued modern warfare had gone through three generations of war in which the battlefield had become ever more dispersed, and was now entering a fourth generation where there are no definable boundaries between the military battlefield and the civilian and political sphere. Fourth Generation Warfare, scholars argue, is a modern form of insurgency in which the "battlefield" is the whole of the enemy's society and the goal is to collapse the enemy internally, rather than physically destroying him.[25] The fundamental thinking behind 4GW tactics is the belief that superior political will on the part of insurgents can defeat a greater economic and military power. Thus suicide bombers cannot destroy the military capability of coalition forces in Afghanistan, but they can target the political will of countries to maintain their forces there, much as America's will to continue the Vietnam War was fought on the "battlefield" of its university campuses.

Fourth Generation Warfare draws attention to the need for interagency solutions to intractable military conflicts. With a primary objective of creating paralysis in the target nation and in international organizations, 4GW tactics and timelines are very different from those of conventional war. Violent tactics may include a range of activities from complex low-intensity conflict to video images of beheadings and targeting UN offices or oil infrastructure with bombs, while nonviolent tactics will center on things like the use of the Internet and other media to appeal, for example, to members of Congress who hold the purse strings for military funding. At the same time, while the United States and its allies conceive of warfare timelines in months or years at most, 4GW practitioners measure their struggle in decades. The nature of 4GW, notes one scholar in the area, is such that it encompasses the fields of diplomacy, defense, intelligence, law enforcement, and economic and social development. "Fourth generation opponents are not invincible. They can be beaten, but only by coherent, patient actions that encompass all agencies of the government and elements of the private sector."[26]

Planning for "How We Fight"

The United States and its allies have responded to the complex and changing nature of the international security environment with a shift from threat-based to capabilities-based military planning. The idea here is that it is difficult to predict what specific threats or which particular adversaries might emerge, but it may be possible to anticipate what types of capabilities an adversary—whomever it may be—might employ, and therefore to develop the necessary range of activities to counter these capabilities. A "capabilities based approach," therefore, focuses more on "how an adversary might fight than who the adversary might be and where a war might occur."[27]

The importance of nonmilitary instruments is highlighted in a new way of thinking about military operations known as Effects-Based Operations (EBO). Joint Forces Command defines EBO as "a process for obtaining a desired *strategic* outcome or 'effect' on the enemy, through the synergistic, multiplicative, and cumulative application of the *full range of military and nonmilitary capabilities* at the tactical, operational, and strategic levels [emphasis added]."[28] Similarly, Germany's defense white paper sees EBO as comprising the "planning and interaction of military capabilities in concert with other instruments of states, alliances, and organizations. They embrace all the factors [not just military] necessary for achieving political and military-strategic objectives."[29] And Britain's defense white paper argues "Effects-Based Operations is a new phrase, but it describes an approach to the use of military force that is well established—that military force exists to serve political or strategic ends . . . Strategic effects are designed to deliver the *military contribution to a wider cross-governmental strategy* and are focused on desired outcomes [emphasis added]."[30] For Britain, capabilities-based planning is linked to EBO in that a force development process which focuses on capability, rather than "like for like platform replacements," will lead to forces that can contribute to a range of military effects.

The idea behind EBO, then, is that a combination of military and nonmilitary instruments, like diplomacy and economic and development assistance, can help bring about the desired results in a particular military mission. Effectively fighting modern insurgents, for example, might involve interaction between military forces, diplomats, intelligence officers, law enforcement officials, and those responsible for economic and social development. Indeed, EBO is seen as particularly relevant to asymmetric warfare. A "less sophisticated adversary can function effectively, even when outnumbered and outmatched" notes one analyst; EBO responds to this by pursuing "a higher order of effects beyond the physical results achieved from applying military to military objectives."[31] Others argue EBO can also be applied to more conventional operations. The point is made, for example, that while it may have made sense in military terms to target Iraq's electrical system in the opening days of the 1991 Gulf War so as to destroy Saddam Hussein's command and control system, the move had unwanted effects. Electricity was required for water purification and its disruption led to a public health crisis.

Critics argue that the notion of EBO is too simplistic. Because military forces are operating in such complex environments, and because intelligence is always imperfect, it is difficult to know what will be the effect of a particular action. "When you enter into the areas where human beings—with their willpower, their imagination, their courage, their fears, their cultural tendencies—all come to bear," argues the former commander of Marine Corps Combat Development Command, "the idea that you can put an algebraic equals sign between something you do and the response that you're going to get is not born out by at least 5,000 years of human interaction."[32] Indeed, the concept of EBO may exaggerate the capacity to control outcomes, implicitly downplaying the role of friction in war and Clausewitz's caution that "in the whole range of human activities, war most closely resembles a game of cards."[33] Yet the approach is also useful in that it explicitly calls for the incorporation of a wide range of instruments, not just military, into the attempt to achieve a desired result.

Wider Understandings of Transformation

Wider aspects of military transformation have been driven by a growing sense of vulnerability. America's adversaries, it was argued from roughly the mid-1990s onward, had learned from the 1991 Gulf War and again from the war in and around Kosovo that it was futile to combat the United States "symmetrically" with conventional capabilities. They were therefore developing "asymmetric" means to target U.S. weaknesses and vulnerabilities, two of which were identified as being its open homeland and its growing dependence on space assets for civilian life and military operations. The 1997 report of the National Defense Panel on Transforming Defense recommended the creation of RMA forces that could project military power, but it also discussed homeland defense as a key national security challenge in the period to 2020 and it made recommendations as to how U.S. military forces should be transformed for this mission. Part of the requirement was to deploy a missile defense system capable of defeating limited attacks. The report also focused to a significant degree on space, identifying the unrestricted use of space as a major strategic interest of the United States.

In the 2001 Quadrennial Defense Review, and again in a 2002 *Foreign Affairs* article on transforming the U.S. military, former Secretary of Defense Rumsfeld echoed these concerns. The specific transformation goals that he identified included familiar RMA ideas, like using information technology to link forces together so they can fight jointly, and projecting and sustaining power in distant theaters. But he also specified the need to be able to protect critical bases of operations, like the U.S. homeland, and to maintain unhindered access to space. In addition, the 2001 review indicated that transforming U.S. forces included the development of new ways to deter conflict, such as conventional expeditionary forces and ballistic missile defense.

A fundamental characteristic underlying military transformation in all its dimensions is the idea that transformation is, at its core, characterized by flexibility and ingenuity in how forces are organized and equipped for war, and how they carry out operations. This idea has been captured in a number of phrases, including "new ways of thinking,"[34] an "adaptive and creative mindset,"[35] and "a culture of command where change is welcomed and rewarded, not dreaded."[36] "Transformation is as much a mindset and a culture as it is a technology or platform," argues the Chairman of the Joint Chiefs of Staff in an assessment appearing at the end of the Quadrennial Defense Review of 2006. An eclectic package of concrete examples that have been given by various U.S. and allied political and military leaders include addressing the problem of improvised explosive devices using a more holistic approach than simply tracking down the bomb and the cell phone that set it off; U.S. Special Operations Forces winning the battle for Mazar-i-Sahrif in Afghanistan in the winter of 2002 by riding horseback while calling in PGMs; the army's decision to break its long-standing division structure in favor of smaller brigade combat teams; changes in the U.S. military's Unified Command Plan and in the global distribution of U.S. military forces as part of the Global Defense Posture Review; and reshaping America's nuclear force posture in the context of a New Triad for defense and deterrence.

What Is Military Transformation?

This book starts from the premise that military transformation encompasses the range of transformation understandings discussed above. Military transformation is in part a change from the cumbersome "in place" armies of the Cold War to the more agile and deployable expeditionary forces of the post–Cold War and post-9/11 eras, and it includes all of the aspects of what used to be called the RMA. Military transformation must also account for further changes in "how we fight"—the requirements for which first emerged in the 1990s with the NATO mission in the Balkans, but have been highlighted repeatedly in the post-9/11 era. Indeed, "it is the very persistence of such missions that is forcing a broader understanding of what transformation means."[37] Stabilization and reconstruction operations, counterinsurgency missions, and special operations forces have become central to military transformation, and are generally captured by the phrase "transforming transformation." Finally, military transformation includes the still wider understandings of transformation such as homeland defense, maintaining unhindered access to space, and new approaches to defense and deterrence. The next chapter examines measures the United States has undertaken in all of the "how we fight" components of military transformation, while Chapter 3 is devoted to U.S. developments in transformation's wider dimensions.

Notes

1. See William Perry, "Desert Storm and Deterrence," *Foreign Affairs* 70(4) (Fall 1991).

2. James R. Blaker, *Understanding the Revolution in Military Affairs* (Washington, DC: Progressive Policy Institute, January 1997), pp. 3–7.

3. Michael J. Mazarr, Jeffrey Shaffer, and Benjamin Ederington, *The Military Technical Revolution* (Washington, DC: Center for Strategic and International Studies, March 1993), p. 1.

4. As quoted in Richard Szafranski, "Peer Competitors, the RMA, and New Concepts: Some Questions," *Naval War College Review* 49(2) (Spring 1996), 118.

5. See "Joint Vision 2010: America's Military Preparing for Tomorrow," *Joint Force Quarterly* (Summer 1996).

6. For a more detailed assessment of *Joint Vision 2010* and *Joint Vision 2020* please see my *Revolution in Military Affairs* (Montreal: McGill-Queen's University Press, 2002), pp. 33–35.

7. William A. Owens, "The Emerging System of Systems," *Military Review* (May/June 1995), 16.

8. As quoted in Mackubin Thomas Owens, "Technology, the RMA and Future War," *Strategic Review* (Spring 1998), 67.

9. Terry J. Pudas, "Disruptive Challenges and Accelerating Force Transformation," *Joint Forces Quarterly* 42 (July 2006), 47.

10. Richard O. Hundley, *Past Revolutions, Future Transformations: What Can the History of Revolutions in Military Affairs Tell Us About Transforming the US Military?* (Santa Monica, CA: RAND Corporation, 1999), p. 9.

11. J.O. Michel Maisonneuve, "NATO's Allied Command Transformation: A Permanent Multinational Coalition's Change Agent," *On Track* 11(2) (Summer 2006), 13.

12. Office of Force Transformation, *Military Transformation: A Strategic Approach* (Washington, DC: Department of Defense, Fall 2003), p. 9.

13. National Defense Panel, *Transforming Defense: National Security in the 21st Century* (Washington, DC, December 1997), p. 57.

14. Maisonneuve, "NATO's Allied Command Transformation," p. 14.

15. Donald H. Rumsfeld, "Transforming the Military," *Foreign Affairs* 81(3) (May/June 2002), 21, 27.

16. Office of Force Transformation, *Military Transformation*, p. 7.

17. James Jones, "NATO Transformation and Challenges," *RUSI Journal* 150(2) (April 2005), 15.

18. Jaap de Hoop Scheffer, speech at the Canadian War Museum, June 15, 2006.

19. Mark Joyce, "Transforming Transformation: American Trends and Transatlantic Implications," *RUSI Newsbrief* 24(7) (July 2004).

20. Max Boot, "The Struggle to Transform the Military," *Foreign Affairs* 84(2) (March/April 2005).

21. James Bergeron, "Transformation and the Future of 'Berlin Plus'," *RUSI Journal* 149(5) (October 2004), 38.

22. Stephen J. Cimbala, "Transformation in Concept and Policy," *Joint Force Quarterly* 38 (Summer 2005), 28.

23. For example, Canada has created a new Special Operations Regiment to support its special operations force, Joint Task Force 2.

24. Ian Roxborough, "From Revolution to Transformation: The State of the Field," *Joint Force Quarterly* 32 (Autumn 2002), 70.

25. William S. Lind, Keith M. Nightengale, John Schmitt, Joseph W. Sutton, and G.I. Wilson, "The Changing Face of War: Into the Fourth Generation," *Military Review* (October 1989), 5, 8.

26. Thomas X. Hammes, "Insurgency: Modern Warfare Evolves into a Fourth Generation," *Strategic Forum* No.215 (January 2005), 7.

27. As quoted in Christopher Lamb, M. Elaine Bunn, Charles Lutes, and Christopher Cavoli, *Transforming Defense* (Washington, DC: National Defense University, September 2005), p. 13.

28. As quoted in ibid., p. 34n8.

29. *White Paper 2006 on German Security Policy and the Future of the Bundeswehr* (Berlin: Ministry of Defence, October 2006), p. 78.

30. *Delivering Security in a Changing World: Defence White Paper* (London: Ministry of Defence, December 2003), p. 10.

31. Michael L. McGinnis, "A Deployable Joint Headquarters for the NATO Response Force," *Joint Forces Quarterly* (July 2005), 62.

32. Lieutenant-General James Mattis, as quoted in "'Effects-Based Operations' Under Fire," *Inside the Pentagon* 20 (April 2006).

33. Carl Von Clausewitz, *On War*, ed. and trans. by Michael Howard and Peter Paret (Princeton, NJ: Princeton University Press, 1976), p. 86.

34. Rumsfeld, "Transforming the Military," 21.

35. Admiral Sir Mark Stanhope, Deputy Supreme Allied Commander Transformation, "Organizational Transformation: Projecting Stability and Global Coalitions," speech to a conference on NATO Transformation: Revitalization for the Future, Calgary, November 3, 2006.

36. George W. Bush, as quoted in Thomas E. Ricks and Josh White, "Scope of Change in Military Is Ambiguous," *Washington Post* (August 1, 2004), A06.

37. Bergeron, "Transformation and the Future of 'Berlin Plus'," 44.

CHAPTER 2

U.S. Military Transformation in "How We Fight"

Of all the Western countries, military transformation has proceeded perhaps most extensively in the United States. This is particularly so with regard to aspects associated with the original revolution in military affairs concept, but progress is also being made in those areas that relate to "transforming transformation" to meet the challenges made evident by experiences in Afghanistan and Iraq.

This chapter examines the concrete changes that have been made, and future changes that are anticipated, in the U.S. military that are associated with the "how we fight" component of military transformation. It begins by outlining technological, doctrinal, and organizational developments in the U.S. military that are now considered part of transformation, but first emerged as Revolution in Military Affairs (RMA) concepts. It goes on to highlight how the U.S. military is responding to new military requirements, including a greater use of Special Operations Forces (SOFs), and an increased attention to counterinsurgency operations and stabilization and reconstruction missions.

Changes Associated with the Revolution in Military Affairs

New Technologies

Technological advances that figure in U.S. military transformation include (but are not limited to) those that were part of the earlier RMA concept. These are advances in: precision-guided munitions; intelligence, surveillance and reconnaissance (ISR) capabilities; and, command, control, communications, computing, and intelligence processing (C4I).

Precision-Guided Weapons. The U.S. military's precision force capabilities first became apparent around the world during the 1991 Gulf War. In the years since then there have been dramatic advances in the precision and range of weapons, and a significant increase in the number of weapons systems that have precision capability. Changes have also come in the type of precision: laser-guided technology, which is dependent on the laser being able to "see" the target and is therefore disrupted by bad weather, has increasingly been replaced with satellite-guided technology. Satellite-guided weapons use the Global Positioning System of satellites, which now consists of twenty-four satellites and is constantly upgraded with each satellite launch. Yesterday's unique characteristic, today precision technology is the growing norm for America's weapons systems. Whereas only 2 percent of the bombs dropped during the Gulf War were smart weapons, almost all that have been used in recent conflicts have been precision-guided.

The U.S. Air Force and U.S. Navy are at the forefront of precision technology. The Air Force has used its Joint Direct Attack Munitions (JDAMs) and Hellfire missiles, and the Navy has used its Tomahawk cruise missiles and JDAMs, in all recent conflicts. These systems are all satellite guided. Hellfire missiles have been launched from Predator unmanned aerial vehicles (UAVs) and Apache attack helicopters. JDAMs, which are Air Force guidance kits that are attached to existing "dumb bombs" to convert them into smart weapons, are compatible with all Air Force and Navy fighter aircraft, including the future Joint Strike Fighter in its Navy, Air Force, and Marine Corps versions. JDAMs guidance kits are being made even smarter with technologies that allow the munitions to send back to theatre commanders continuously updated sensor information and to be retargeted in mid-flight if necessary. Other Air Force and Navy precision munitions include the Joint Standoff Weapon, and the Joint Air-to-Surface Standoff Missile.

Precision-guided technology is now making the leap to the U.S. Army, the last of the U.S. services to embrace it. Adopting the JDAMs idea, the U.S. Army has developed the Excalibur projectile, designed to attach to decades old self-propelled howitzer munitions and turn them into precision weapons. The Marine Corps will also use the Excalibur. In future, the U.S. Army foresees satellite-guided artillery rounds and laser-guided mortar rounds directed by battlefield UAVs. In about 2015 it is also expected the Mounted Combat System variant of the Future Combat System (FCS) (see later), which is meant to replace the M1 Abrams tank, will be equipped with precision-guided shells called Mid-Range Munitions. The Army is also following the Air Force lead in developing precision munitions that can be launched from existing UAVs. Viper Strike precision munitions, for example, are laser-guided anti-armor weapons that can be launched from Hunter UAVs.

ISR. The U.S. military's ISR capabilities encompass manned aircraft, unmanned aircraft, and satellites with advanced sensor systems. Many of these platforms have been in existence for several years or even decades but their capabilities have advanced significantly since they first appeared. First deployed operationally in the 1991 Gulf War, Joint Surveillance and Target Attack Radar System (JSTARS) aircraft have been upgraded in recent years such that they can provide air force and army commanders with real-time high-resolution imaging of moving objects to ground commanders. Airborne Warning and Control System (AWACS) aircraft, which first made their debut in the late 1970s, provide commanders with information about all activity in the airspace for hundreds of miles, from the lowest flying aircraft to the stratosphere. The AWACS is not only a sensor system but also a command and control platform capable directing several hundred aircraft at a time.

Unmanned aerial vehicles were first developed in the 1980s and have been used with increasing frequency in various conflicts since that time, including the Gulf War and in the Balkans, Afghanistan, and Iraq. Once seen as an "add on" military capability, UAVs have now become integral to military operations. Two mainstays of U.S. military operations are the U.S. Air Force's medium-altitude Predator UAV and its strategic Global Hawk UAV, both of which have been used extensively in Afghanistan and Iraq. These platforms can loiter for up to thirty-six hours at a time at around 30,000 and 65,000 feet respectively and, through satellite links, can provide real-time ground imagery to military commanders thousands of miles away. The U.S. Army's veteran Hunter and newer Shadow 200 tactical UAVs are also used extensively by ground forces in all current and recent operations to assist them in "seeing over the next hill," while the U.S. Navy and Marine Corps use their Pioneer UAVs. The army is also developing an extended range multipurpose UAV called the Warrior, similar to the Air Force's Predator, as its next generation tactical unmanned battlefield drone. The brigade-level, medium-range Warrior will replace the Hunter UAV and its ISR capability. Beginning next decade the Army plans to field hundreds of unmanned aircraft of various sizes and capabilities as part of its FCS project. At the same time, the Quadrennial Defense Review (QDR) of 2006 has called for the Air Force to establish a Special Operations Forces (SOFs) UAV squadron under U.S. Special Operations Command, and to nearly double its UAV coverage capacity by accelerating the acquisition of more Predator and Global Hawk UAVs.

The U.S. military's space-based sensing system for looking down at the earth is the Defense Support Program (DSP) system of satellites, first deployed in the early 1970s to detect Soviet ballistic missile launches. The system comprises between eight and ten satellites at any one time, with the last one launched in 2007, and these heat-seeking satellites provide missile warning by detecting the infrared radiation in its exhaust trail. They operate in geosynchronous orbit, meaning they are high enough above the earth (approximately 22,000 miles) that they have the same orbital period as the earth and therefore they appear to stay in a fixed position above the earth. Since the mid-1990s plans have been underway to replace the DSP with a more advanced Space-Based Infrared System (SBIRS) of six satellites, four in geosynchronous orbit and two in highly elliptical orbit. Once launched, the SBIRS will significantly improve current ISR capabilities by providing both strategic and tactical information about ballistic missile launches. But the technological challenge of adding tactical monitoring to strategic warning has proven difficult, and the first of the SBIRS satellites will not be launched until late 2008 at the earliest.

At the same time, the U.S. military is pursuing satellite-based sensing capabilities to detect and track objects other than ballistic missiles. America's

Space Radar program, formerly known as Space Based Radar and prior to that Discoverer II, seeks to deploy a system of satellites in low earth orbit to detect and track enemy forces and vehicles, as well as low flying aircraft, drones, cruise missiles, and ships. Space radar can best be described as a system which will take the capabilities of America's JSTARS to the level of space. Instead of surveying hundreds of square miles of territory, space radar will be able to watch thousands. Unbroken coverage of the earth's surface by satellites in low-earth orbit would require between twenty and twenty-five satellites, however a smaller number of satellites can provide near-continuous coverage. Discoverer II called for a system of twenty-four satellites, but the Space Radar program is now likely to consist of nine satellites, with the resulting gaps in coverage filled with airborne ISR assets such as the Global Hawk UAV. Program managers must also contend with a tradeoff in terms of whether the emphasis is placed on obtaining high-resolution imagery or on achieving a Ground Moving Target Indicator capability. In this regard, the program is to be re-examined in 2009, with full deployment unlikely before the end of the next decade. Apart from Space Radar, the United States also has a series of highly secret LaCrosse radar imaging and Keyhole optical imaging intelligence satellites.

Command, Control, Communications, Computing and Intelligence Processing. Significant advances are also underway or already in place in C4I, which involves translating the voluminous sensor data that is gathered, often in real time, into knowledge and then being able to act on this information. Some advances involve straightforward improvements in the speed with which information can be transferred from one player to the next within the observe-orient-decide-act (OODA) loop, say from JSTARS sensor to theatre commander to Air Force or Navy strike platform. Here the most important technological development is the Link 16 data link that allows for the secure transmission of broadband data. Originally a U.S. Navy system, most, if not all, U.S. Navy and Air Force platforms have now been equipped with the Link 16 data link, enabling these services to interoperate. Future army platforms will also have this capability. In addition, some platforms are already being upgraded with the link 22 tactical data link, which is compatible/interoperable with link 16.

Link 16 alone does not enable the platforms to communicate with one another. Rather, they must have compatible software that allows them to rapidly transfer information among themselves and among the platforms of other services. In this way, advanced C4I in U.S. military transformation efforts is closely connected with the idea of network-centric warfare (see Chapter 1). The U.S. Navy is seeking to bring their ships and munitions together into an ever more integrated battlefield network through compatible command and control systems on existing and future vessels and aircraft. And the Air Force is moving to a web-based system that will connect all users and will enable all airmen to have access to the information they need.

The U.S. Army has undertaken a number of measures to advance its C4I and network-centric capability. It has deployed its LandWarNet to Iraq, a network that interfaces with already-existing networks to connect soldiers to combat and support personnel. It also has its satellite-based Battle Command, Brigade and Below system, known as the "blue force tracker" that allows soldiers to differentiate between enemy (red) and friendly (blue) forces. Indeed a key aspect of all the service systems is that they will be able to display the location of both friendly and enemy forces in real time. Information from the Battle Command, Brigade and Below system, which is usually only available at fixed-site command centers, will soon be available to mobile forces through the Army's Mounted Battle Command program, which involves installing the necessary technology in ground vehicles. A new satellite-linked planning system, known as Command Post of the Future, has also been deployed to Iraq. It allows soldiers at fixed sites around the country to collaborate on battle plans through interconnected computer screens and real-time information exchange, thereby eliminating the need for planners to make risky journeys to a central battle planning location. Finally, the Army's FCS of Vehicles will also use a distributed network to connect all of the platforms involved in that system. The service systems of each of the Navy, Army, and Air Force are also being designed so that they can "speak" to the systems of the other services. The overall objective is a massive Global Information Grid, a seamless, secure, and joint network into which will feed the Navy, Army, and Air Force systems.[1]

In many cases military satellite communications will be involved in advanced C4I. America's secure, dedicated military satellite communications system is the MILSTAR system of five satellites, launched between 1994 and 2003. Like all communications satellites, those belonging to MILSTAR are in geosynchronous orbit. The U.S. military's next generation follow-on satellite communications capability is the Advanced Extremely High Frequency (AEHF) satellite system of three satellites, the first of which scheduled for launch in 2008. AEHF will provide U.S. warfighters with ten times greater total capacity, and data transmission rates six times higher, than that of MILSTAR, thereby allowing the transmission of tactical military communications such as battlefield maps and images. Other planned systems include the Wideband Gapfiller system of six satellites, operating in a higher frequency than the AEHF system and therefore somewhat less reliable or robust (see later), and the Transformational Satellite System (TSAT) of five or six satellites. Intended as the backbone of the Global Information Grid, TSAT is "transformational" because its satellite will communicate by laser pulses rather than radio waves, thereby enabling the transmission of images in a fraction of the time of even the AEHF system. The Wideband Gapfiller satellites are being launched between 2007 and 2012 and will remain operational until at least 2024, while TSAT is likely to be in place by the end of the coming decade.

Although the U.S. military has made significant strides in incorporating advanced C4I and network centric warfare technologies, there remain problems to be resolved. Exercises have shown that as network centric warfare pulls together sensor imagery from many platforms and sends it to theatre commanders in real time, operational and tactical commanders could be micromanaged by senior commanders and/or hesitate to act even in situations where they clearly have the authority to take decisions because they know they are being monitored.[2] Others have noted the large amount of time senior officers at the Pentagon spent watching live Predator UAV footage during the 2001–2002 war in Afghanistan, a poor use of time that revealed the requirement for some "need to know" monitoring guidelines.[3]

A further and significant problem emerged in the Iraq war when it became clear that network centric information was only as good as the system for accessing it. One U.S. ground force unit was taken by enemy surprise at a bridge south of Baghdad in April 2003 because the means by which they had to access the data base of friendly and enemy forces was too time consuming to set up, given the speed of the advance. "In what should have been the showcase for the concept of network-centric warfare—a high-intensity, conventional battle between opposing armored forces—the information keystone failed."[4] Enemy forces were concealed from sophisticated American sensors by simple camouflage, and information about forces that were detected could not be translated from UAVs and other airborne sensors to ground unit battle command systems in time. The net result was that "During the Iraq war many units found out where the enemy was just as soldiers have for thousands of years: by … running into your foes."[5]

Bandwidth. Advanced C4ISR and the degree to which the concept of network centric warfare can be implemented is limited or at least challenged by the requirement for a finite and highly desirable resource: bandwidth. Electromagnetic impulses can travel through cables or through the air (wireless) at a range of frequencies or waves per second, from the "slowest" radio waves in the high (HF), very high (VHF), and ultra high (UHF) frequencies, to the much faster micro waves classified as super high frequency (SHF) and encompassing the L-, C-, X-, and Ku-bands, or as Extremely High Frequency (EHF) encompassing Ka-band. The lower bands are more reliable in that they are not disrupted by weather, but because they travel at slower speeds, more of the band is needed to transmit information. In addition, images (especially color images) take more bandwidth to transmit than does data, which in turn takes more than voice communications.

There is enormous and growing demand among military users for wireless bandwidth. The demand is being driven by at least three important factors: concepts of network-centric warfare which require, for example, the wireless transmission of information among ships and airborne platforms; the growing dispersion of military operations, which means that the overwhelming ground force requirement is now for wireless communications; and the proliferation of remote controlled sensors on and above the battlefield. UAVs, for example, "not only generate digital rivers of photographs and full-motion video, but also demand clear channels to take directions from their operators back on U.S. soil."[6] Overall, the U.S. military's bandwidth needs grew five fold between the 1991 Gulf War and the 2003 war in Iraq, and it continues to climb. There is also competition between civilian and military users for bandwidth, however this is offset by the fact that some bandwidths, such as X-band, are designated for military or government use, and that the military leases commercial bandwidth from commercial satellite operators.

The struggle for bandwidth is a factor behind many of the delays in communications systems, from the AEHF satellite system down to the Joint Tactical Radio System. Not surprisingly, defense industries and militaries, including NATO, are examining technological solutions as to how better to transmit information, and allocate and prioritize bandwidth. The TSAT concept of using lasers and routers to provide more bandwidth is just one outcome of that kind of thinking. Nonetheless, all discussions of C4ISR—from advanced tactical radios to UAVs to JSTARS to space radar and satellite communications—continue to be framed by the fact that the transmission of images, voice communications, and data (such as fire control data and blue force tracking information) is dependent on the availability of bandwidth, and this "like oil or gold [is] a finite resource...there is only so much of it."[7]

New Doctrines

Standoff Precision Force. Advances in military technologies have facilitated the emergence of some new military doctrines and accompanying organizational changes. One of these, first seen most vividly in CNN coverage of the 1991 Gulf War, is the idea of standoff precision force. In the American context, this has been achieved with tomahawk cruise missiles launched from ships and submarines, as well as Joint Standoff Weapons, Joint Air-to-Surface Standoff Missiles, and JDAM equipped dumb bombs launched from long-range bombers like the B1 bomber and the B2 stealth bomber, and from navy and air force air-to-ground strike aircraft.

Unmanned Combat. A significant development in warfare in recent years has been the move toward unmanned combat aerial vehicles. Just as warfare changed when manned aircraft started to be used in combat roles, so too does unmanned combat hold the potential to revolutionize warfare. UAVs were first used in a combat role in the 2001–2002 war in Afghanistan when the U.S. Air Force armed its Predator UAVs with hellfire precision-guided missiles and successfully struck many Taliban targets. Predator UAVs also carried out combat operations in Iraq.

The Predator was originally designed as a UAV and was modified to conduct strike operations; similarly, the Army's Hunter UAV has now been fitted with precision-guided weapons. But the Pentagon is now developing UAVs that have been conceived from the start as an unmanned combat aerial vehicle (UCAV). The idea is that these will be able to fill a gap between cruise missiles and manned strike systems. The Joint Unmanned Combat Air System (J-UCAS) comprises two experimental UAVs: Boeing's X-45C, an earlier version of which was part of an Air Force UCAV program; and, Northrop Grumman's X-47B, which is designed to conduct ISR and strike operations from an aircraft carrier and is the successor to an earlier U.S. Navy UCAV program. A new version of the Predator, the Predator B or Reaper, is also armed and has been deployed to Iraq and Afghanistan, while the U.S. Army's Warrior, noted earlier, will also be capable of air-to-ground strike operations. Meanwhile, calls to arm the Global Hawk for combat missions have been rejected by Pentagon officials. Once updated with more sophisticated sensors this platform is thought to be a good replacement for the decades-old manned U-2 spy planes, which enjoy special over flight rights from some countries that the United States would not get for combat aircraft.

To date UAVs have performed ISR and strike roles, but in future their missions could broaden to include aerial refueling and air-to-air combat, among other things. Already U.S. SOFs are using their Snow Goose and Onyx UAVs for "dirty and dangerous missions" like dropping psychological operations leaflets and delivering supplies to commando units.[8] The Pentagon has begun studying how the J-UCAS's capabilities may be able to trade off against or replace some of those offered by combat, transport, and refueling aircraft in the period beyond 2015. And Lockheed Martin has proposed developing an unmanned version of its Joint Strike Fighter. The U.S. Army is also thinking about unmanned combat in the form of unmanned ground combat vehicles. Under its FCS program it is developing vehicles that will be able to carry gear, breach doors and generate smoke, and find and destroy targets. A special emphasis is being placed on robotic vehicles for logistics, mine detection, and reconnaissance tasks on the battlefield.

The move toward unmanned combat would seem to indicate that the days of manned combat aircraft are numbered. The Air Force has been criticized for continuing to support two large fighter aircraft projects, the FA-22 Raptor and the F-35 Joint Strike Fighter. The F-22 is a particular target since it was originally designed during the Cold War as a powerful air-to-air combat aircraft, a conflict scenario that is unlikely in the contemporary security environment. Although the F-22 has subsequently been modified to carry out air-to-ground strike operations in support of ground forces—a key air force mission in most recent conflicts, including Bosnia, Kosovo, Afghanistan, and Iraq—the Pentagon has still dramatically reduced the number of originally planned F-22 buys from several hundred to a current figure of about 180. In an era where the primary role of navies and air forces is to support friendly ground forces and target enemy ground forces rather than battle enemy navies and air forces, and where land bases may be hard to establish near the conflict, the Joint Strike Fighter is seen as much more relevant. The F-35 has been designed from the start as an air-to-ground strike platform and its naval version operates from aircraft carriers in international waters.

The future use and value of UAVs must be tempered against operational experiences that indicate these platforms are not yet resilient enough to carry out some combat missions. Although the armed Predators performed very well in Afghanistan, launching more than 100 missiles, their combat role in Iraq was scaled back significantly as a result of a shortage of radio frequencies with which to remotely control the platforms and, more importantly, of weather that was too windy and turbulent for UAV operations. Thus while UCAVs have an important and growing role to play, manned aircraft will continue to be used in certain operational circumstances, at least for the foreseeable future. Similarly, developing ground robots that can navigate the many possible ground surfaces is proving very difficult (far more difficult than developing unmanned vehicles that fly through air) and it is likely to be some time before robots are used in battlefield situations.

Expeditionary and Highly Mobile Forces. A further doctrinal change associated with the RMA and now central to conceptions of military transformation is that of a rapidly deployable (to the battlefield) and highly mobile (on the battlefield) ground force. Rapid deployability depends in part on the existence of strategic air and sealift and this is an area in which the U.S military, with more than 150 Air Force C-17 Globemaster III strategic lift aircraft, and plans for a total of 180, far surpasses any other country in the world. In addition, the U.S. military has numerous sealift ships, including fast sealift ships, medium-speed roll-on roll-off ships (which do not require port facilities), and maritime pre-positioning ships.

Rapid deployability, as well as battlefield mobility, also requires lighter, more agile equipment. To this end, the U.S. Army is developing and deploying lighter, wheeled vehicles. The Stryker Mobile Gun System is a 19-ton, eight-wheeled vehicle that can carry eleven soldiers and weapons and travel at speeds of up to seventy miles an hour. Deployed in Iraq since 2003, the platform has proven highly mobile but also increasingly vulnerable to roadside bombs, known as Improvised Explosive Devices (IEDs). Strykers are not as heavily armed as a tank and are not intended as a front line combat replacement for the Abrams tank. Rather, this capability is to come as part of the FCS of Vehicles. Launched soon after the turn of the century, the FCS program comprises more than a dozen platforms, including unmanned aerial vehicles, and unmanned and manned ground vehicles. The FCS close combat vehicle is meant to be just as survivable as a tank but at a fraction of the weight. Whereas an Abrams tank weighs about 60 tons, FCS manned ground vehicles have been given a 20-ton limit to ensure that they can be rapidly deployed by air. The first batch of manned FCS vehicles, called Non-Line-of-Sight Cannons, are to be delivered in 2010.

Organizationally, an expeditionary capability requires units that are small enough to be suited to rapid deployment. Stung by the length of time it took to deploy Apache helicopter units to Kosovo during Operation Allied Force in 1999, the Army undertook to transform itself into a more rapidly deployable force. Part of this involved developing lighter weapons systems like the Stryker and FCS, but the army also launched organizational changes. A first step was to create a handful of Stryker brigade combat teams, units based on that platform and comprising about 3,600 soldiers. The first of these teams deployed to Iraq in late 2003. The Stryker has performed well in Iraq in the roles it has been assigned; its ability to move rapidly on improved roads from one part of the country to another is seen as especially useful.[9] Originally conceived as an interim force until such time as the FCS could be fielded, Stryker Combat Brigade Teams are likely to continue operations even as the FCS enters service early next decade.

In the aftermath of the Iraq war the U.S. Army leadership decided that far more extensive organizational changes were required. Between 2003 and 2010, the Army will have reorganized all ten of its large, heavy, slow-moving divisions, previously comprising between 15,000 and 20,000 troops, into 42 mobile brigades as small as 3,500 soldiers. These brigades will be divided into three types: light, armed with the Stryker; heavy, armed with M-1A Abrams tanks and Bradley Fighting Vehicles until the FCS can be fielded; and airborne, armed with Apache helicopters.

The idea behind the reorganization has been to make the Army more expeditionary in terms of speed and precision of deployment, and to increase its combat capacity. Units have been made modular so that companies and battalions can be mixed and matched according to the needs of the mission. The reorganization also gives the army more usable combat power because previously the U.S. Army had to deploy a large force even when a smaller force would have sufficed. The new, smaller brigades have been designed to be self-sustaining, incorporating all the necessary logistics and support requirements that previously would have been supplied at division level. Unlike past practice, personnel will also stay with the same unit for three years, increasing their operational effectiveness by training together for an extended period of time before being deployed.

The Army's transformation efforts have not been without their difficulties. One is the growing concern that military technology simply has not advanced enough to allow the FCS to live up to its original billing, at least in the short term. Originally, the goal was to develop FCS platforms that were light enough to be transported on a C-130 Hercules cargo plane. But the new Army standard is that three FCS vehicles must be able to fit on the much larger (and far less plentiful) C-17 Globemaster III. Some argue that this indicates the Army does not have the technology to allow lighter vehicles to survive anti-armor threats.[10] In other areas the technology is proceeding, but not as quickly as originally envisioned. The timeline for fielding the first brigade equipped with a full suite of FCS platforms is now set at around the middle of the 2010s. In the meantime, the 2006 QDR states that FCS technological advances will be incorporated "into the modular force through a spiral development effort that will introduce new technologies as they are developed." To promote jointness and streamline research and development efforts, the Army and Marine Corps are now working together to field their next generation ground vehicles and have formed a FCS Joint Program Office. This approach mirrors that which the Navy and Air Force took with respect to UCAVs, where two previously separate program offices were amalgamated into a joint endeavor.

An ongoing and unresolved debate facing Army transformation proponents is whether the U.S. Army's re-equipment component is appropriate to real world operational experiences faced by U.S. forces. Some see the FCS as unsuited to the most likely future warfare situations. Planners preparing for the 2006 QDR looked at four kinds of warfare—conventional or traditional, irregular or insurgency, catastrophic, and disruptive—and found that the FCS is well-suited only to the first of these, traditional warfare.[11]

While the tank has often been characterized as a Cold War system unsuited to contemporary and future warfare requirements, the Iraq conflict and its aftermath have demonstrated the continued value of heavy forces. Operation Enduring Freedom in spring 2003 revealed that close combat is still possible in modern conflicts and that heavy armor is still vital both for force protection and for having a psychological impact on the adversary. Indeed, for some Pentagon officials, the experience of Iraq highlighted that the new requirement is not so much rapid deployability, but maneuverability and survivability on the battlefield.[12] Subsequent events in Iraq over the past several years have made evident the need for heavy forces that are less susceptible to roadside bombs. Tanks are much less vulnerable than other platforms and, as a result, are likely to be used in some scenarios in the future. Already the U.S. Army has reversed plans to retire its Abrams tanks, planning now to upgrade them so that they can operate until 2050.

The development of highly mobile, sustainable expeditionary forces is most often associated with the U.S. Army but this overall objective has also figured in the organizational plans of the other services. In 2000 the U.S. Air Force reconstituted itself into ten Air Expeditionary Forces, which are self-contained packages with strategic and tactical aircraft, and command and control and logistics support, drawn from throughout the Air Force that can deploy on short notice around the world. The U.S. Navy is also building deployment flexibility into its plans, changing its previous practice of maintaining carrier groups on deployment as long as possible in favor of more specific, targeted, missions. This practice, as well as new maintenance practices and the fact that carrier based planes armed with satellite guided bombs are far more combat effective than their predecessors, has enabled the U.S. Navy to reduce its carrier fleet numbers to eleven from twelve—a level that had been maintained for half a century.

Littoral Warfare. Post–Cold War changes in the international security environment prompted a move away from deep-ocean U.S. naval operations and toward littoral warfare, which essentially means operations along coastal areas. This doctrinal change, originally part of the RMA, is also central to post-9/11 conceptions of military transformation.

One component of littoral warfare is maritime interdiction missions. Terrorists, like criminals and drug smugglers, often move along the coasts transporting supplies, weapons, and personnel. Frigates are thought to be the existing naval platform that is best suited to the "global coast guard role" of maritime interdiction,[13] but these are thought to be impractical for patrolling close to shore because of their size and associated cost. To fill the gap where its blue-water warships are less effective or too expensive to be risked the U.S. Navy is developing a new class of ship, the Littoral Combat Ship (LCS). This is a smaller, much faster vessel specifically designed for terrorist interdiction, anti-mining operations, and anti-submarine warfare along the coasts. The LCS program, which has been plagued by cost overruns, calls for a fleet of 55 ships. Organizationally, the U.S. Navy has formed a command that will facilitate the conduct of warfare in coastal areas. The new Navy Expeditionary Combat Command will bring together a number of pre-existing naval units designed to operate in "brown water" coastal areas and rivers.

Another element of littoral warfare is amphibious warfare, that is, the ability to transport Marines ashore in combat situations or in support of humanitarian operations. To increase its ability to carry out amphibious operations, the U.S. military is building some 30 amphibious assault ships. It is also developing the ability to land SOFs ashore and to support these forces with conventional precision force. The U.S. Navy is transforming four of its oldest Trident nuclear ballistic missile submarines into platforms capable of carrying Tomahawk cruise missiles and SOFs. SOF on the submarines will be able to gain access to denied areas, locate high value individuals, designate precision strike targets, or conduct direct action missions.

The U.S. Navy is doing some innovative thinking about how to support these forces ashore. A first step was the creation of new Expeditionary Strike Groups made up of Marine Corps and Navy personnel and assets. Like their predecessor amphibious groups, these strike groups focus on landing Marines on distant shores, but in addition to amphibious ships they also include a frigate, destroyer, attack submarine, and cruiser to provide supporting firepower using Tomahawk cruise missiles and antiaircraft rockets and guns. The idea is to combine amphibious capabilities with substantial naval combat force to better respond to the spectrum of warfare.

But the Navy's most ambitious doctrinal change related to littoral warfare is its Sea Base concept. The Sea Base will not be a massive floating island but rather a collection of ships including at least one Expeditionary Strike Group, one Carrier Strike Group, as well as ships from the Maritime Prepositioning Force. The primary difference between the Expeditionary Strike Group formation and that of a Sea Base is that the latter would be able to sustain marines and soldiers ashore after they go into combat, shuttling supplies to land while continuing to provide aerial support. The concept, which will not be fully in place until about the end of the next decade, is driven by the post-9/11 U.S. military requirement to be able to support joint military forces ashore from ships offshore rather than from bases on land.

Jointness. Underlying all of these changes has been an increased focus on "jointness" or the ability of sea, land, and air forces to work together in military operations. Although the idea of different services collaborating in operations has been around for decades—the Normandy landings during World War II involved both land and sea power—in the post–Cold War era the concept of jointness has reached a qualitatively new level, placing a premium on interoperability among services. Advanced ISR and C4I are pursued with a view to ensuring that platforms from the different services can communicate with one another. New doctrinal concepts are being developed by joint offices, rather than by a single service.

During conflict operations, front line troops receive their support from whichever service can provide it. Central to military transformation, and the RMA before it, is the idea that there is one battlefield and that the services work seamlessly together within that battlefield. An example was the U.S. Marine Corps' November 2004 offensive on Fallujah, during which marines under mortar fire received back up support not from fellow marines but from an Air Force Predator UAV "piloted" from a command center in Nevada.

Changes Associated with "Transforming Transformation"

Special Operations Forces

Most of the technological, doctrinal, and organizational changes that first figured in the RMA vision of the 1990s continue to be part of current conceptions of military transformation. But there are also new ideas in the U.S. military which were not stressed during the 1990s and which have become central to military transformation in the post-9/11 era. One is the significantly increased importance and focus on special operations forces, or SOF.

America's SOF include "a range of soldiers from the Army, Navy, and Air Force who are specially trained for sensitive missions, typically secret in nature, and frequently involving rescues or assaults on high-value enemy targets."[14] Their increased use responds to the requirement for ever-greater precision in warfare where the enemy is not a division, a brigade, or even a smaller unit, but rather a handful of individuals. In this sense, precision warfare, which under the RMA encompassed navy and air force precision-guided weapons, must now incorporate what may be characterized as precision ground force operations. Part of this change is accommodated by the U.S. Army's move toward smaller, modular units equipped with precision guided weapons, but SOFs, even more so, "fit precisely into the model of a leaner, more flexible military" that transformation advocates have been trying to create.[15]

After the 2001–2002 war in Afghanistan, when U.S. conventional forces appeared to be slow and cumbersome by failing to capture Osama bin Laden or any of his close advisors, the Pentagon took a number of steps to increase the role of SOF in U.S. military strategy. In 2003 it elevated the status of U.S. Special Operations Command (SOCOM) from that of a supporting command or force provider to other U.S. Commands, to one that had the authority to plan and carry out its own operations. In the new Unified Command Plan the following year, SOCOM was assigned as the lead Combatant Command for planning, synchronizing, and executing global operations against terrorist networks. In the five-year period after 9/11, SOCOM's budget nearly doubled and its size increased by almost 6,000 troops to roughly 55,000 personnel. The 2006 QDR mandated the Department increase Special Operations Forces by 15 percent, increase the number of Army Special Forces battalions by one third, and create a new Marine Corps Special Operations Command of some 2,600 Marine Corps and Navy personnel.

The United States is also enhancing its special operations capability by training conventional ground forces in SOF techniques. The 2006 QDR states that general purpose ground forces, in their new modular, self-sustaining composition, will increasingly take on the tasks traditionally performed by SOFs, becoming capable of conducting long-duration irregular operations. Part of this will involve developing a better understanding of foreign languages and cultures. Other changes include moving almost all psychological operations and civil affairs units out of SOCOM and into the Army's conventional force structure.[16] Similarly, the Marine Corps is modifying existing units for irregular operations like civil-military operations and assisting indigenous security forces.

Although SOFs have proven highly relevant to the contemporary security environment, their missions have not been without their problems. Some of these pertain to concerns about the overall ability of SOCOM to take the lead on the war on terror. As a new operational command there was a lack of experience at SOCOM headquarters in developing long-term plans and coordinating with regional commands and other government organizations.[17] To address this concern, SOCOM developed a plan that established procedures for how SOF will work with the forces of the other warfighting commands, which are divided up regionally around the world.

SOCOM is also stretched for personnel, despite the 10 percent troop level increase since 9/11. With ongoing conflicts in Iraq and Afghanistan, almost 90 percent of SOCOM's resources are dedicated to just two countries. And yet al-Qaeda cells operate in about sixty countries and there are Islamic insurgencies in almost 20. This is leading to a capability shortfall involving SOCOM's ability to locate and track terrorists, and to conduct secret air operations over countries with advanced air defenses. Notwithstanding the troop shortage, plans are underway to increase the U.S. SOF presence around the world. Elite special operations troops are to be posted at U.S. embassies in a dozen countries in Asia and Latin America, as well as the Middle East, to do intelligence gathering and conduct operational planning for military operations where the U.S. is not at war, thereby strengthening America's capabilities in areas previously dominated by the CIA and State Department.

Finally, concerns have been raised about whether the right emphasis is being placed on the types of special operations missions. SOF are divided into two different types of combat teams: those that conduct direct action hits on targets, known as Special Mission Units, and those that develop long-term relationships with local villagers, take on their customs and attire, and gain intelligence information from them. This is known as counterinsurgency work. Some experts have argued that too much emphasis is being placed on the "kick down the door" direct action approach as opposed to the counterinsurgency operations that are key to gaining information on the whereabouts of terrorists and their supporters.[18] The 2006 QDR appears to respond to these concerns, stating that SOF will "increase their capacity to perform more demanding and specialized tasks, especially long-duration, indirect and clandestine operations."

Counterinsurgency Operations (COIN)

The nature of the contemporary security environment is driving an increased emphasis on counterinsurgency operations on the part of the U.S. and Western militaries. Rather than traditional, conventional, state-based militaries, the United States is facing irregular fighters—or insurgents—in Afghanistan and Iraq; Israel similarly faced Islamic guerrilla fighters in Lebanon in the summer of 2006. The U.S. military defines an insurgency as "an organized movement aimed at the overthrow of a constituted government through the use of subversion and armed conflict."[19] Every insurgency is unique in that it emerges from its own historical circumstances. Nonetheless, there are some common characteristics that all or most irregular fighters share. Today's insurgents: draw on popular support; use improvised explosive devices as a means of achieving media coverage of casualties, not military goals; understand the local terrain; blend into the local population; are patient and intent on wearing down the opponent's will to fight; are sophisticated in the use of technology and the internet; and, are highly adaptive, changing tactics continually.[20]

In late 2006 the Army and Marine Corps released a new counterinsurgency manual for fighting irregular wars. The manual defines counterinsurgency as "those political, economic, military, paramilitary, psychological, and civic actions taken by a government to defeat an insurgency."[21] Thus, although the U.S. military continues to view combat operations as an important component of counterinsurgency efforts, it is also placing greater emphasis than in the past on the nonmilitary aspects of counterinsurgency. The manual stresses the importance of achieving legitimacy among the people of a host nation, and of ensuring a unity of effort among military and nonmilitary agencies, including governmental, non-governmental, and international organizations. It also highlights a number "paradoxes" of counterinsurgency, including: "the more you protect your force, the less secure you are," meaning forces should mingle with the population, not stay in fortified bases; "the more force you use, the less secure you are," referring to the practice of insurgents using propaganda to portray the lethal use of force against insurgents as being directed against the entire population; "the best weapons for COIN do not shoot," meaning counterinsurgents can best defeat insurgents not by killing them but by focusing on gaining popular support and legitimacy for the host government; and "tactical success guarantees nothing," referring to the well-known post-Vietnam dictum that winning all the battles does not guarantee winning the overall war.

For some, America's new counterinsurgency manual over-stresses winning "hearts and minds"—that is, the political, economic, and social tactics aimed at gaining popular support. "Soft power tactics are not the only keys to victory," argues one counterinsurgency expert, "An insurgency is still war, and the key is finding and capturing or killing terrorist and militia leaders."[22] Others argue the manual places too much emphasis on combat operations. But perhaps the most notable characteristic of the manual is that it reflects a more holistic approach to U.S. military missions than has previously been the case. Earlier U.S. military doctrine divided the Army's duties into roughly two categories: conventional warfighting operations and Operations Other Than War (OOTW), which included things like stability and peacekeeping operations, but also things like evacuating citizens. The 2001 QDR replaced this latter terminology with that of Smaller Scale Contingencies (SSC), but it did not significantly change the U.S. military's conceptual approach.

The 2006 QDR, by contrast, discusses irregular warfare and describes this as encompassing counterinsurgency operations against insurgents, guerrilla warfare, and irregular fighters, as well as military support to stabilization and reconstruction efforts. The U.S. Army and Marine Corps manual on counterinsurgency elaborates that a counterinsurgency campaign includes "a mix of offensive, defensive, and stability operations." Under this more comprehensive approach "land forces use offensive combat operations to disrupt insurgent efforts to establish base areas and consolidate their forces. They conduct defensive operations to provide area and local security. They conduct stability operations to thwart insurgent efforts to control or disrupt people's lives." The manual stresses that even while conducting offensive operations the Army needs to be ready to conduct stability operations.

In equipment terms, the U.S. military is responding to the counterinsurgency requirement by developing technologies and platforms to meet the nature of the threat. The Pentagon, for example, is accelerating the fielding of a new 15-ton Mine Resistant Ambush Protected (MRAP) armored vehicle that, with its V shaped hull, is specifically designed to defeat IEDs. Some 20,000 of these vehicles are to be deployed to Iraq by 2009. Meanwhile, the U.S. Air Force is considering a dedicated aircraft fleet mix specially designed for counterinsurgency operations. These would mostly consist of transport planes, helicopters, and lower, slower flying turboprop aircraft, rather than the bombers and fighter jets of conventional operations.

Stabilization and Reconstruction Missions

A third and related key element of transforming transformation is an increased focus on stability and reconstruction missions (a subset of counterinsurgency in the U.S. military's conceptualization). These sorts of missions have in the past been variously referred to as peacekeeping, peacebuilding, or peace support operations, but today's such missions are much different from and far more dangerous than those to which these terms were first applied during the Cold War and early post–Cold War period.

The United States has historically shied away from stabilization missions, preferring to focus its military efforts on how to win wars fast, rather than on postwar stabilization and peacekeeping. But, as is the case with counterinsurgency and SOF, real-life events have been forcing a change in emphasis. As early as 1997 the National Defense Panel recommended the United States restructure some of its military units to deal with smaller scale contingencies such as stability operations.

This idea was taken up in late 2003 when the Pentagon's Office of Force Transformation, which had previously focused on high-tech network-centric warfare, emerged as a leading advocate of designing forces for postwar stability operations. Studies written and sponsored by the office detailed what may be the components of new stabilization and reconstruction divisions.[23]

These proposals did not go any further, primarily because it was felt within the Pentagon that it was best to give all troops new skills in conducting stabilization missions, rather than only designating specific military units.[24] In addition, combat veterans have indicated it is easier for troops trained in high-intensity combat to switch to peacekeeping than they other way around, and since the nature of missions can change rapidly it is best to err on the side of warfighting capability.[25] Nonetheless, the proposals did indicate the beginnings of an interest at high levels in the Pentagon in shifting some of the focus from conventional warfare to nation-building and stabilization requirements. Over the next few years the Pentagon's attention to stability missions increased. This was in part because the ongoing situation in Iraq made it increasingly clear that the Pentagon was ill-equipped to establish postwar peace in that country, but also because of a growing recognition that failing states and ungoverned areas need to be addressed if the United States is to prevent terrorists from using such places as havens for training and for launching terrorist attacks. The result was a landmark change in the use of U.S. military forces, at least in stated doctrinal terms.

In Department of Defense directive 3000 on Military Support for Stability, Security, Transition, and Reconstruction Operations, issued late in 2005, the Pentagon elevated stability operations to the status of a core U.S. military mission. The directive states that U.S. forces will now accord combat and stability operations the same priority, and that the U.S. military services and U.S. military commanders around the world should plan accordingly. It defines stability operations as "military and civilian activities conducted across the spectrum from peace to conflict to establish or maintain order in States and regions." In peace-building terms this is a somewhat narrow definition of stability operations, which has been defined elsewhere as "comprehensive efforts after major combat operations to establish security and rebuild state institutions."[26] But the directive gets to the same point when it argues U.S. military forces must be ready not only for war but also for things like developing democratic political institutions, establishing judicial systems, training security forces, and reviving economic activities. U.S. military commanders are to incorporate postwar stability plans into every war plan, and are to coordinate with civilians at the U.S. State Department early on to develop nation-building teams. The goal is to make sure there is a plan to restore security quickly after major combat operations end, and that funds are in place to begin rebuilding.

Releasing the directive on stability operations is only the first step; implementation will be a long-term process and compliance is to be monitored by the Pentagon's policy office. An encouraging sign is that the change in mindset appears to have taken hold at the upper levels of the Pentagon. The 2006 QDR concedes that "operational end-states defined in terms of 'swiftly defeating' or 'winning decisively' against adversaries may be less useful for some types of operations." Defeating terrorist networks requires combat strike capabilities but also multipurpose forces to conduct stability and reconstruction operations. This thinking has been reflected in and reinforced by the more recent Army and Marine Corps counterinsurgency manual. The QDR also states that the Department's force planning construct will be adjusted to place a greater emphasis on long-duration unconventional warfare. The long-duration, and potentially large-scale, component is to be accommodated by developing a "surge capacity" for campaigns that is over and above what would normally take place under steady state operations. Examples of irregular surge campaigns are the operations in Iraq and Afghanistan. Finally, the QDR notes that part of the Army transition to modular brigades involves a "rebalancing" of combat and combat support capabilities so that there is a relatively greater emphasis on the support units (e.g. logistics, military police, medic, communications, combat engineers) that are key for stabilization missions, than was previously the case.

A further encouraging sign is that the U.S. military is already implementing some aspects of the directive on stability operations. Most notably, the directive stresses that military-civilian teams are critical tools for stability operations, and that the Department of Defense will continue to lead and support the development of such teams. This is no doubt a reference to the Provincial Reconstruction Teams (PRTs) that the United States established in Afghanistan in 2003, and that have subsequently been transferred to the International Security Assistance Force (ISAF) under NATO command. The U.S. Army and Marine Corps manual on counterinsurgency highlights the PRTs in Afghanistan as being a model for civil-military cooperation in counterinsurgency and stability operations.

The move to fully incorporate the idea of stabilization and reconstruction into U.S. military doctrine may also be seen in the decision to increase the size of the U.S. Army and Marine Corps. For some years after 9/11 former Secretary of Defense Rumsfeld insisted that advanced military technologies could compensate for a larger military force, even in the face of growing commitments in Iraq. The February 2006 Quadrennial Defense Review included force reductions of about 75,000 in the Navy and Air Force combined. But after the Secretary's departure later that year the President announced a nearly 15 percent increase in the size of the Army and Marine Corps over the period to 2012—some 65,000 troops for the Army and 27,000 troops for the Marine Corps. In 2007 the plan was expanded and accelerated such that the Army will add 74,000 soldiers to its ranks by 2010.

But the real test is whether the new requirements come to be reflected in budgetary priorities, and in particular whether or not the Pentagon reduces funding for so-called "legacy systems," meaning ships, aircraft, and army platforms that were originally conceived during the Cold War. "[The U.S. Department of Defense] is way over-invested in capabilities for conventional warfighting," but un-equipped to respond to such threats as terrorism, insurgency and attacks with weapons of mass destruction," noted defense analyst Michelle Flourney in

2005.[27] Efforts are being taken to address low-tech threats, such as new platforms like the MRAP and new technologies like electronic countermeasures against remote controlled IEDs and lasers that can detect IEDs hidden in the ground. The United States is also deploying thousands of new bomb-detecting robots to Iraq and Afghanistan, and it uses UAVs in Iraq and Afghanistan to track insurgents as they plant devices on convoy routes. Nonetheless, recent budgets have failed to significantly reduce major programs that would be only tangentially useful if not irrelevant to irregular war, such as the Navy's DDX destroyer and the Air Force's F-22 fighter. Human intelligence, not high-tech gadgetry, is what is need for counterinsurgency and rooting out terrorists, analysts argue, and this is where the budgetary emphasis should be.

Reconciling Transformation Components

Challenges lie ahead in reconciling the two parts of the "how we fight" component of military transformation. The first is to find the appropriate mix of military capabilities to respond to both conventional and unconventional war. Some of the changes associated with the original RMA are relevant to the missions the United States and its allies are carrying out in Iraq and Afghanistan. The U.S. Army's organizational shift from division-based to battle group-based units is important for the range of contemporary missions. In addition, tanks and especially their follow-on FCS platforms could play a role in future urban conflict environments. Advances in C4ISR are arguably equally important across the range of military missions.

But other changes advanced by the RMA component of transformation are largely irrelevant to, or worse incompatible with, the counterinsurgency missions associated with transforming transformation. The kind of force that is optimized for contemporary war, as demonstrated by the Iraq War of 2003 and even the war in Afghanistan in late 2001 and early 2002, is a small, dispersed, rapidly deployable force with access to aerial sensors and standoff precision strike. Yet satellite guided weapons can do little against low-tech IEDs and rocket-propelled grenades in the often-dense urban areas of counterinsurgency work. Moreover, such operations require a much larger force that relies less on combat strike and more on building relationships with, and gathering intelligence from, the local population.

It is not possible to simply build a force for counterinsurgency missions. Although in the post-Iraq War time period irregular war has become the predominant form of military operation, one cannot rule out the possibility of more traditional, conventional wars in the future. "Future operations are going to be full-spectrum, so you can't just pick a category and you can't build a force for just one category of operations."[28] At the same time, few countries can afford to build, in essence, two militaries—one for conventional war and one for irregular war. The United States is the one country that could potentially do so by optimizing its 15 FCS-equipped brigades for conventional war, while developing its light-infantry, Stryker-equipped brigades for counterinsurgency operations. This would involve including in the Stryker brigades more soldiers that are trained in civil affairs, military police work, construction engineering, and human intelligence. Even so, it is not unlikely that FCS-equipped units could be called upon to play a role in counterinsurgency missions, or that Stryker-equipped units could be needed for warfighting (as they were in the 2003 Iraq War). And the Apache-equipped paratrooper units could be called upon to participate in the range of conflicts. Ultimately, many would argue, the United States will need to "build a force that can do it all."[29]

The second and no less daunting challenge is to prepare the same soldier for what are, broadly speaking, two different types of missions. This will require considerable skill and mental flexibility on the part of the soldier to shift from one kind of operation to another. "Can a soldier be world class at both [counterinsurgency warfare and conventional warfare]?" asks Andrew Krepinevich, Director of the Center for Strategic and Budgetary Assessments, "Probably not. But the Army is going to have to do both."[30] To do so successfully will require almost continuous individual and organizational adaptation and learning.

This realization is likely to have an impact on training. For half a century Western militaries have followed the dictum that if a force is well trained for major war it will also be able to handle peacekeeping or counterinsurgency missions. This assumption was challenged in Iraq when it became clear that well-honed tactics for warfighting provided soldiers with little guidance on how to respond to the circumstances they were facing. The Army and Marine Corps' new counterinsurgency manual maintains the case that units must be able to carry out both types of missions. But in a departure from previous practice, it states that training for a primarily offensive force will now differ from training for stability operations.

Conclusion

The "how we fight" component of military transformation comprises both the technological, doctrinal, and organizational elements of the RMA that the U.S. military began pursuing in the 1990s, and the "transforming transformation" ideas of the post-9/11 and especially the post-Iraq War (2003) period. Given the timelines, it is perhaps not surprising that progress has been most significant in areas associated with the RMA, although some of the organizational and equipment aspects are still several years from fruition. The second set of ideas remains largely that—stated changes for the future with regard to counterinsurgency and stability operations that have been written into policy and doctrine but await tangible implementation. Concrete steps to date include the changes in funding, size, and mission of U.S. SOFs, the deployment of provincial reconstruction teams to Afghanistan, and the increased force size projected for the Army and Marine Corps.

The two parts of the "how we fight" component of military transformation are to certain degree in tension with one another. The technology and equipment of a military force meant for combat, and the training its personnel receive, are not always suited to counterinsurgency and stability operations. In some cases they are irrelevant; in the worst case they are counterproductive. Yet the U.S. military must prepare for both broad categories of mission. The challenge is to find the right balance of forces, and to appropriately train soldiers, sailors, and airmen to carry out the spectrum of operations. The next chapter examines some wider aspects of military transformation, including homeland defense, changes in the U.S. military's global force posture, maintaining unhindered access to space, and America's adoption of a New Triad for defense and deterrence.

Notes

1. Megan Scully, Laura M. Colarusso, and Christopher P. Cavas, "U.S. Slowly Shifts Its War Approach," *Defense News* (October 18, 2004), 28.

2. David Pugliese, "Human Factor Slows Battlefield System," *Defense News* (October 18, 2004), 25.

3. Andrew Chuter, "U.K. Strike Chief Notes UAVs' Shortcomings," *Defense News* (August 4, 2003), 8.

4. Greg Grant, "Network Centric Blindspot: Intelligence Failed to Detect Massive Iraqi Counterattack," *Defense News* (September 12, 2005), 1.

5. Max Boot, "The Struggle to Transform the Military," *Foreign Affairs* 84(2) (March/April 2005).

6. Gopal Ratnam, "Bandwidth Battle," *Defense News* (October 9, 2006), 37.

7. U.S. Vice Admiral Lewis Crenshaw, as quoted in ibid., 40.

8. Gopal Ratnam and Michael Fabey, "UAVs vs. Manned Aircraft?: New Road Map Sees Larger Roles for Robot Planes," *Defense News* (August 15, 2006), 8.

9. Greg Grant, "U.S. Army Drops C-130 Requirement for FCS," *Defense News* (September 26, 2005), 4.

10. Ibid.

11. Greg Grant, "Full FCS Fielding Slips 5 Years," *Defense News* (October 3, 2005), 1.

12. Grant, "U.S. Army Drops," 4.

13. Melana Zyla Vickers, "LCS Could Bolster Defense Against Terror," *Defense News* (July 14, 2003), 28.

14. Gregory L. Vistica, "Military Split On How to Use Special Forces in Terror War," *Washington Post* (January 5, 2004), 1.

15. Jennifer D. Kibbe, "The Rise of the Shadow Warriors," *Foreign Affairs* 83(2) (March/April 2004), 102.

16. Michèle Flournoy and Shawn Brimley, "Irregular Transformation," *Defense News* (July 10, 2006), 44.

17. Bradley Graham, "Shortfalls of Special Operations Command Are Cited," *Washington Post* (November 17, 2005), 2.

18. Vistica, "Military Split On How to Use Special Forces in Terror War," 1.

19. U.S. Army manual FM 3-24, *Counterinsurgency* (2006), p. 1-1.

20. NATO Supreme Allied Commander Transformation, General Lance Smith, as paraphrased in Pierre Tran, "Shape of Success Unclear in Irregular War," *Defense News* (October 9, 2006), 69.

21. U.S. Army manual FM 3-24, p. 1-1.

22. Richard H. Schultz, Jr. and Andrea J. Dew, "Counterinsurgency, by the Book," *The New York Times* (August 7, 2006).

23. See, for example, Hans Binnendijk and Stuart Johnson, eds., *Transforming for Stabilization and Reconstruction Operations* (Washington, DC: National Defense University, 2003).

24. Bradley Graham, "U.S. Directive Prioritizes Post-Conflict Stability," *Washington Post* (December 1, 2005), 21.

25. Boot, "The Struggle to Transform the Military." 108.

26. Seth G. Jones, "Averting Failure in Afghanistan," *Survival* 48(1) (Spring 2006), fn 1, 123.

27. As quoted in William Matthews, "Less Is More? Funding Request Supports Push to Restructure Forces," *Defense News* (February 14, 2005), 14.

28. A high-ranking U.S. Army officer as quoted in Greg Grant, "U.S. Creates 'Iraq Study Group'," *Defense News* (October 9, 2006), 8.

29. Ibid.

30. As quoted in ibid.

CHAPTER 3

Wider Aspects of U.S. Military Transformation

"It is not just an away game for the U.S. Navy any longer," a high-ranking U.S. officer has argued," and it is not a home game either. Rather, the two roles are merging into "one game."[1] Indeed, one of the most important facets of a wider understanding of military transformation is that it involves an integrated approach to security that encompasses measures abroad and measures at home. This reorientation is most obvious in an increased attention to homeland defense measures, but it is also inherent in America's change in overseas force posture, its emphasis on maintaining unhindered access to space, and its adoption of a "new triad" for defense and deterrence.

This chapter examines activities beyond narrower changes in "how we fight" that are nevertheless included by many as part of U.S. military transformation. It begins by discussing America's slow but progressive rhetorical orientation toward homeland defense issues in the years leading up to 9/11 in the context of official government statements and bipartisan reports. It then identifies important themes in post-9/11 security strategies, before looking at developments in a number of key areas of the wider transformation agenda: repositioning the U.S. military's overseas base structure; developments in homeland defense and military support to homeland security; the release of a new space policy; and adopting a new triad. It concludes that in contrast to the "transforming transformation" agenda, much has already been accomplished with regard to those changes associated with a wider view of military transformation.

Antecedents: The Homeland Dimension Before 9/11

Greater attention to the U.S. homeland first emerged in rhetorical terms in U.S. defense policy in the Quadrennial Defense Review (QDR) of 1997. The previous defense review, the Bottom-Up Review of 1993, had made no reference to direct threats to the U.S. homeland, beyond lingering concerns about intercontinental ballistic missiles held by Russia. For the Bottom-Up Review, the new era of dangers included the proliferation of weapons of mass destruction (WMD), including nuclear, biological, chemical or radiological weapons, regional threats like large-scale aggression by major regional powers or ethnic and civil strife, threats to democracy and reform in the former eastern bloc, and economic threats to national security. The 1997 QDR included a similar range of concerns, focusing first on the dangers posed by aspiring regional powers and the instabilities created by failed and failing states, and then on the destabilizing consequences of the proliferation of weapons and especially WMD. But its third and fourth concerns went well beyond the earlier framework. The 1997 QDR said that the United States would be challenged by transnational dangers such as terrorism over the following fifteen to twenty years, and that unconventional means of attack would threaten Americans not only overseas but also at home.

Over the next few years two prescient, congressionally mandated bipartisan commissions pushed forward the change in thinking that was first reflected in the May 1997 QDR. The National Defense Panel (NDP), meeting during a time period that partially overlapped with those writing the 1997 QDR, issued its report at the end of 1997. In a notable contrast to earlier U.S. security and defense reports, the Report of the NDP placed homeland defense as the number one U.S. national security challenge over the period to 2020, with the more familiar concern about regional stability figuring second on the list. The change in the type and degree of threats to the United States, the Panel argued, was such that U.S. national territory faced an increased danger from terrorism, information warfare, WMD, and cruise and ballistic missiles.

The NDP report not only identified the increased threat to the homeland but also, unlike the 1997 QDR, gave specific organizational prescriptions for how it should be addressed. The Panel argued the U.S. military should break with Cold War practice and establish a military command specifically charged with the homeland defense of the United States. Previously, the U.S. Military's Unified Command Plan had assigned all areas of the world to a geographic command *except* North America and the Soviet Union/Russia. The NDP recommended North America and the pre-existing Southern Command (essentially covering South America and the Caribbean) be amalgamated into one America's Command, with Southern Command and a new Homeland Defense Command being established as subordinate commands.[2]

The Clinton administration's *National Security Strategy for a New Century*, which was produced—like all U.S. National Security Strategies—in the White House by the National Security Council, did not heed the NDP's advice on threat priorities. It returned to the BUR and 1997 QDR framework of placing regional and state-centered actors first on the list of threats to U.S. interests. But transnational threats, including the threat posed to the U.S. homeland by terrorists and other nonstate actors, did place second, followed by the proliferation of WMD, foreign intelligence collection, and failed states. In addition, the security strategy outlined a number of initiatives that had been undertaken to address "emerging threats at home" including, among other things, Presidential Decision Directives on combating terrorism and protecting critical infrastructure.

The second bipartisan commission was the U.S. Commission on National Security/21st Century. The commission issued three reports over the period 1999 to early 2001 that proved to be even more prescient than the earlier NDP report. The first focused on the major themes and implications of the emerging global security environment and concluded "Americans will likely die on American soil, possibly in large numbers." The second devised a national strategy for addressing the new challenges, stating that the first objective must be to take measures to defend the U.S. homeland because "Americans are less secure than they believe themselves to be." And the third centered on more specific proposals for the creation of appropriate institutional structures, most notably the establishment of a new National Homeland Security Agency.

When the terrorists struck on 9/11, 2001, the QDR of 2001 was all but completed. Due to be submitted to Congress by the end of the month, the report was hastily revisited—but not significantly changed—to accommodate the new security environment. Whereas the Bottom-Up Review focused on four key "dangers to U.S. interests," and the 1997 QDR centered on four "challenges to U.S. security," the 2001 QDR allowed only that "the global security environment involves a great deal of uncertainty about the potential sources of military threats, the conduct of war in the future, and the form that threats and attacks will take." Compared to previous defense reviews, the 2001 QDR adopted the somewhat softer language of identifying key security geopolitical "trends," including: diminishing protection afforded by geographic distance; regional security developments; increasing challenges and threats emanating from the territories of weak and failing states; the diffusion of power and military capabilities to nonstate actors; developing and sustaining regional security arrangements; and, increasing diversity in the sources and unpredictability of the locations of conflict.

Given the events of 9/11, the fact that the 2001 QDR placed failing states and nonstate actors as third and fourth on the list of important security trends was perhaps surprising. But in a later section, appropriately titled "paradigm shift in force planning," the QDR more directly accommodates the new security environment. The report notes that the Department of Defense has adopted a new force-sizing construct designed, first and foremost, to defend the United States. The construct, states the report "places new emphasis on the unique operational demands associated with the defense of the United States and restores the defense of the United States as the department's primary mission." The report included a brief overview of the issues that needed to be addressed in order to effectively defend the United States and noted, at this early juncture, that measures to defend the United would be a crucial component of the Pentagon's transformation efforts.

America's Post-9/11 Security Strategies

The September 2002 National Security Strategy of the United States marked a reordering of threats to the United States from those that had appeared in previous official security and defense documents. The first threat it mentions is "shadowy networks of individuals" that can bring chaos and great suffering to U.S. shores. To defeat this threat, President Bush argues in his opening letter, the United States will use military power, but it will also focus on better homeland defenses, law enforcement, intelligence, and efforts to cut off terrorist financing. The second, and "gravest" threat the document mentions is one that "lies at the crossroads of radicalism and technology." The reference is to both terrorists and the prospect they may acquire WMD, but also rogue states and their ambitions to acquire such weapons. For these latter threats the strategy is broader, involving the use of military force (perhaps preemptively) but also ballistic missile defenses and cooperation with allies. The National Security Strategy discusses regional conflicts, like the Israeli-Palestinian conflict, and acknowledges the United States is "attentive to the possible renewal of old patterns of great power competition," yet generally speaking it does not see notable threats to the United States beyond those posed by terrorism and rogue states. To meet the challenges of this new security environment the strategy talks about transforming national security institutions, including the U.S. military which should focus on expeditionary forces but also on military capabilities to defend the homeland, and protect critical U.S. infrastructure and U.S. assets in space.

The National Security Strategy of the United States released in March 2006 is in many ways an update of the earlier Bush administration document. As with the National Security Strategy of 2002 (and in contrast to previous American national security strategies), the current strategy does not "list" threats to the United States; rather, they emerge in the context of the overall approach to national security. The greatest and most immediate threats to U.S. security interests are global terrorist networks, especially a terrorist attack with WMD, and tyrannies (i.e. rogue states) that pursue WMD or sponsor terrorism. Regional conflicts, both intrastate (like Darfur) and interstate (like Ethiopia and Eritrea) can lead to long-term threats, should they result in failed states and ungoverned areas that can become havens for terrorists. As the same time, great power tensions remain a possibility. Indeed, this strategy includes a small but palpable increase in emphasis on great power rivalry as result of China's "non-transparent" military expansion and, notably, growing competition for energy supplies. The United States, the strategy states, will encourage political freedom for China while at the same time "hedg[ing] against other possibilities."

To address terrorism the strategy highlights "the genius of democracy" which, in the Bush administration's view, can ameliorate many of the factors that underlie the terrorist threat. In order to create the long-term window for democracy to take root, four necessary short-term steps are listed: prevent attacks by terrorist networks, deny WMD to rogue states and terrorists, deny terrorists the support and sanctuary of rogue states, and deny the terrorists control of any nation which can act as a base and from which it can launch operations. When it comes to tyrannies, the strategy outlines a "new triad" for strengthening deterrence and defense, comprised of offensive strike systems, active and passive defenses, and a responsive infrastructure (discussed below).

Like its predecessor, the security strategy of 2006 highlights the need to focus on homeland security and defense requirements when transforming America's national security institutions to meet immediate and potential long-term threats. It also goes beyond the 2002 document by giving more detailed guidance to the Department of Defense. The U.S. military, the strategy states, must prepare for four categories of challenges: traditional, meaning states using conventional arms; irregular, referring to state and nonstate actors using methods like terrorism and insurgency; catastrophic, involving WMD, including biological pandemics; and disruptive, like cyber and space operations to counter America's technological advantage. These four security challenges were also listed and elaborated in the March 2005 National Defense Strategy of the United States, which provided the strategic foundation for work surrounding the 2006 QDR. It is left to the QDR itself, released a month before the 2006 national security strategy, to "operationalize" the four categories of challenges first enunciated in the National Defense Strategy.

The Quadrennial Defense Review of 2006

The QDR of 2006 begins by arguing that the United States is engaged in what will be a Long War. While the Cold War was a standoff between two conventionally-armed camps of nation states that never went hot, the Long War went hot some time ago and is characterized by traditional states facing irregular forces of dispersed, global terrorist networks. Just as the Cold War was with us for decades, the Long War can be expected to last at least one, if not two, generations. Americans, the QDR states, should not expect one battle but a lengthy campaign. Iraq and Afghanistan are only the first two battlegrounds; over the coming years and decades the United States can be expected to wage this war simultaneously in many locations around the world, at varying degrees of intensity.

The opening pages of the QDR also give a simple, yet useful, statement of what senior Pentagon leaders view to be military transformation—"a shift of emphasis to meet the new strategic environment." It lists numerous examples of this shift in emphasis, all of which are consistent with narrower and broader interpretations of military transformation. They include (among several others) a move: from threat-based planning to capabilities based planning; from "one size fits all" deterrence to tailored deterrence (the new triad); from a focus on kinetics to a focus on effects (effects-based operations); from Department of Defense solutions to interagency approaches; from static defense, garrison forces to mobile, expeditionary operations [Revolution in Military Affairs (RMA) forces]; from exposed forces forward to reaching back to the continental United States to support expeditionary forces (global defense posture review); and, from fragmented homeland assistance to integrated homeland security.

The QDR "operationalizes" the security challenges identified in both the National Defense Strategy of 2005 and the National Security Strategy of 2006 by identifying four priorities for the U.S. military: defeating terrorist networks, defending the homeland in depth, shaping the choices of countries at a strategic crossroads, and preventing hostile states and nonstate actors from acquiring or using WMD. The first two priorities pertain to the Long War. For the first, the QDR places a strong emphasis on hunting down and rooting out terrorists—on "relentlessly finding, attacking and disrupting terrorist networks." It identifies specific military capabilities associated with this power-projection, precision warfighting approach, such as special operations forces, persistent surveillance, and global strike capabilities, while at the same time stressing the need to be able to carry out irregular operations, urban and riverine warfare, and long-term stabilization and reconstruction operations to defeat terrorist networks.

Measures to defeat terrorist networks, in turn, are linked to the notion of defending the homeland in depth. The "in depth" component refers to the need to be able to defeat threats at as great a distance as possible from the United States. To this end, the QDR notes, the United States has adopted a "tailored" approach to deterrence that involves "prompt global strike" as well as air and missile defenses and other defensive measures. The latter are divided into three roles: those where the Department of Defense takes the lead, notably defending U.S. airspace and air and maritime approaches; those where the Pentagon acts in support of other government departments, as was the case with Hurricanes Katrina and Rita; and those where the U.S. military enables other departments to respond to threats to the homeland, but does not actually take part. The overall goal, notes the QDR, is "to maintain a deterrent posture [that] persuade[s] potential aggressors that their objectives in attacking would be denied and that any attack on U.S. territory . . . could result in overwhelming response" through global strike.

Shaping the choices of countries at a strategic crossroads centers on the challenges and possible threat posed by major and emerging powers. Major powers include Russia and, most notably, China, which is the country the Pentagon singles out as possessing the greatest potential to compete militarily with the United States. Emerging powers include India, but also countries in the Middle East, Central Asia, and Latin America. America's overall objective in this regard is the promotion of democracy, but role of the U.S. military is to "dissuade major and emerging powers from developing capabilities that could threaten regional stability." This approach aligns with the National Security Strategy of 2006, which says the Pentagon is building a future force that will dissuade potential competitors and is, in turn, a toned down version of a statement in the National Security Strategy of 2002 that said U.S. forces would "be strong enough to dissuade potential adversaries from pursuing a military build-up in hopes of surpassing, or equaling, the power of the United States." The notion of going beyond deterrence to dissuade adversaries, in fact, first appeared officially in the 2001 Nuclear Posture Review.[3] A key aspect of dissuasion, the QDR notes, is a diversification of the U.S. military's basing posture (see later). Moreover, it involves many of the military force characteristics, such as persistent surveillance and rapid, global strike capabilities, which are identified as necessary for defeating terrorist networks.

The goal of preventing hostile states and nonstate actors from acquiring or using WMD cuts across the "defeating terrorist networks" and "shaping the choices of countries" priorities. States like Iran (identified as an emerging power) and North Korea could pose a direct threat to the United States, or they may pose an indirect threat by transferring WMD to a terrorist organization. The QDR talks about preventative measures to stop the proliferation of WMD and, should preventative measures fail, responding with diplomacy and the use of force if necessary. These "WMD elimination operations" may involve, among other things, special operations forces, persistent surveillance capabilities, and interdiction operations to stop air, ground, and maritime shipments of WMD.

America's Global Defense Posture Review

America's security and defense policy statements draw out many elements of a broader transformation agenda, one of which is changes in the U.S. military's overseas base structure. "Transformational change," argues the 2006 QDR, involves a shift "from dependence on large, permanent overseas garrisons toward expeditionary operations utilizing more austere bases abroad." This change is part of official government policy, but it has arguably been underway since the 9/11 attacks.

In August 2004 President Bush announced a Global Defense Posture Review that called for the most significant redeployment of American armed forces since the 1950s. One part of the plan is a smaller global footprint in terms of overall force size. The United States has withdrawn its forces from Saudi Arabia and it is also bringing home thousands of troops and family members from large bases in Europe and South Korea. This includes its major bases in Germany, although in 2007 these plans were scaled back because the forces here have been rotating into Iraq and Afghanistan.

Another part of the review is a more globally distributed footprint. In a pattern that has been compared to the Roman Empire's dozens of frontier posts, and the British Empire's worldwide system of naval bases, the United States is in the process of establishing numerous small bases throughout an "arc of instability" that stretches from the Balkans to the Caucasus and around the Asian shore.[4] The idea is that by having a network of smaller bases closer to areas of instability or projected "hotspots" the U.S. military will be better able to respond to any unpredictable threats that emanate from these regions. According to the plan, American bases in Germany, Italy, the United Kingdom, Japan, and South Korea are being maintained but reduced in size. They are to be key nodes or hubs in a network of smaller bases that will include numerous "forward operating bases" and "cooperative security locations" in southern Europe, Africa, the Middle East, and Asia. The forward operating bases will be lightly-manned U.S. military installations that can accommodate a large surge in American power should the need arise, while the cooperative security locations will be host-nation facilities with equipment and logistical capabilities, but no permanently stationed U.S. military forces.

As a result of the war on terrorism, the United States dramatically increased its military presence in the "arc of instability" in the years after 9/11. In Central Asia, it established military installations in Afghanistan, Kyrgyzstan, Pakistan, Tajikistan, and Uzbekistan. The United States was forced to withdraw from Uzbekistan in 2005, but has explored options in Kazakhstan, Turkmenistan, Azerbaijan, and Georgia. In the Middle East, the United States withdrew its forces from Saudi Arabia in spring 2003, but it consolidated its military presence in Qatar, Kuwait and Bahrain (and Iraq). In Eastern Europe, the United States has signed basing agreements with Bulgaria and Romania. Further West, America still has troops and facilities in Bosnia and Kosovo. In Africa, negotiations have taken place for cooperative security locations in ten African countries, including Algeria, Djibouti, Gabon, Ghana, Kenya, Mali, Sao Tome and Principe, Senegal, and Uganda.[5]

Most recently, the United States has decided to create an Africa Command, to be headquartered in Africa and to be fully operational by the end of 2008. After 9/11 the United States established a combined joint task force of about 2,000 personnel based in Djibouti to carry out humanitarian assistance and intelligence operations in northeastern Africa, and to provide military training to local security forces to assist them in their abilities to keep terrorist groups from operating in the region. Building on this, and reflecting the requirements of addressing fourth generation warfare, AFRICOM will comprise a unique blend of U.S. military forces and civilian personnel from the State Department and the U.S. Agency for International Development, as well as African nation exchange officers. The QDR stressed the need to integrate with other U.S. agencies and friendly governments, noting that "to address more effectively many security challenges" the Pentagon would have to "shift its emphasis from Department-centric approaches to interagency solutions." The creation AFRICOM as a model of interagency cooperation combining diplomacy, humanitarian aid, and counterterrorism operations is one of the U.S. military's more visible attempts to move in this direction.

The QDR discusses the defense posture review's changes as a way of shaping the choices of major and emerging powers—of increasing the U.S. military's ability to promote bilateral relations, deter regional conflict, and defeat aggression should deterrence fail. But when the review was first released in 2004, its changes were also presented as a means of responding to and defeating terrorists throughout the "arc of instability." Thus, this aspect of military transformation is relevant not only to addressing major and emerging powers but also defending the homeland in depth against terrorist networks.

Military Transformation for Homeland Security and Defense

The other aspect of defending the homeland in depth, or what the QDR calls a "layered" approach to protecting the homeland, is homeland security and defense. Homeland security refers to the prevention, preemption, and deterrence of, and defense against, threats to a country's territory, sovereignty, domestic population, and critical infrastructure, as well as the management of the consequences of such threats, whether they are manmade or natural. Homeland security missions are civilian-led and may or may not include a military component that reports to the civilian lead agency. Homeland defense is a sub-set of homeland security and refers to military-led missions to protect the people, property, and systems of a country. In this context, military transformation for homeland security and defense includes both measures to improve the U.S. military's ability to carry out its military missions to defend the United States, and its ability to work with and support other government departments in homeland security missions.

U.S. Northern Command (NORTHCOM) fills both these bills. NORTHCOM was established in October 2002 to create a single locus of authority for the military-led mission of defending the United States. Its conceptual genesis could be found in the NDP's proposal, some five years earlier, to create an Americas Command and subordinate Homeland Defense Command. Under the U.S. Military's Unified Command Plan, NORTHCOM is responsible for all of the land, sea, and air approaches to the United States. Its geographic area of concern is the continental United States, Canada, Mexico, and parts of the Caribbean. For the air approaches, the commander of NORTHCOM is "double-hatted" as the commander of the North American Aerospace Defense Command (NORAD), which for fifty years has been responsible for the air defense of North America. NORAD has traditionally looked outward at aerospace threats approaching the continent, but in the wake of 9/11 its mandate was broadened to include an inward focus, enabling it to respond to airborne threats that may arise from within the continent.

NORTHCOM was also created to establish a one-stop conduit for U.S. military support to civilian authorities and specifically to the Department of Homeland Security (DHS), established in March 2003. Previously, several of America's combatant commands[6] performed various homeland security missions. Today, NORTHCOM could be called upon to provide support to DHS for a wide range of missions, from hurricane and disaster relief to counter-drug operations and mitigating the consequences of the terrorist use of a weapon of mass destruction. The command's relatively few dedicated military forces are made up primarily of the Joint Task Force Civil Support Units that had previously been assigned to Joint Forces Command. In providing support to DHS, NORTHCOM operates through these established task forces; should additional forces be necessary for either the homeland defense or support to homeland security mission, the President and Secretary of Defense would assign the command forces from other commands on a temporary basis.

Unhindered Access to Space

A growing sense of vulnerability is behind the increased attention to homeland security and defense as well as another area associated with broader conceptions of military transformation: maintaining unhindered access to space. As America's national and homeland security has become ever more dependent on satellite capabilities, it has become increasing concerned that these assets will be the target of hostile activity. The United States is therefore seeking "space control" or what can be defined as guaranteed access to its satellite capabilities, and the ability to effectively counter its adversaries' space assets.

Ensuring access to satellite capabilities involves tracking all objects in space, identifying those that could pose a threat to U.S. satellites and defending them against attacks. Tracking objects in space is something that America has done for decades. The U.S. space surveillance network (SSN) dates to the late 1950s when the U.S. Navy and the U.S. Air Force began to establish land based sensor systems that could track space objects (the SPASUR and Spacetrack systems, respectively). These systems, combined, made up the Space Detection and Tracking System, or SPADATS which was further expanded in the 1980s and renamed the SSN. Today the SSN consists of ground-based radars and optical sensors operated by the navy, army, and air force at more than two-dozen locations around the world.

More recently, officials have argued that it is not enough to "detect and catalog" objects in space; rather, it is also necessary to assess "what a space object is and what it can do."[7] Achieving this new level of situational awareness is likely to involve space-based space surveillance. Other than an experimental space sensor launched in the mid-1990s, to date the United States has only had ground-based space surveillance sensors. But U.S. Strategic Command is in the process of examining whether it would be useful to put new sensors on existing satellites, or to launch new satellites with a space-sensing capability. A more immediate capability in this area will be Canada's Sapphire mission, a space-based electro-optical sensor scheduled for launch in 2010 that will feed information into the SSN.

Threats to U.S. satellite capabilities could come in a number of forms. Low-tech jamming could occur, taking to the level of space long-standing military practices of emitting radio frequencies to disrupt an opponent's communications signals. The United States is already engaged in developing satellite-jamming capabilities of its own. In 2004 it deployed its CounterCom system, which is a mobile, ground-based antenna that can jam the signals from a single satellite in geosynchronous orbit.[8] The system is to be upgraded and the Air Force will be fielding additional antennas to carry out the counter-space mission in the future. Longer-term threats to U.S. systems could include the use of microsatellites for direct physical attack, antisatellite weapons launched from earth (direct ascent weapons), and ground based lasers that could be used to flood or dazzle an imaging satellite's optical sensors, effectively blinding it. In January 2007 China used a (ground based) missile to destroy one of its old weather satellites operating in low-earth orbit, demonstrating the potential threat to U.S. systems in this same orbit. In addition, in fall 2006 the Chinese military "painted" or illuminated a U.S. satellite with a laser beam.

In 2006 the United States released a new National Space Policy that states the United States reserves the right to deny access to space to anyone hostile to U.S. interests, and to retaliate if its own space assets are subject to hostile attacks or interference. Such retaliation could take the form of attacks on ground stations, but some argue the United States should also develop space-based systems such as lasers or small maneuverable satellites to target enemy satellites. Already Lockheed Martin has developed and launched an experimental small satellite, the XSS-11, which is a highly maneuverable spacecraft that demonstrated the ability to navigate around other satellites in low earth orbit, conducting applications such as space servicing and maintenance. The success of the mission has led to a further experimental nanosatellite program called Angels that is being designed for use in geosynchronous orbit.

If such satellites were given the ability to ram enemy spacecraft or attack them with weapons this would constitute the "weaponization" of space, a highly contentious—and unresolved—issue both within and outside the United States. Some American experts argue the United States needs to develop orbital weapons to prevent other countries, such as China and India, from doing it first and therefore placing at risk U.S. satellites. Others argue this is a threshold that the United States should not be the first to pass and that America can effectively defend its satellites from the ground.[9] The space policy itself appears to leave the matter open, with some administration officials interpreting the classified document as indicating the United States will use military force in space to protect satellites, and others saying the policy revisions are in no way a prelude to introducing weapons into Earth orbit.[10] In any case, the United States has explicitly rejected participation in arms control agreements that might limit U.S. flexibility to deploy weapons in space.

Military Transformation in Defense and Deterrence

A final aspect of a broader understanding of military transformation is a move from the "one size fits all" deterrence of the Cold War to tailored deterrence and a new triad for the contemporary era. "Today our adversaries have changed—and so has the deterrence calculus," argued Donald Rumsfeld in his 2002 article on military transformation, "We need to find better ways to deter new adversaries."[11] Tailored deterrence refers to the ability to respond to aggressors in a range of ways that are specific to the threat at hand, while the new triad is designed to increase the range of choices that are available. In place of the "old triad" of bombers, intercontinental ballistic missiles (ICBMs), and submarine-launched ballistic missiles (SLBMs) that formed the basis of deterrence during the Cold War, the new triad includes: offensive strike systems encompassing everything that was in the old triad (i.e. nuclear capabilities) *and* improved long-range conventional strike capabilities; active and passive defenses, most notably missile defenses; and, a "responsive infrastructure," meaning a research, development and industrial infrastructure that is robust enough to maintain offensive and defensive forces. The new triad includes in its concept of non-nuclear strike forces not only "kinetic" systems like missiles or "things that go boom," but also "non-kinetic" weapons such as information operation assets capable of computer network attacks.[12]

Although referenced in the 2006 QDR, the shift to the new triad, like the change in force posture, has been underway for some time. The 2001 Nuclear Posture Review, which began well before 9/11 but was released in December of that year, adopted a capabilities-based approach (discussed in Chapter 1) to force planning. Such an approach is inherently "tailored." Rather than building forces for one type of threat using a threat-based approach—that would then by default have to be used against other types of threats—it develops different capabilities for a range of possible types of threats. "Although the United States may not know with confidence what threats a state, combinations of states, or nonstate actors pose to U.S. interests," elaborated the 2005 Doctrine for Joint Nuclear Operations, "it is possible to anticipate the [range of] capabilities an adversary might use."[13] The result was the new triad approach. The idea behind integrating conventional and nuclear attacks into one leg of the triad is to provide leaders with a broader range of strike options to address threats.

Many of the changes in conventional force characteristics associated with the RMA component of military transformation are relevant to the new triad, most notably long-range precision strike using manned and unmanned platforms and precision-guided munitions. Conventionally armed Tomahawk cruise missiles and JDAM-equipped conventional bombs launched from long-range bombers, for example, would be considered part of the new triad. In addition, the United States is placing precision-guided conventional warheads on some of its SLBMs to further increase the range of its non-nuclear deterrence options.

The United States also maintains its strategic nuclear forces, at reduced numbers in accordance with the Nuclear Posture Review and the Strategic Offensive Reductions Treaty (SORT) agreed with Russia in 2002. This is an almost two-thirds reduction in operationally deployed nuclear warheads over the decade ending in 2012, to a level of between 1700 and 2200 warheads deployed on Trident submarines, Minuteman III ICBMs, and B-52 and B-1 bombers. Still, there are ongoing debates as to just how large a nuclear arsenal the United States will need in the future security environment; some experts contend that as few as 1,000 warheads would be sufficient for deterrence and response.[14] Because the Nuclear Posture Review is, in essence, a pre-9/11 document, the House of Representatives has launched a bipartisan commission to reevaluate the U.S. nuclear posture for the post-9/11 world.

A further debate in this area is whether the U.S. military needs new, low-yield nuclear weapons to target underground facilities suspected of being used to produce nuclear weapons. The issue here is that existing strategic nuclear forces may be too powerful to pose a credible threat of use against a rogue state's facilities, yet conventional forces may not be sufficiently powerful. Therefore, low-yield, earth-penetrating nuclear weapons—known officially as the Robust Nuclear Earth Penetrator—may be necessary to create a credible deterrent.[15] To date, Congress has not agreed to fund the development of so-called "bunker busters" for fear of the impact on the global nonproliferation regime. The Nuclear Posture Review identified shortfalls in U.S. capabilities concerning hardened and deeply buried targets, but it did not go so far as to call for new nuclear warhead designs.[16] The United States is, however, proceeding with upgrades to its existing nuclear warheads under the Reliable Replacement Warhead program.

For the defense aspect of the new triad the United States is deploying a global ballistic missile defense system designed to provide a limited missile defense against long-range missile threats to the United States and its allies. To date a number of countries have agreed to take part, including Japan, Australia, India, and Britain. The primary threat is thought to be rogue states like Iran and North Korea, but the system is also meant to defend against the accidental launch of a missile from China or Russia. By about 2012, the system is expected to consist of: ground-based interceptors at sites in California, Alaska, and Europe (probably Britain and Poland); sea-based interceptors on Aegis cruisers in the North Pacific and the Sea of Japan; Patriot air defense missiles at various sites; upgraded sensors in Alaska, Greenland, and Britain; a new tracking radar at a European site (probably the Czech Republic); a huge X-band radar on a converted, self-propelled oilrig off the Aleutian Islands; and new satellite-based ballistic missile detection sensors. Many of these elements are already in place, although some areas remain problematic. The X-band radar, for example, has had technical problems and has yet to be deployed. The proposed radar and interceptors in the Czech Republic and Poland respectively have raised concerns with Russia (see Chapters 5 and 7) and with the Democratic controlled Congress, which has sought to delay funding out of foreign policy considerations and also because of technical issues surrounding the interceptors.

To tie together the offensive and defensive aspects of the new triad, the offensive strike mission—both conventional and nuclear—as well as the missile defense mission, have been integrated organizationally. U.S. Strategic Command has been assigned responsibility for both the global strike and global missile defense missions. Within this overall framework NORTHCOM has been assigned the missile defense mission for the North American continent specifically, with NORAD providing aerospace warning information to NORTHCOM about approaching ballistic missiles.

Conclusion

The Pentagon's broader military transformation agenda includes many elements beyond the narrower "how we fight" conception of transformation. Some of the more significant aspects are changes in America's global force posture, an increased emphasis on the U.S. military's ability to assist civilian authorities in homeland security activities, a focus on maintaining unhindered access to space, and a new approach to deterrence which conceptually links together measures at home and those abroad in the context of a new triad. These aspects, which have arguably seen greater progress than ideas associated with "transforming transformation," are the result of an increasingly globalized and interconnected world that is erasing lines between home and abroad, driving and necessitating an integrated approach to security. The next chapter examines the range of military transformation efforts undertaken by Australia and some of America's NATO allies.

Notes

1. As quoted in Christopher P. Cavas, "New Missions Will Rely on Sea Basing," *Defense News* (January 17, 2005), 4.

2. The NDP also recommended Russia and a number of other former Soviet republics become part of European Command.

3. David S. Yost, "The U.S. Nuclear Posture Review and the NATO Allies," *International Affairs* 80(4) (2004), 707.

4. "The Next American Empire," *Economist* (March 20, 2004), 34.

5. Alexander Cooley, "Base Politics," *Foreign Affairs* 84(6) (November/December 2005), 85.

6. There are currently ten U.S. military commands: Strategic Command, Joint Forces Command, Special Operations Command, Transportation Command, European Command, Pacific Command, Central Command, Southern Command, Northern Command and the newly created Africa Command.

7. The Vice Commander of U.S. Air Force Space Command as quoted in Gopal Ratnam, "U.S. STRATCOM Launches Space Control Plan," *Defense News* (October 16, 2006), 7.

8. Jeremy Singer, "USAF To Upgrade Satcom Jamming," *Defense News* (March 5, 2007), 34.

9. Gopal Ratnam, "To 'Militarize' or 'Weaponize' Space? U.S. Debate Begins," *Defense News* (May 23, 2005), 1.

10. The undersecretary of state for arms control and international security, as quoted in Bill Gertz, "U.S. to Defend Space With Military Force," *Washington Times* (December 14, 2006); National Security Council spokesman as quoted in Marc Kaufman, "Bush Sets Defense as Space Priority," *Washington Post* (October 18, 2006), A01.

11. Donald H. Rumsfeld, "Transforming the Military," *Foreign Affairs* 81(3) (May/June 2002), 28.

12. Yost, "The U.S. Nuclear Posture Review and the NATO Allies," 716.

13. Department of Defense, *Doctrine for Joint Nuclear Operations* (Washington, DC: Joint Publication 3–12, March 15, 2005), p. ix.

14. See John M. Deutch, "A Nuclear Posture For Today," *Foreign Affairs* 84(1) (January/February 2005).

15. Robert R. Monroe, "Defining Deterrence," *Washington Times* (September 29, 2005).

16. Yost, "The U.S. Nuclear Posture Review and the NATO Allies," 717, fn 33.

CHAPTER 4

Allied Approaches to Military Transformation

Military transformation is a U.S.-led phenomenon, driven by the changing military requirements to meet ongoing developments in the international security environment. But America cannot always or even mainly operate alone in the world. It is to the benefit of the United States that countries that share its values and interests are capable of making a valuable contribution to international operations. Conversely, it is in the interests of those allies that they have sufficient military capability to address threats, influence the nature of the American response, and adequately defend their own homelands. As a result, many of America's allies are also engaged in military transformation efforts, and in some cases they are well advanced along a transformation path. This chapter examines military transformation in five countries allied with the United States—Australia, Britain, Canada, France, and Germany—drawing out, with respect to each, changes in both the narrower and wider aspects of transformation.

Australia

Geographically located in a potentially dangerous area of the world, possessing a strong alliance with the United States, and amenable to America's desire that Australia assume greater responsibility for regional security, Australia has been engaged in military transformation efforts for some years. Its official thinking with respect to transformation and its precursor, the Revolution in Military Affairs, dates to a policy document it released in 1997. Australia's Strategic Policy equated the Revolution in Military Affairs (RMA) to the information revolution— a narrow interpretation of the RMA—and argued the exploitation of information technologies to create a "knowledge edge" would be the capability development priority of the Australian Defense Force (ADF). The second area of emphasis was on continuous, real-time surveillance of Australia and its maritime approaches, with strike capabilities for overseas missions figuring third on the priority list, followed by land forces with sufficient firepower, mobility, and rapid reaction capability to prevail over potential enemy forces that may land somewhere on Australia's vast territory. In 2000 Australia published a defense white paper that echoed this approach, stating the ADF's three defense priorities as: the defense of Australia; contributing to the security of its neighborhood; and, contributing effectively to international coalitions of forces to meet crises beyond its immediate neighborhood.

Australia's strategic thinking has been impacted by the 9/11 attacks, the terrorist bombings in Bali against Australian citizens, and the war in Iraq. Whereas primary attention had been given to defeating attacks against Australian territory, post-9/11, and especially since the Iraq war, Australia has emphasized expeditionary operations in multinational coalitions. "Australia must have the capacity to lead or contribute to coalitions in our region, while at the same time providing capacity to contribute to coalitions in areas further afield where our interests may be at stake," argues Australia's 2005 Defense Update. The lesson of Iraq, especially, was that Australia needed a defense force that was more mobile and better prepared for combat operations overseas than was previously thought to be necessary. But the reordering of strategic priorities has not rendered irrelevant previous initiatives. Indeed most, if not all of the previous plans accord with current requirements. The post-9/11 environment has identified additional, not replacement, areas of focus and these are consistent with elements of "transforming transformation." Moreover, the wider understanding of military transformation that encompasses homeland defense measures meshes well with Australia's previous emphasis on the defense of the homeland.

Changes Associated with the Revolution in Military Affairs

Since the mid-1990s Australia has emphasized the importance of advanced intelligence, surveillance, and reconnaissance capabilities, with a particular focus on long range and long endurance unmanned aerial vehicles to compliment and perhaps replace its AP-3C Orion maritime patrol aircraft. Unmanned Aerial Vehicles (UAVs) figured significantly in Australia's Strategic Policy and have continued to do so in all subsequent official statements and plans including the most recent, the Defense Capability Plan of 2006. This ten-year road map for Australian defense acquisitions places High Altitude Long Endurance UAVs high on the priority list, with the expected purchase being America's Global Hawk UAV. Australia plans a squadron of strategic UAVs, which will carry out maritime patrol and land surveillance roles with respect to Australian territory, provide a continuous surveillance capacity for military missions abroad, and assist with aide of the civil power tasks like detecting and responding to forest fires. In addition, the Australian army is purchasing tactical UAVs (TUAVs) to provide its land forces on deployed operations with battlefield surveillance information. Both programs are expected to be in service by about 2010.

For advanced command and control, Australia is taking delivery of six Airborne Warning and Control System (AWACS) aircraft starting in 2008. It is also integrating the link 16 and eventually the link 22 tactical data links into its naval vessels and other platforms. A 2007 version of its Network Centric Warfare Roadmap foresees a joint, seamless, network centric capability by 2020 that will include a range of platforms. The core of the Royal Australian Navy's network centric capability, for example, will be new Air Warfare Destroyers (see later) that will network with Joint Strike Fighters, AWACS, and ground-based air defense, in addition to integrating with other naval vessels. At the most strategic level, Australia is upgrading its military satellite communications capability. The ADF already has its own satellite communications capability—a dedicated payload on board a commercial satellite that was launched in 2003 and is due to retire in 2013. In 2007 Australia joined the U.S. Air Force's Wideband Gapfiller satellite communications system (see Chapter 2), agreeing to provide the sixth and final satellite in the system.

One of Australia's main areas of command, control, communications, computing, and intelligence processing (C4I) emphasis is on networking its army platforms, including its tanks, helicopters, light armored vehicles (LAVs), and future TUAVs. The Battlespace Communications System (Land) will provide wireless communications and networking infrastructure for all Army combat units. This system is central to Australia's plans to transform its Army from a light infantry force to a hard-hitting, networked, mobile, and deployable medium weight force. Under the Hardened and Networked Army program Australia is undertaking the C4I changes, as well as replacing or upgrading many of its army platforms. The service is in the process of acquiring new tanks (the Abrams main battle tank), armed reconnaissance helicopters (the Eurocopter Tiger armed with precision-guided hellfire anti-tank missiles), and troop lift helicopters (the MRH 90 based on the Eurocopter NH90). It is also upgrading and increasing the number of its armored personnel carriers. Australia's acquisition of America's Abrams tank is consistent with allied and coalition experience in Afghanistan and Iraq where the tank is conceived not as a platform to engage in broad, sweeping tank battles, but rather as an infantry support platform necessary for meeting the dangerous operating environment of contemporary stabilization operations.

To deploy and sustain a significant expeditionary force the ADF is acquiring both strategic sea- and airlift. It is taking delivery of four of America's giant C-17 Globemaster air transporters and by the middle of the coming decade will have two amphibious landing ships. These ships will be used for the full range of missions, from peacekeeping and regional disaster relief to combat operations; they will be able transport a battalion of troops (approximately 1,000 personnel) and 150 vehicles, including the heavy tanks, and be equipped with six helicopter landing pads. The ADF is also in the early stages of considering replacements for its tactical lift aircraft, with options being either new Hercules aircraft to replace the old, or perhaps the Airbus A400M strategic air transporter which is roughly midway in size between the large C-17 and smaller C-130 Hercules.

In the area of standoff precision force Australia has in place a Follow-On Stand-Off Weapon program that is evaluating replacements to the F-111 strategic bomber, to be retired starting in 2010. The almost certain purchase will be the land variant of America's F-35 Joint Strike Fighter, armed with satellite-guided precision munitions such as the Joint Stand-Off Weapon or, more likely, the Joint Air-to-Surface Standoff Missile (JASSM). The first Royal Australian Air Force F-35 squadron is tentatively scheduled to become operational sometime after 2014. To bridge the gap between F-111 retirement and F-35 delivery, Australia is upgrading its F-18 fighter aircraft with the JASSM. The ADF has also left open the possibility of buying unmanned combat aerial vehicles in the next decade to provide a standoff precision strike capability. To increase the range of the F-18s as well as the F-35 in the future, Australia has begun taking delivery of five new air-to-air refueling tankers. The decision to purchase these tankers, as well as strategic airlift, underscores Australia's determination that in the new strategic environment it is necessary to operate in distant theatres with coalition forces.

Apart from strategic lift, the ADF's two new amphibious ships will contribute to its littoral warfare capabilities, which was identified in the early post-9/11 period as an important shift in emphasis on the part of the Royal Australian Navy. In addition to transporting troops and vehicles, the ships will have landing craft for amphibious assault and command and control facilities to support forces ashore. Beyond this, however, Australia is limited in its sea-to-land capability. The Australian Navy currently has no submarine or ship-launched land attack missiles necessary for littoral warfare nor—given priorities and costs—any plans for acquisition. But it is acquiring three new air warfare destroyers in the middle of the coming decade. The Spanish built Hobart class ships will include a version of America's Aegis air warfare system, and will be designed to work alongside the navy's frigates and Collins class submarines in maritime interdiction roles and to protect the amphibious ships during deployments. The Royal Australian Navy is also studying the U.S. Navy's Littoral Combat Ship program.

Changes Associated with "Transforming Transformation"

The ADF is undertaking measures to transform its forces that go beyond those associated with the earlier RMA. In response to the post-9/11 requirement for the increased use of special operations forces the ADF formed a new Special Operations Command (SOCOM) in 2003 and began expanding its special forces strength. The SOCOM has been formed as a separate arm of the ADF, alongside the army, navy, and air force. It consists of two anti-terrorism tactical assault groups, a special air service regiment, the 4th battalion of the Royal Australian Regiment (4RAR), a commando unit made up of reservists, and an Incidence Response Regiment designed to respond to nuclear, chemical, and biological warfare attacks. Australia's special forces command now has approximately 2,500 personnel, double the size of the special forces community at end of the 1990s, and some 300 of these are deployed in Afghanistan.

Beyond the significant measures it is taking in the area of special operations force (SOF), Australia is responding to the requirement for larger ground forces to carry out stabilization and reconstruction missions. Under its Enhanced Land Force program, the Australian Army will grow by more than 20 percent, from 25,000 to 30,000 troops by the middle of the coming decade. The Army's infantry force is due to expand from six battalions to eight by about 2011. Although certainly a post-9/11 requirement, the increased ground force size is something the Australian army had actually been arguing for since 1999 when the ADF led the intervention into East Timor.

Wider Aspects of Australian Military Transformation

Australia's 2005 Defense Update states the ADF must be able to respond to the range of potential domestic, regional, and global scenarios, providing response options from expeditionary forces to domestic security. Indeed, Australia has stressed that despite the expeditionary emphasis, its defense forces must maintain its support for domestic security and border protection activities. In this sense, Australia has moved beyond the "how we fight" aspect of military transformation to include wider elements that integrate the "home game" with the "away game."

Efforts to strengthen the ADF's capacity to contribute to domestic security include, in part, the measures that are being taken to increase its special forces capability. The Incident Response Regiment was originally created to respond to possible WMD threats during the 2000 Sydney Olympics, but then it was reestablished after 9/11. In addition, the Royal Australian Navy is acquiring a new fleet of Armidale patrol boats to enhance border patrol capabilities. In other areas, notes the Defense Update, the ADF's domestic response contribution encompasses secure facilities, command, control and communication systems, integrated intelligence, surveillance, and reconnaissance systems, dedicated lift for medical evacuation, and bomb disposal.[1] Meanwhile, on the civilian side of homeland security Australia has significantly increased the funds devoted to its security and intelligence services, as well as to other departments that conduct anti-terrorist measures such as Immigration, Customs, and Transport.

Britain

Britain's efforts to transform its military forces began in various areas soon after the end of the Cold War but they were first given comprehensive expression in official policy with the Strategic Defense Review (SDR) of 1998. In it, the Secretary of Defense stressed that the British are by instinct an internationalist people who must be able to defend their own country and also discharge their responsibilities around the world—sentiments which no doubt continue to inform Britain's approach to military transformation. The SDR placed its emphasis in particular on ensuring the British Armed Forces had the ability to carry out expeditionary operations. This would be done through the creation of Joint Rapid Reaction Forces comprising all services. Ground forces would be modernized and rapidly deployable; naval forces would project power with aircraft carriers and roll-on roll-off ships and focus on littoral operations; air forces would be equipped for standoff precision strike and contribute to expeditionary capability with the acquisition of strategic airlift. Reductions would come in the areas of heavy tanks, land based aircraft and ships for open-ocean submarine warfare.

All of these trends were consistent with the RMA core of military transformation. The SDR's New Chapter, released in July 2002, argued that the expeditionary strategy outlined in the SDR remained sound, as did many decisions surrounding that document. For Britain, much like the Australian experience, the post-9/11 security environment revealed the requirement not so much for a change in direction as for additional areas of emphasis over and above initiatives already in train. The major conceptual difference was that while the SDR, written in the midst of the British experience in the Balkans, foresaw operations in Europe and around its periphery, more recent policy documents stress the need to be able to operate more widely. "The potential for instability and crises occurring across sub-Saharan Africa and South Asia," notes the Defense White Paper of December 2003, "and the wider threat from international terrorism will require us . . . [to] extend our ability to project force further afield than the SDR envisaged." The SDR New Chapter, the Defense White Paper, and further announcements since that time have reinforced RMA-related ideas while at the same time emphasizing changes that accord with both "transforming transformation" and with a wider approach to military change.

Changes Associated with the Revolution in Military Affairs

British military transformation efforts are focused on creating a networked, expeditionary force that can operate with U.S. troops. Command, control, communications, computing, intelligence, surveillance, and reconnaissance (C4ISR) systems that can gather, analyze, and distribute information provide the networked capability and in this regard Britain is pursuing advanced C4ISR capabilities at the tactical, operational, and strategic level. Strategically, Britain launched the first of a new generation of Skynet secure military communications satellites in 2007. Skynet 5, which will comprise three military satellites and associated ground stations, is unique in that it is not owned by the government but rather is "out sourced" to industry. Britain is also examining the use of low-Earth micro-satellites as part of a mix of assets that would provide persistent intelligence, surveillance, target acquisition, and reconnaissance. At the more operational level, Britain is deploying its Airborne Standoff Radar (ASTOR) system, which is similar in function to America's Joint Surveillance and Target Attack Radar System (JSTARS). Consisting of five aircraft that operate at 40,000 feet, ASTOR looks down on hundreds of square miles of territory, through any type of weather, giving commanders real time information about objects on the ground. Each aircraft is equipped with synthetic aperture radar to distinguish objects from their background, and a ground moving target indicator capability to track them. ASTOR was pressed into service in 2006, three years ahead of its scheduled deployment, to scan the borders of Iraq and Afghanistan and detect insurgents entering from Iran and Pakistan respectively.

Britain's tactical standoff sensor capability centers on its Watchkeeper battlefield surveillance system. Based on the Hermes 450 tactical unmanned aerial vehicle, the Watchkeeper system will provide the British army with the Intelligence, Surveillance, Target Acquisition, and Reconnaissance (ISTAR) capability that was first identified as a force requirement in the 1998 Strategic Defense Review. Watchkeeper is to enter service around 2010; until then Britain's UAV assets are limited to its declining stock of Phoenix UAVs, deployed with the Royal Artillery, and mini-UAVs purchased for British operations in Iraq. Hermes 450s are also being purchased as an emergency operational requirement for forces in Iraq and Afghanistan. Although the Watchkeeper is intended to increase the Army's ability to see the battlefield, in future it could be expanded to include a capability to relay information to maritime aircraft, attack helicopters, and electronic warfare aircraft. Britain may also pursue UAV capabilities beyond the Watchkeeper and has established a joint UAV experimentation program to test UAVs ranging from handheld micro UAVs to high-altitude strategic UAVs like America's Global Hawk.

For tactical command, control, and communications among its troops, the British Army has deployed its new Bowman secure, digitized, voice, data and situational awareness communication system. The Bowman program, which encompasses more than 40,000 radios of various frequencies for individual soldier and vehicle use, including approximately 10,000 operational-level Falcon II radios, is to be the backbone of the British Army's network-enabled effort (see later) over the next two decades. Late next decade soldiers will also be equipped with Future Infantry Soldier Technology which will enhance capabilities in five areas: C4I, lethality, sustainability, survivability, and mobility. Bowman technology will be part of the C4I component, but the advancements under FIST will also include, among other things, a range of attributes from better sighting systems, GPS, helmet-mounted displays, a highly accurate grenade launcher and a laser aimer, all wired together and powered by lithium batteries.

Network-enabled or network-enhanced capability (NEC) is the UK's term for the increased effect achieved by linking platforms and people through a network. To this end, the Royal Air Force and Royal Navy have installed the link 16 communications system on most aircraft, helicopters, and vessels. As outlined in the 2003 Defense White Paper, NEC depends on the provision of a digitized communications network and the appropriate sensors to gather the information, as well as forces that "have the appropriate reach and deployability to achieve rapid effect."[2] In this sense, advancements in both the sensor and command and control components of C4ISR are linked to changes in military force structure and strategic lift acquisitions that facilitate rapid deployment.

The most substantial military force structure changes are underway in the Army. To accommodate the contemporary requirement for rapidly deployable yet still highly lethal, survivable, and combat capable forces Britain is reconfiguring its army so it includes medium-weight brigades, rather than only light and heavy brigades. As Britain's defense minister explained early on, "Our current light forces cannot provide the combat power required by some of the more demanding operations in which rapid deployment is needed, so we must move...to a more graduated structure."[3] The new structure is to comprise two heavy armored brigades, three medium-weight brigades, and two light brigades. The medium weight brigades are to be equipped with the Future Rapid Effects System (FRES) family of vehicles that, like America's Future Combat System, will encompass platforms with roles that range from armored personnel carrier to variants carrying 120mm guns and missiles. The latter will be designed to combine the firepower and survivability of a tank with the ability, by virtue of being much lighter, of rapid deployability. Of the up to 16 variants of FRES vehicles, it is expected the armored personnel carrier will enter service first, sometime after 2012, while the most sophisticated variants will not be in place until closer to the end of the decade.

Britain's 2003 Defense White Paper notes that the addition of medium weight forces does not remove the requirement for heavier armored forces. Indeed, British commanders in Afghanistan have called for their paratroopers and light infantry to be reinforced with Challenger tanks and Warrior fighting vehicles. Consistent with developments in countries like Australia and Canada, and in response to "lessons learned" in Iraq and Afghanistan, Britain is retaining its armored warfare capability, albeit at reduced levels. It is cutting its number of heavy brigades from three to two, and reducing the number of Challenger 2 main battle tanks and Warrior infantry fighting vehicles, but at the same time is upgrading the platforms that remain and indeed has plans to keep them in service until 2025. Finally, for increased land force firepower and mobility in theatre, Britain is acquiring Apache combat helicopters and has begun to think about new battlefield support helicopters.

The rapid deployment of combat power is dependent on the availability of airlift and sealift and Britain has taken measures in both these areas. It has purchased five C-17 air transporters from the United States, and as part of the Airbus A400M project that includes nine mainly European countries Britain is purchasing 25 of these medium-size air transporters. They will begin to replace its older C-130 Hercules tactical lift aircraft early next decade. For sealift Britain now has six roll-on/roll-off vessels, which are ships that can transport heavy vehicles (and troops) to almost any location because they are not dependent on the existence of sophisticated port facilities. It is also receiving four new landing ships for delivering logistics items like stores, as well as vehicles.

Britain's expeditionary capability will be enhanced by the middle of the coming decade with two new 50,000-ton aircraft carriers. These ships, from which the Joint Strike Fighter will operate, will be indispensable for those situations where there is no friendly territory nearby on which to base fighter aircraft. The carriers will also be central to Britain's ability to project force from the sea onto land—one of the key military requirements for naval forces since the early post–Cold

War period. Britain's capability in this area currently consists of two smaller aircraft carriers, as well as nuclear-powered submarines equipped with land attack Tomahawk cruise missiles. In addition, it has purchased two new amphibious assault ships, called Landing Platform Docks, for power projection onto land. Meanwhile, the British navy has slightly reduced the number of its frigates, arguably the current vessel best suited for maritime interdiction operations in the open ocean. These naval equipment trends are consistent with the 2003 Defense White paper's statement that Britain would focus on "delivering effect from the sea onto land, which includes a land attack capability [and] supporting forces ashore."

The Royal Air Force's precision air to ground strike capabilities currently center on the Tornado GR4 strike aircraft armed with Paveway IV satellite-guided precision bombs, and Storm Shadow precision-guided cruise missiles for long-range standoff strike. In addition, its new Typhoon (Eurofighter) aircraft will be upgraded with a land-attack capability. But for some years Britain has been examining future requirements in the context of its Future Offensive Air System (FOAS) program. Conceived in the early 1990s as a straightforward Tornado replacement program, by the turn of the century it had become clear that the new requirement was for a "strike capability" consisting of many platforms—some old, some new—all connected via a "systems of systems." Just as the Army is putting in place a network to link new and existing platforms, FOAS is now expected to encompass a mix of combat aircraft, missiles, and unmanned aerial vehicles linked by a digitized command and control network. The Joint Strike Fighter armed with the Paveway IV is likely to fulfill a large part of the FOAS requirement. Britain has committed to 150 of the aircraft, which are intended to replace the Harriers in service with the Royal Air Force and Royal Navy, but there is a possibility the number of land-based variants will be reduced. In addition, Britain is examining the role that unmanned combat aerial vehicles could play in FOAS, which is slated for fielding toward the end of the coming decade.

Changes Associated with "Transforming Transformation"

As with other Western countries, Britain has responded to the post-9/11 environment by increasing its special forces capability. Influenced by the 2001–2002 war in Afghanistan, where SOF were highly effective in pinpointing targets for standoff precision strike, Britain stated in the SDR New Chapter its plans to enhance the capabilities of its special forces to maximize their flexibility and utility, particularly with regard to target acquisition and strike. To this end, in 2005 and as part of the overall army restructuring discussed above, Britain created a new special forces regiment for covert reconnaissance and intelligence gathering. The Special Reconnaissance Regiment comprises about 400 troops and is one of three major units that are part of the U.K. Special Forces Group, the other two being the Special Air Service and the Royal Marines' Special Boat Service. Britain is also developing new urban warfare weapons for its special forces to improve their ability to fight terrorists and other land forces in built-up areas.

Although stressing in its policy documents the importance of stabilization missions, Britain is not increasing the size of its army to accommodate the increased manpower demands of these missions. In accordance with plans announced in 2004, the infantry is being reorganized to reduce the number of battalions from forty to thirty-six, and overall the army's force numbers are going down by a small amount. A 2005 assessment of the SDR New Chapter found that the document "gave greater emphasis to the ideas of the revolution in military affairs than did [the] SDR," emphasizing warfighting "over wider soft security issues such as nation building."[4] Some critics have argued Britain has placed too much emphasis on the potential multiplier effect of network-enabled (technological) capabilities and not enough on troops.[5]

Wider Aspects of British Military Transformation

The SDR New Chapter drew out the necessity of adopting a wider approach to military transformation, devoting an entire section to home defense and security and measures to improve the British Armed Forces' ability to contribute in these areas. Since that time, Britain has created 14 Civil Contingency Reaction Forces (CCRFs) to cover the different regions of the U.K. Each CCRF comprises a pool of about 500 volunteers drawn from the voluntary reserves of all three services that can provide assistance to civil authorities in emergency situations, if so requested. These personnel are trained in particular to help civil authorities to deal with chemical, biological, nuclear, and radiological attacks.

Early post-9/11 scholarly discussion raised the possibility of Britain establishing a military command for homeland protection[6], much as the United States has created Northern Command to defend its homeland, and Canada has similarly created a Canada Command. But, given its experience over thirty years in combating Irish terrorism and the existence of the Home Office to lead in this endeavor, it was felt that an office of homeland defense already existed in the form of the Home Office.[7] In 2007 the Home Office was streamlined and reorganized to increase its focus on terrorism, especially combating al Qaeda and homegrown terrorists.

Canada

Canada is driven to transform its military forces, the Canadian Forces or CF, for two distinct yet inter-related reasons. The first is to take the measures that are necessary to build a military force appropriate for addressing contemporary threats, and the Canadian government often mentions that some two-dozen Canadians were killed in the World Trade Center on 9/11. The second is to be in a position to contribute to international peace and security, and this is framed more in terms of Canada's longstanding tradition of multilateral engagement in the world. But Canada lives in a peaceful area of the world and enjoys the benefits of membership in the North Atlantic Treaty Organization (NATO). As a result, in comparison to a similar sized country, Australia, it has not fielded as wide a range of military platforms for independent action, such as AWACS, ground attack helicopters, and LDH amphibious landing vessels. Canada's geopolitical position is such that Canadian governments have had the luxury of being able to cut defense spending as part of any cost cutting exercise. Many Canadians, in fact, feel there is very little threat to the country. As a result, investments in defense depend to a significant degree on the platform of the political party in power and the personal preferences of the Prime Minister and his leading ministers. It is the degree to which these players want to expend their political will on making the case for Canada to take an active role in the world, and to maintain the necessary military forces for that role, that determines investments in defense and ultimately advancements in military transformation.

In 1994 the Canadian government released a defense white paper that called for the maintenance of a force that could fight "alongside the best, against the best" in military operations around the world. But budgetary pressures meant that much of the document was never implemented. Over the next several years the individual military services released a number of vision statements, all of which implicitly or explicitly outlined goals that were consistent with the RMA component of military transformation, but again many of these ideas were not backed up with sufficient government funding. These trends began to change post-9/11 and with the arrival of a new Prime Minister. In 2005 the Canadian government released a Defense Policy Statement, the first since 1994, which promised to rebuild the Canadian Forces. But the quick succession of minority governments meant that a Defense Capability Plan designed to implement the statement was never approved, and it also called into question the status of the policy statement. The result is that Canada has neither a defense policy nor a defense capability plan officially approved by the current government. But because governments since late 2003 have been generally in favor of a strong Canadian Forces, military transformation is well underway.

Changes Associated with the Revolution in Military Affairs

The Defense Policy Statement of 2005 set in train one of the most significant military reorganizational efforts in Canadian history. In place of a military force structured around the three traditional services, Canada has established four combined commands[8], one of which is Expeditionary Forces Command. This command is responsible for all of Canada's international operations, with the exception of those controlled directly by Special Operations Command (see later). Previously, all operations, both domestic and international, were directed by a Deputy Chief of Defense Staff who, in the event of a crisis, had to engage in an often time consuming process of requesting forces from the Navy, Army, and Air Force. With the new structure, the services are force generators only, responsible for recruiting and training, and these forces are then made available to the unified commands. The intention is to boost the expeditionary capability of the CF—a longstanding and core element of military transformation.

In contrast to those of France and Germany (see later) and even the United States, Canada's individual services themselves did not need to undergo significant organizational change to become rapidly deployable. The army, for example, is and has been for some decades structured around brigade groups, which is the organizational unit to which the United States is moving. Its nine battalions (three for each brigade group) often form the basis of Canada's contribution to a multinational operation. In the late 1990s the Army began a process of making its forces even more deployable by replacing heavy main battle tanks with lighter, wheeled equipment like the Light Armored Vehicle (LAV) III and the Coyote reconnaissance vehicle. In 2003 it also announced plans to purchase the Stryker Mobile Gun System, which would have led to an armed force that mirrored America's Stryker brigade combat teams. But the conflicts in Iraq and especially Afghanistan, where Canada is heavily engaged, revealed the need for heavy armor to protect its troops. In fall 2006, Canadians carrying out combat operations against the Taliban in Afghanistan as part of the NATO mission there were surprised to encounter a "semi-conventional" enemy with dug-in lines of defenses.[9] Canada responded by deploying its Cold War era main battle tanks to Afghanistan. In a significant reversal of position, the Canadian government has indicated it will cancel the Mobile Gun System and in 2007 it announced plans to lease twenty Leopard II tanks from Germany, as well as to purchase, in the long term, up to hundred Leopard II tanks from the Dutch. Beyond this, Canada also has long-term plans for a Family of Future Combat Vehicles, much like America's Future Combat System of Vehicles.

The Canadian Forces is undertaking measures to make its units both rapidly deployable to theater and highly mobile in theater. It is purchasing four C-17 strategic transporters, with all four to be in service by the end of 2008. These aircraft will be able to transport even Canada's heaviest military equipment, the Leopard tanks, to overseas crises. Canada is also replacing its aging fleet of C130 Hercules tactical lift planes with 17 C-130J Hercules', having chosen this aircraft over the A400M air transporter. The deployability of Canada's forces will also be enhanced by the acquisition of three multi-role Joint Support Ships (see later) that, among other things, will have sealift capacity for vehicles and troops and, as result, will reduce Canada's reliance on chartered sealift. For increased battlefield mobility, Canada's Army is to receive sixteen medium-lift Chinook helicopters starting in about 2011. This is a critical capability shortfall for Canada, which for a decade and a half has had no troop lift helicopters appropriate to combat situations and has therefore been dependent on its allies for battlefield mobility in places like Afghanistan. Unlike many of its allies, Canada has no current plans to purchase an armed combat helicopter like the Apache or Eurocopter Tiger, but it is considering an armed escort or reconnaissance helicopter designed not as an attack helicopter but rather to protect the Chinooks. Finally, to reduce weight and improve mobility the Army has deployed new battlefield artillery, the air portable

M777 Howitzer, armed with Excalibur GPS-guided artillery rounds. Its acquisition will increase interoperability with the U.S. Army and U.S. Marine Corps, which use the same artillery system.

In 2006 Canada announced the acquisition of three Joint Support Ships, with the first to arrive in 2012. These ships will greatly enhance Canada's capabilities in two naval doctrinal areas associated with the RMA: maritime interdiction operations and support to forces ashore. Canada carries out maritime interdiction operations—for example in the Arabian Gulf after 9/11—in the context of naval task groups made up of destroyers, frigates, and replenishment vessels that enable the task group to remain deployed for months at a time. But its Auxiliary Oil Replenishment vessels are almost four decades old and thus the Joint Support Ships, which have fleet replenishment at sea as one of their three roles, will provide an important capability. The next step in this area must necessarily be a replacement of the Canadian Navy's command and control destroyers (also almost four decades old) and the eventual replacement of its frigates. Current plans are to develop, for deployment around 2020, a common hull ship to replace both the destroyers and the frigates. This may be accompanied by an interim upgrade of the frigates to include a command and control capability since it is unlikely the destroyers can be maintained beyond 2015.

The Joint Support Ship will provide support to forces ashore in a number of ways. In the first instance they will provide command and control capabilities for directing deployed ground forces. The ships will be designed to function as a Joint Task Force Headquarters in conflict areas where it may be impossible to establish a headquarters ashore. In addition, the ships will have a roll-on roll-off capability for cargo, enabling them to unload in places where there are no modern port facilities. Finally, each ship will be equipped with three or four maritime helicopters for transporting forces and cargo ashore. To this end, Canada's aging Sea King maritime helicopters are being replaced with almost 30 new Sikorsky H92 Cyclone helicopters, with the first to begin arriving in 2008.

But Canada's Navy has no capability for projecting force ashore. Ever since precision strike from sea onto land was proven useful in the Balkan wars of the mid-1990s Canada's naval leadership has been arguing for some sort of land strike capability. The 2005 Defense Policy Statement stated that Canada's naval task groups should be capable of precision fire, but the present government has not approved concrete action in this area. The policy statement also included a far more ambitious plan centered on the acquisition of at least one amphibious assault ship. The proposal was to create a standing contingency task force made up of navy, army, (including special operations forces) and air force (up to six troop-carrying helicopters) elements that would be ready to deploy anywhere around the world within ten days notice. Missions would involve things like sending troops ashore to secure a failing state. In 2006 the CF conducted an exercises with an American amphibious assault ship to develop the necessary skills. But budgetary pressures as a result of the Afghanistan deployment, where Canada has had between 800 and 2,500 troops since 2002, have delayed this vision by several years. Canada will not be further pursuing an amphibious assault capability until sometime after 2010.

In the Air Force doctrinal area of standoff precision force Canada has taken a number of important steps. Its CF-18 Hornet fighter aircraft date to the 1980s but these have been subject to significant upgrades over the years. In 1999 the Canadian Air Force was able to make a significant contribution to the Operation Allied Force in and around Kosovo because its CF-18s had been equipped with laser-guided weapons. The 2005 Defense Policy Statement further signaled moving these aircraft, which were originally Cold War air-to-air fighters, to a ground attack role. The associated upgrades, to be completed in 2008, include state of the art targeting pods that will allow weapons to change direction mid-flight, hitting targets that have moved, and Enhanced Paveway 2 kits that will transform the CF-18's Mk82 "dumb" bombs into satellite guided precision weapons. Yet no amount of upgrades can reverse the fact that the CF-18s' airframes will come to the end of their operational life around 2020. Canada has participated in, and contributed to financially, the U.S. Joint Strike Fighter program for some years and it is likely that this will be its future generation strike aircraft. Indeed, it has tentatively decided to purchase 80 Joint Strike Fighters, with delivery to begin in 2016. But a firm decision does not have to be made until 2012 and until then Canada's Next Generation Fighter Capability office will be determining exact requirements, including a possible mix of manned and unmanned strike aircraft.

Canada's advanced ISR capabilities are centered primarily in the tactical and most strategic domains. Tactically, the Canadian Army has battlefield unmanned aerial vehicles for situational awareness, including Sperwer tactical UAVs and mini-UAVs used to gather intelligence for individual units. Both systems have been acquired in recent years for the Afghanistan mission. The Air Force's plans to sole source purchase Predator B UAVs from the United States were cancelled in 2007; however, it still plans to purchase more than a dozen medium- or high-altitude UAVs early in the coming decade. As an interim step, by 2009 Canada plans to acquire aerial drones with an ISR capability that would enable the platform both to track insurgents on the ground and to direct precision-guided munitions launched from Canada's army howitzers or CF-18 fighter aircraft. The Canadian Navy, too, has begun to think about UAVs. It is looking at whether Canada's frigates could carry, launch, and recover UAVs, and may also be considering fitting UAVs on its new arctic patrol vessels.

Strategically, the Canadian Forces is experimenting with a ground moving target indicator capability in space. Under project Polar Epsilon the Canadian Forces will have a military payload on the commercial earth-imaging satellite, RADARSAT II, operational in 2008. The satellite will keep watch on Canada's polar regions, providing 3-meter resolution imagery of ships or low-flying aircraft, and it will also conduct an experiment to see if objects can be indirectly tracked from space by comparing their location from one satellite pass to the next. Beyond this, Canada is taking steps to provide nearly instant, in-theatre, commercial satellite imagery. Under the Joint Space Support Project the Air Force is developing a mobile antenna and receiver terminal, deployable by C-130 Hercules, that can download satellite imagery for use in mission planning, tactical reconnaissance, target acquisition, and battle damage assessment.

All three of Canada's services are pursuing advanced command and control capabilities. The Canadian Navy is already highly interoperable with that of the United States, having worked closely with the U.S. Navy throughout the Cold War. Canadian naval vessels have been upgraded with link 16, and they are capable of being integrated seamlessly into U.S. carrier battle groups. Canada's Air Force has historically been somewhat less interoperable with that of the United States, despite decades of working with the U.S. Air Force through the North American Aerospace Defense Agreement (NORAD). But its CF-18s have now been fully upgraded with link 16, allowing secure communications between Canadian fighters and American fighters and AWACS. Canada has no AWACS of its own, but its does provide crews for NATO's common-funded AWACS operating out of Germany. Meanwhile, the Canadian Army is pursuing a network centric capability through its Intelligence, Surveillance, Target Acquisition, and Reconnaissance (ISTAR) program. Approved in 2003, the ISTAR program is developing an integrated, interoperable ISTAR capability that is linking together all battlefield platforms, including the UAVs. Under its Land Command Support System program the Army is also pursuing a capability to integrate information from the navy and air force—the recognized maritime picture and the recognized air picture—into their own systems. The goal is to create a joint picture of the battlespace to include maritime, land, and air assets. Finally, at the most strategic level, Canada will receive its first dedicated military satellite communications capability in 2010 by virtue of a payload on America's Advanced Extremely High Frequency (AEHF) satellite system. Satellite receivers for the Canadian Army and Victoria-class submarines have already been selected, however Canada's surface fleet will be equipped with whichever AEHF receiver the U.S. Navy ultimately selects, thereby ensuring interoperability.

Changes Associated with Transforming Transformation

Canada has taken a number of steps to respond to the requirements of "transforming transformation." In recognition of the growing role of manpower-intense stabilization and reconstruction missions, the Canadian Forces is growing in size for the first time since the post–Cold War cuts of the early 1990s. Under the current government's plans the CF's regular forces are expanding by some 12,000 troops over the next several years, to a force level of 75,000. Canada's reserve force of some 25,000 soldiers is also being increased. Canada, like the United States, has also begun to incorporate counterinsurgency operations into its official military doctrine. In 2007 it published its first ever counterinsurgency manual to give troops and their commanders insight into how to fight wars against insurgents and win the support of the population. These insights will be, and are already being, incorporated into its mission in Afghanistan.

Canada's most concrete "transforming transformation" efforts pertain to special operations forces. In 2006 it created a Special Operations Command to integrate four special forces formations: Joint Task Force 2, Canada's longstanding special operations force which has been doubled in size since 9/11; a Joint Nuclear, Biological, and Chemical Defense Company that has its antecedents in the Cold War but was significantly enhanced post-9/11; a new "tier 2" Canadian Special Operations Regiment (CSOR) of some 750 troops that is being trained to support JTF 2; and, an aviation squadron that has been reassigned to provide dedicated special operations aviation support, and will eventually be equipped with Canada's new battlefield troop lift helicopters. It is expected that Special Operations Command will comprise about 2,500 troops by early next decade. Forming the tier 2 CSOR to support the "tier 1" JTF 2 will make Canada's special forces more interoperable with those of its allies, most of which already have tier 2 and even tier 3 SOFs. The CSOR, which will not reach full strength until at least 2010, is best compared to the U.S. Army's Green Berets and Rangers, and Australia's 4RAR. In addition, the unit is being trained with the same "communications requirements, weapons, tactics, techniques and procedures" to ensure it can work within a coalition special operations setting involving American, British, and Australian tier 2 Special Forces.[10]

Wider Aspects of Military Transformation

Canada's expansion in its special forces capability is linked to new homeland defense roles associated with a wider perspective on military transformation. Indeed, while Expeditionary Forces Command is dedicated to overseas operations, and Canada Command (see later) is concerned exclusively with defending the homeland, Special Operations Command has responsibilities in both the domestic and overseas realms. To this end, the military is prepositioning special forces equipment at sites around the country to facilitate a quicker response to a terror attack, and it is also considering the creation of a special forces unit based on the West Coast to deal with maritime threats like coastal disasters. Beyond this, elements of Canada's conventional land force reserves are being reorganized into territorial defense battalions of some 500 personnel located in and around six major Canadian cities to assist in responding to crises, especially those involving weapons of mass destruction.

In 2006 Canada created a new military command dedicated to the military defense of the country. The idea behind the creation of Canada Command was to have a single locus of authority for responding to a domestic emergency. As was the case with America and the Northern Command it created in 2002, this is the first time Canada has had such a command. Previously, forces were structured for overseas operations and whenever there was a need for a domestic operation, the force was put together on an ad hoc basis. As part of the new organization the CF has created six regional headquarters across the country, each of which integrates navy, army, and air force assets for quick response to crises. Canada

Command is the country's primary point of contact with Northern Command for the defense of North America and like Northern Command it includes within its area of responsibility both military-led missions for the defense of North America, and support to civilian lead agencies for homeland security missions. In 2003 Canada created Public Safety Canada (PSC), which can be broadly compared to the Department of Homeland Security (DHS) with the major exceptions being that unlike DHS, PSC encompasses Canada's intelligence organizations, and unlike PSC, DHS includes the Coast Guard.

France

France's desire to define itself as a great power, and to maintain an autonomous and independent position from the United States, have been factors behind a significant transformation in French military forces since the mid-1990s. Its efforts began in earnest in 1996 when President Jacques Chirac announced a plan for modernizing the French military known as Model 2015. Informed by the experience of the 1991 Gulf War, when despite having an army of over 250,000 France struggled to deploy 10,000 troops to take part in coalition operations, the overall emphasis of Model 2015 has been to create a highly capable, expeditionary force to project military power worldwide. The plan is being carried out in the context of three Defense Program Laws, one each for the periods 1997 to 2002, 2003 to 2008, and 2009 to 2015. A 2006 report to Parliament on the status of the second program law underscored four priorities for French military reform: capabilities in the area of command and control and battlespace awareness; reducing the shortfall in the deployability and mobility of forces; increased flexibility and precision in deep-strike capacity; and, protection of deployed troops against weapons of mass destruction. The new conservative government of Nicholas Sarkozy is conducting an internal defense review of budgetary priorities, and could also draft a white paper setting out the government's thinking on defense matters.

Because its conscript soldiers focused on Cold War territorial defense and could not be deployed outside Europe without parliamentary approval, France's first order of business in the 1990s was to downsize and professionalize the French military. This was the overall of focus of the first Defense Program Law, which sought to fully professionalize the French military by 2002. The goal was accomplished slightly ahead of schedule, with the last drafted forces leaving their barracks in November 2001. The French army now comprises some 135,000 professional soldiers, somewhat less than the 170,000 originally envisaged in 1996. During this period the Army itself also underwent significant restructuring. In a process that brings to mind America's post-9/11 Army organizational changes, France swept away its previous divisional structure in favor of smaller, more flexible brigades. Its nine mobile brigades are now made up of fifty-one maneuver regiments. Some elements of this force are special operations forces. Indeed, France is one of the few countries in Europe with a significant special operations force capability and these forces have been operating under U.S. command on the Afghan-Pakistan border.

Under the second defense program law, approved shortly before 9/11 but modified since that time to reflect operations since 2002, France's restructured army is in the process of receiving many new platforms. Some of these are consistent with the RMA while others (notably the tank) did not figure in the RMA but are considered relevant again, in smaller numbers, in the contemporary security environment. For increased firepower and mobility on the battlefield, France has begun taking delivery of new Tiger combat helicopters and is to start receiving new NH90 troop lift helicopters in 2010. In 2007 delivery was completed for new Leclerc main battle tanks, while its new, wheeled infantry armored combat vehicle (the Véhicule Blindé de Combat d'Infanterie or VBCI) have started being delivered in 2008.

In the area of advanced C4ISR France is creating a network centric capability to link together its army platforms and people. It is integrating into one interoperable system the command and control systems of the dismounted soldier FELIN system, the Leclerc tank, the Tiger attack helicopter, and a new tactical unmanned aerial vehicle to replace the Army's CL289 tactical UAVs. France is already beginning to equip its regiments with the FELIN future soldier system which, like that of the British, will feature a communications system integrated into each soldier's clothing and equipment. Project Scorpion is the name for the French Army's effort to develop a roadmap for creating a network centric armored force. Work is also underway on project Attila, which will be a complete architecture for connecting land, air, and naval communications.

France is investing significantly in satellites for both remote sensing and communications. In fact, it is the only country in Europe to have both satellite-based reconnaissance and satellite-based communications systems. Over the past few years it has launched two next-generation Syracuse III military communications satellites, as well as a Helios II military surveillance earth imaging satellite with a ground resolution of less than one meter. A second Helios II satellite is to be launched in 2008. For earth imaging, France is also part of Germany's SAR Lupe project under which Germany has deployed a five-satellite space based radar system (see later). As part of its Preparatory System for Early Warning network, known by its French acronym SPIRALE, France also plans to launch two micro satellites designed for ballistic missile early warning, the first system of its kind for Europe.

Unlike trends in the United States and Australia, France will not be pursuing a high-altitude unmanned aerial vehicle for remote sensing. However it does operate a range of operational and tactical drones, while its manned C4I platforms include four Air Force AWACS and several E-2C tactical AWACS aircraft operating off its aircraft carrier. In contrast to its ground forces, most French air force assets and almost all its naval assets are interoperable with those of the United States. France's Charles de Gaulle aircraft carrier, E-2C aircraft, and Rafale fighter aircraft, among other platforms, are all equipped with the link 16 data link. France has also deployed the Cooperative Engagement Capability system on several of its naval vessels, a system that is installed on ships of the U.S. Navy and British Royal Navy and allows interoperability in naval air defense.

With its fifty A400M strategic lift aircraft not scheduled to arrive until after 2010, France's ability to rapidly deploy its military forces is hindered by the fact that it has no strategic airlift. But it has increased its capability in the maritime dimension to project power and sustain its military forces overseas with the delivery of two new amphibious assault ships, also known as Command and Projection Ships. These vessels, ideal for expeditionary operations, are command and control vessels that can direct multinational forces on shore, carry sixteen helicopters, have a significant capability for medical support, and can transport up to 450 fully equipped troops as well as heavy equipment like the Leclerc main battle tank. But perhaps the most significant development in the area of power projection was the 2002 decision on the part of the new center-right government—after years of declining defense budgets—to proceed with a second aircraft carrier. Both the new carrier and the existing Charles de Gaulle are to be equipped with the Rafale fighter aircraft armed with the precision-guided Scalp cruise missile. The aircraft carrier was the single largest item in France's 2006 defense budget and is expected to survive the 2007 change in government. During the French Presidential campaign Nicolas Sarkozy argued that there is no logic in having just one aircraft carrier, and that he would press ahead with two. Beyond this, the French Navy has ordered eight new multi-mission frigates, with the first scheduled to enter service in 2011. These will be well suited to maritime interdiction operations, but are also likely to be equipped with a naval version of the Scalp missile for land attacks roles.

France's standoff precision-strike capability centers on the naval and air force versions of the new F2 Rafale fighter, armed with precision-guided cruise missiles and air-to-ground missiles. The F2 Rafale fighter-bomber has already seen combat, having launched Paveway 2 precision guided bombs in Afghanistan in 2007. After the 2001–2002 war in Afghanistan France also stepped up measures to develop a long-range unmanned combat aerial vehicle (UCAV) for the ability to project air power in depth. The Defense Ministry's Délégation Générale pour l'Armement awarded a contract to a French company to develop a technology demonstrator for a UCAV and to invite other European countries to become partners in the project—much as the United States is proceeding with the Joint Strike Fighter. The new European combat drone, called the Neuron, is scheduled to carry out flights tests in the first half of 2011 and to be operational about eighteen months later.

Germany

Of America's Western allies Germany faced perhaps the greatest challenges in responding to the new military requirements of the post-Cold War era. Forty years of being the territorial focus of any potential Cold War battle, combined with a post-World War II tradition of conscription to ensure the military remained tied to civilian society, meant that Germany had to undergo a dramatic change in thinking if it were to respond to the doctrinal core of the RMA—a highly mobile expeditionary military capability. The need for such a capability was recognized as early as the 1994 Defense White Paper but, despite a number of initiatives in the 1990s, and the hard-hitting advice of an independent "Blue Ribbon" commission report in 2000, it was not until after the 9/11 attacks that German policy began to fully reflect a view that the country's security lay beyond the direct defense of its territory. Defense policy guidelines released in 2003 argued the notion of defense had to be understood as something much more than traditional conventional attack against Germany or its allies.[11] Rather, security began with crisis management abroad and, as a result, the Bundeswehr (German armed forces) had to be able to take part in the full spectrum of operations beyond German borders. This change in thinking continues to be reflected in the most recent policy document, the 2006 Defense White Paper. Yet at the same time Germany remains wedded to conscription, with the result that while military transformation is underway, it is arguably proceeding at a slower pace than in the other countries examined here.

Army force structural change is at the heart of Germany's military transformation efforts. From a pre-9/11 figure of 340,000, Germany's military force is being reduced to approximately 250,000 troops by 2010. Previously, Germany's military consisted of a 50,000-person Crisis Reaction Force (which included only a small number of ground forces) and a Main Defense Force encompassing the remainder. By contrast, the new structure is to be divided into three categories of soldiers: Intervention or Response Forces of 35,000 troops for high-intensity combat operations; Stabilization Forces of 70,000 troops designed for multinational operations of low or medium intensity; and Support Forces of 147,500 troops to train new troops and to provide support to response and stabilization forces prior to and during operations. The 2006 Defense White Paper stresses that response and stabilization forces must be able to interact in operations. Nonetheless, the German decision to create two forces for two different missions is unique among the Western allies. Most countries start from the premise that a well-trained soldier is the best peacekeeper; all soldiers are trained for high-intensity conflict and those same soldiers then undergo training specific to stabilization and reconstruction missions prior to deployment. In 2003 the United States briefly considered creating separate stabilization and reconstruction divisions, but this idea was not pursued.

In stark contrast to developments in France, Germany has decided to maintain conscription. Many would argue that these forces are ill-suited to the post–Cold War world and certainly to the ability to rapidly deploy military forces to trouble spots around the world. Moreover, maintaining conscription arguably holds back capability advancements in Germany's professional all-volunteer forces because funds are devoted to the conscript army that could otherwise be allocated to new technology and equipment. Since suspending conscription in 1996, for example,

France's military personnel costs have dropped by over 15 percent, allowing these extra funds to be devoted to modernization projects.[12] But in its 2006 defense white paper the German government stresses that universal conscription provides a guaranteed pool of resources to protect Germany and its citizens, and notes that conscripts willing to go on operations abroad can opt for up to fourteen months additional military service.

Given the increased focus on the homeland as part of a wider conceptualization of military transformation, Germany's retention of forces for territorial defense is not entirely out of step with contemporary security trends. The white paper notes that "the Armed Forces must be able to make their capabilities available in the homeland, too, in support of the security and protection of our citizens"—a sentiment that all of Germany's allies would share. Rather, the issue is more one of degree: while Britain has established Civil Contingency Reaction Forces totaling about 6,000 troops, and Canada is developing territorial defense battalions of some 3,000 personnel, Germany is devoting tens of thousands of soldiers to homeland defense.

Notwithstanding the continued strong emphasis, in personnel terms, on territorial defense, the Bundeswehr is placing its rhetorical and some tangible emphasis on military transformation. The German defense white paper specifically includes a section titled "transformation," which it defines as a process of permanent adaptation on the part of the Bundeswehr to changing political, societal, economic, and technological parameters. The armed forces have established a Center for Transformation and within this center, which advises military leaders on transformation issues, there is a Concept Development and Experimentation division. For Germany, the overriding goal of transformation is to "improve and sustain the operational capability of the Bundeswehr in a changing environment."[13] To this end, the Bundeswehr is focusing on developing capabilities in six specific areas: command and control, intelligence collection and reconnaissance, mobility, effective engagement, support and sustainability, and survivability and protection—all areas associated with the RMA component of military transformation.

For advanced command and control at the strategic level Germany is receiving its first-ever dedicated military communications satellites. Under the SATCOMBw program, which is to be operational in 2009, the German armed forces will have a secure information network for use by soldiers on deployed operations to transmit voice, data, and video images, considered central to the Bundeswehr's ability to push forward a network centric warfare capability. At the tactical level Germany's outdated battlefield command and control system is being replaced with state-of-the-art networkable radio equipment that is "software defined," meaning that the radio hardware is not limited to a specific frequency but rather has software which allows the radio to tune into any frequency within a wide band. It is also implementing a new command, control and information system for its armed forces, based on a NATO-wide effort known as Multifunctional Information Distribution System to incorporate the link 16 data link into a wide range of air force, navy, and potentially army platforms.

Germany is making significant advances in the area of intelligence, surveillance, and reconnaissance. Most notable is the fact that it is already deploying a Space-Based Radar (SBR) system—well ahead of a similar effort on the part of the United States. Germany's five-satellite SAR-Lupe SBR system is designed to provide surveillance coverage world wide through any kind of weather. Operating in low-earth orbit, each satellite's Synthetic Aperture Radar monitors relatively large areas at low resolution and can then switch to a magnifying glass—or lupe—to hone in on smaller areas to a resolution of one meter. The constellation is to be fully deployed in 2008 and is meant to provide German forces with high-resolution (less than one meter) radar imagery over a period of ten years. France is contributing financially to the project and therefore will also receive such imagery. In addition, the ground segments for the SAR-Lupe satellites and France's Helios II earth observation satellites will be linked so that each country can task the other's satellites and receive imagery. In other areas of ISR, Germany is participating in NATO's Air Ground Surveillance System, it has recently upgraded its CL289 tactical reconnaissance drones, and it is pushing forward with the more strategic Euro Hawk UAV program. Germany hopes to field a fleet of Euro Hawks (which is based on America's Global Hawk) by the middle of the coming decade.

Part of Germany's increased force mobility effort involves the organizational changes that the Bundeswehr is undertaking, noted above. Germany's pool of rapidly deployable response forces will include special operations forces capable of "particularly rapid operations."[14] The Special Forces have been organized into a Special Operations Division that comprises a 1,000 strong Special Forces Command and two airborne brigades. The range of missions for Germany's SOF include relatively low-risk tasks like gathering information, through to countering terrorist threats and carrying out combat missions on enemy territory. Beyond these organizational changes, the Bundeswehr is promoting mobility by significantly reducing the size of its main battle tank fleet and taking steps to incorporate lighter yet still combat-capable platforms into its army, like the Fennek reconnaissance vehicle and the Puma air-transportable infantry-fighting vehicle. But the rapid deployability of Germany's armed forces is significantly hindered by a lack of strategic lift. The 2006 white paper notes that contracts for civilian air- and sealift will be used to close capability gaps in the area of mobility. Germany is also part of the A400M airlift program, under which it will begin to receive 60 aircraft in about 2010, and it is leading the effort at NATO to create an Alliance airlift capability. Meanwhile, Germany is enhancing its tactical mobility in theatre by buying NH90 (army and air force) and MH90 (navy) troop transport helicopters.

"Effective engagement" is the term used by the United States and its NATO allies to refer to a precision strike capability using a wide range of military platforms. The 2006 German defense white paper states that in developing the response forces, special emphasis will be placed on improving force protection and standoff and precision force capabilities—the same two areas on which France is placing its greatest emphasis. In Germany's case, its effective engagement capacity has been significantly limited by the fact that it has few precision-guided munitions in its arsenal. The Bundeswehr is in the process of buying 180 land-based Eurofighter aircraft, armed with laser- and satellite-guided air-to-ground precision munitions as well as air-to-air missiles. These will be given greater range with the conversion of a number of Airbus A310s into air-to-air refueling aircraft. Meanwhile, the army will increase its ability to carry out air to ground assault operations with the acquisition of 80 Tiger attack helicopters armed with precision munitions. Beyond this, the German army is conducting trials with the Tares unmanned combat aerial vehicle. With regards to naval power projection from the sea onto land Germany is acquiring new type K-130 corvettes that, similar in function to America's Littoral Combat Ship, will be capable of precision target engagement ashore. Next decade it also plans to develop and procure a new class of frigate that will be especially geared toward long-term stabilization operations by being able to remain on station for up to two years at a time.

Conclusion

Although military transformation is thought of as a U.S.-led phenomenon, the allies that have been examined here have adopted approaches that are broadly similar. Each is at a different stage along the transformation path. Britain has a military force that in many ways is a smaller version of America's, with the exception that its does not yet have the fully digitized ground force or range of precision munitions that does the U.S. military. Australia too, with plans for AWACS, amphibious vessels, combat helicopters, and the joint strike fighter, is a small yet increasingly capable force, reflecting the fact that this country lives in a dangerous area of the world and may need to take independent action. France's longstanding desire to maintain independent and autonomous military capabilities has meant that it is the only country, other than America, that has invested almost across the board in defense technologies. Canada's transformation measures have come primarily in organizational change, with associated capital acquisitions just beginning, while Germany is still struggling to transform its military forces. In many ways, because of its history, it is difficult to discuss German force transformation without reference to NATO. The next chapter examines overall Alliance efforts to pursue military transformation.

Notes

1. Australia's Defense Update 2005, p. 11.
2. Britain's Defense White Paper 2003, p. 11.
3. Defense Secretary Geoff Hoon as quoted in Andrew Chuter, "Middleweight: Britain's Army Slowly Rolls Toward Lighter Force," *Defense News* (November 10, 2003), 15.

4. Andrew Dorman, "Transformation and the United Kingdom," *Joint Forces Quarterly* 37 (April 2005), 30.

5. Andrew Chuter, "UK Chops Forces," *Defense News* (July 26, 2004), 1.

6. Michael Codner, "British Military Strategy Home and Away, " *RUSI Journal* (April 2002), 80.

7. Andrew Chuter, "New U.K. Defense Unit to Guard Homeland," *Defense News* (June 17–23, 2002), 6.

8. They are: Expeditionary Forces Command, Special Operations Command, Canada Command, and Operational Support Command.

9. Graeme Smith, "Conquering Canadians Take Stock," *Toronto Globe and Mail* (September 13, 2006).

10. Commander Canadian Special Operations Regiment as quoted in David Pugliese, "New Canadian Force Ready for Action While Training," *Defense News* (June 5, 2006), 11.

11. For a detailed discussion of German reform efforts please see Kerry Longhurst, "Endeavors to Restructure the *Bundeswehr*: The Reform of the German Armed Forces 1990–2003," *Defense & Security Analysis* 21(1) (March 2005).

12. Ibid., 33.

13. Germany's White Paper on Defense 2006, p. 74.

14. Ibid., p. 78.

CHAPTER 5

NATO and Military Transformation

The North Atlantic Treaty Organization's (NATO) military transformation process has been inextricably linked to a broader process of political transformation that began soon after the Soviet Union disintegrated. Over the course of a decade NATO looked progressively outward, holding on to its traditional collective defense mandate yet at the same time increasingly recognizing that the security of its members depended on its ability to conduct crises management operations beyond its borders. The 9/11 attacks confirmed a political direction already in train, and did away with any lingering arguments against these developments. It also prompted a reinvigorated process of military transformation that, as with the political dimension, had well predated the attacks.

This chapter draws out those political developments within NATO that have formed the backdrop to military transformation, and discusses initiatives that have been taken since the late 1990s to advance NATO transformation. It examines NATO's current and projected capabilities in the Revolution in Military Affairs (RMA) component of military transformation, before highlighting what has been done in aspects associated with "transforming transformation." Finally, it addresses NATO's wider transformation role, particularly with regards to cooperation with the European Union on homeland security and defense, and as it pertains to a potential ballistic missile defense system to protect alliance territory.

Military Transformation: The Political Backdrop

NATO's military transformation efforts have been undertaken against the political backdrop of a slow but progressive acceptance that the security of its members depends on military action that goes well beyond that which is prescribed by the North Atlantic Treaty. Article V commits Alliance members to act together should there be an armed attack against one of its members, while Article VI defines this as being an armed attack against the member's territory (or military assets in and around Europe). As recently as November 1991 NATO held fast to the territorial specifications of the Treaty. Yet at the same time it revealed signs of mixed minds as to where to draw the defensive line. "The Alliance is purely defensive in purpose: none of its weapons will ever be used except in self-defense," stated the new Alliance Strategic Concept agreed by NATO Heads of State and Government in Rome, "however, Alliance security must also take account of the global context ... including [wider risks like] proliferation of weapons of mass destruction, disruption of the flow of vital resources and actions of terrorism and sabotage."

Driven by the dramatically new post–Cold War security environment, soon after the Soviet Union disintegrated NATO began to envision circumstances where it would have to undertake military activities on territory that did not belong to one of its members, that is, military action "out of area." The impetus in this regard was not the USSR's disappearance per se, although this was an enabling factor, rather it was the growing carnage in the Balkans. As war spread from Slovenia to Croatia and finally to Bosnia, NATO announced, in 1992, that it would be prepared to support, on a case-by case basis, peacekeeping activities under the auspices of the Conference on Security and Cooperation in Europe and the United Nations.[1] This support came in the form of NATO air and naval assets; NATO ground forces did not deploy out of area until acting under NATO auspices in the implementation force (IFOR) of 1996, and subsequent stabilization force (SFOR) (although ground forces of NATO member countries made up the bulk of the UN force, UNPROFOR). The Alliance Strategic Concept that was approved at NATO's fiftieth anniversary celebrations in Washington in 1999 reflected the change in Alliance emphasis. Gone was the statement that the Alliance would only use weapons in self-defense; kept were the words that the Alliance had to take account of the global context and the various risks mentioned in 1991. While in 1991 NATO needed to maintain the necessary forces to effect deterrence,[2] in 1999 the Alliance needed military capabilities "to accomplish the full range of NATO missions." More specifically, NATO members had to be "prepared to contribute to conflict prevention and to conduct non-Article 5 crisis response operations." Even as the Concept was released, such an operation was already under way in Kosovo.

Yet still the out of area debate continued, with some of the view that while NATO could go out of area into other parts of Europe (i.e. the Balkans), it should not go too far out of area, to places like the Middle East, Africa or Asia. This threshold in thinking was finally and quietly crossed in 2002 when NATO Foreign Ministers agreed "NATO must be able to field forces that can move quickly to wherever they are needed, sustain operations over distance and time, and achieve their objectives."[3] The statement reflected the post-9/11 acknowledgment that NATO needed to address threats to Alliance members wherever they arose—and that this may often be far from the borders of NATO member countries. Since then, with a NATO-led mission in Afghanistan, and requests for Alliance operations in places like Sudan and Lebanon, it is easy to forget that not long ago

NATO struggled with whether the concept of defense could be pushed beyond its members' territorial boundaries.

NATO's Military Transformation Initiatives

The reorientation of NATO thinking from defense in place, to defense by tackling threats as far from Alliance borders as possible is closely linked to, and has had a direct impact on, the content of NATO's various military transformation initiatives. Developing rapidly deployable, combat capable expeditionary forces—the RMA component of military transformation—is reflected in the Defense Capabilities Initiative (DCI) of 1999, the Prague Capabilities Commitment (PCC) of 2002, further commitments made at Istanbul in 2004, and most recently in the Comprehensive Political Guidance of 2006. This latter initiative also reflects ideas that are consistent with the "transforming transformation" aspect of military transformation.

The Defense Capabilities Initiative was conceived by the United States in the fall of 1998, and approved at the Washington summit in April 1999, as a means of addressing the growing gap in military capabilities and technologies between America and its NATO allies. The summit itself took place about a month into NATO's military operation in and around Kosovo, thereby coincidentally giving increased impetus to the need for greater Allied interoperability, and highlighting the shortfalls in European and Canadian military capabilities. The DCI concentrated on five areas of military capability—deployability and mobility; sustainability and logistics; survivability; effective engagement; and command and control and information systems—with each of its fifty-eight capability goals falling into one of these five categories. A high-level steering group was formed to oversee progress in fulfilling the goals, but NATO countries made no specific commitments. After three years it was clear that little had been accomplished.

Meeting at Prague in November 2002, NATO heads of state and government adopted a much different approach from that of the DCI. Rather than trying to fulfill dozens of goals across five categories of capability, under the Prague Capabilities Commitment allies agreed to increase their military capability in one or more of eight specific areas: defense against WMD; intelligence; air-to-ground surveillance; command, control, and communications; combat effectiveness, including precision-guided munitions; airlift and sealift; aerial refueling; and deployable combat support units. In many of these areas a specific country agreed to take the lead in pushing the capability forward: Spain led a group of nations to lease air-to-air refueling tankers; the Netherlands to secure more "smart" weapons; Norway to develop sealift; and Germany to lease airlift. These groups, in turn, were made up of those countries that decided to increase their capability in that particular area. In this way, the PCC's overall approach was one of multinational teaming or pooling, and on role sharing or specialization. The allies made progress in some of the PCC's capability areas (see later) but, generally speaking, four years after the plan's adoption there remained almost as many capability gaps as before. This reflected the fact that the commitments made were still only statements of intent; actual implementation would take many years and would have to be funded by national governments.

The next NATO initiative was still more realistic in that it set out a framework for increasing Alliance military capability over ten to fifteen years. Under the Comprehensive Political Guidance, issued by NATO heads of state and government at Riga in November 2006, allies agreed they needed to "put a premium" on ten capability requirements over the subsequent decade and a half. These included, among other things, the ability to: conduct joint expeditionary operations far from home; identify hostile elements in urban environments; undertake combat, stabilization, reconstruction, reconciliation, and humanitarian activities simultaneously; provide military support to stabilization and reconstruction missions by creating a safe space within which civilian organizations can carry out their tasks; protect Alliance population, territory, and critical infrastructure; and, assist in the "consequence management" of any WMD attack on Alliance territory. The list is notable for the fact that it reflects not just the RMA component of military transformation (which was the primary focus of the DCI and PCC) but also ideas associated with "transforming transformation," and with wider conceptions of military transformation.

Changes Associated with the Revolution in Military Affairs

Organizational Transformation

What was referred to as the revolution in military affairs in the 1990s, and now forms the core of military transformation, contains a package of ideas along technological, doctrinal, and organizational lines, all separate and yet closely interlinked in that each facilitates the others. For NATO, the most significant changes have been in the area of organizational transformation, and specifically in the creation of command and control structures oriented towards rapidly deployable force projection. In 1992 NATO created the Allied Command Europe Rapid Reaction Corps (ARRC), a mobile army headquarters of about 1,000 military personnel, located in Germany but commanded by Britain (and made up largely of British forces), to conduct humanitarian and peacekeeping missions. Building on the ARRC idea, the following year the Alliance introduced the Combined Joint Task Force (CJTF) concept as a means of assisting NATO forces in making the transition from collective defense capabilities to those that are necessary for operations outside the Alliance. "Combined" refers to multinational forces, while "joint" involves more than one of the military services (navy, army, air force and, in the case of Britain and the United States, the marine corps). Thus, under the CJTF concept, which was approved at the NATO summit in January 1994, NATO sought to establish headquarters structures that would enable the forces and services of several NATO nations to be brought together as a task force and undertake various types of operations beyond NATO borders.

Over the next several years the Alliance undertook conceptual work to establish the command and control arrangements for a range of different operations, and exercises were conducted to evaluate proposed structures. The military structure adopted by NATO in IFOR and SFOR also provided practical insight into CJTF development. But it was not until the Prague Summit of November 2002 that ideas that informed the CJTF concept really moved forward. Indeed, while the Prague Capability Commitment was one outcome of the summit, its far more significant and long-lasting decisions centered on NATO organizational change. At the summit, Alliance heads of state and government took two decisions that were significant in military transformation terms: to dramatically reduce and streamline NATO's entire command structure, and in doing so creating a command specifically devoted to thinking about military transformation; and, to create a NATO Response Force or NRF, which is meant to become a catalyst for pushing forward transformation in practice.

NATO's New Command Structure

Under NATO's new command structure the Alliance's previous two operational commands—Allied Command Europe and Allied Command Atlantic—have been amalgamated into one operational command, Allied Command Operations. At the same time, NATO has created a nonoperational command, Allied Command Transformation (ACT) in Norfolk, Virginia, headed by the Supreme Allied Commander Transformation. Tasked with being "NATO's forcing agent for change," ACT assesses the strategic environment the Alliance faces, identifies the need for new capabilities to adapt to those environments, and helps develop capability solutions.[4] It also organizes conferences, joint training, and exercises to further these processes. ACT is, in essence, the long-term strategic thinking arm of NATO—something that could not be done by NATO's operational command, which is taken up in the day-to-day running of military operations. In this regard, its creation "represents a transformation in NATO from being an entity that reacts to imminent threats to an organization that plans for future troop capabilities."[5] ACT's responsibilities are facilitated by the fact that its commander is double-hatted as the commander of U.S. Joint Forces Command, which is charged with the transformation of U.S. military forces.

Allied Command Operations is located in Mons, Belgium, and is headed by a four-star American military officer who, despite the change in the command's name, continues to be known as the Supreme Allied Commander Europe or SACEUR. Allied Command Operations is NATO's most strategic operational level. At the second operational tier, reporting to SACEUR, there are two joint force headquarters, one each in the Netherlands and Italy, as well as a smaller joint headquarters in Portugal. At the third tier there is an air, land, and maritime component reporting to each of the joint force headquarters, one of which is the (land force) ARRC, for a total of six headquarters organizations at this level. These are located in each of Britain, Italy, Spain, and Turkey, as well as two locations in Germany. Overlapping the six tier-three component commands are six High

Readiness Force headquarters, including the ARRC on which they are modeled. Because the tier-two joint headquarters serve to integrate land, sea, and air forces (i.e. joint) from several nations (i.e. combined), they reflect, in essence, an adaptation of the CJTF concept to the entire Alliance. Overall, the number of NATO operational commands at all levels has been reduced from a Cold War high of about sixty to less than a dozen today.

The NATO Response Force

The second significant organizational undertaking at the Prague Summit was the decision to create a NATO Response Force. This force is to consist of up to 25,000 personnel, combine land, sea, air, and special operations forces, be capable of deploying within a five-day notice, and be able to sustain itself for thirty days or longer if re-supplied. Its missions are to include Article V collective defense; non-Article V crisis response such as evacuations and disaster management; responding to humanitarian crises; counterterrorism; and, acting as an "initial entry force" for larger, follow-on forces.[6] Already elements of the NRF have been used to provide humanitarian relief on certain occasions, such as after the earthquake in Pakistan in 2005.

The Alliance's new operational structure is closely linked to the NRF. Operational command of the NRF has rotated among the three second-tier headquarters ever since the force obtained an initial operating capability late in 2002. Under the original NRF concept, NATO member countries commit land, air, navy, or special operations forces to the NRF for a one-year period. These forces first undergo a six-month joint training program, during which they are certified to a certain standard; afterward, they spend six months on "stand-by" as the NRF. The land component of the force is to be a brigade-sized unit (roughly 5,000 troops); the naval component is to comprise a carrier battle group, amphibious task group, and surface action group; the air component is to be capable of 200 combat sorties per day; and the special operations component is to be variable, depending on the mission at hand. The force is truly multinational: an NRF exercise in 2006, for example, included American F-16s, Turkish special forces, a Spanish aircraft carrier, a submarine, several frigates and troops from a dozen different NATO countries, for a total force of about 7,800 personnel.

Although the NRF was declared fully operational at the NATO Summit in Riga in 2006, it has faced challenges in maintaining the necessary force strength. Member nations have had to divert forces originally committed to the NRF to ongoing operations in Iraq, Afghanistan, Lebanon, and Kosovo. This reality prompted NATO defense ministers, at their informal meeting late in 2007, to examine the possibility of revising the NRF concept. The future NRF may consist of a core force on permanent standby which can then be augmented with additional forces, up to an overall size of 25,000 troops, in the event of a crisis.

The NATO Response Force is potentially an important operational tool for addressing crises in the contemporary security environment. But when it was introduced by Secretary Rumsfeld in 2002 it was also meant to be a practical force for transformation. As the different forces from the various NATO countries rotated through the NRF, they would be trained to high standards and be exposed to new concepts and technologies, thereby promoting military transformation. Moreover, the process would be continuous. From one perspective the NRF could be seen as a permanently ongoing NATO military training exercise that would be used to evaluate new concepts and capability improvements. "For NATO," argued NATO's former SACEUR in 2005, "the operational path for transformation lies in the emergence of the NRF."[7] The The difficulties in realizing the NRF vision could raise questions about its ability to act as a vehicle for promoting NATO transformation. But in some respects the missions themselves, to which the NRF forces have been diverted, have taken up this role. "There is a transformation element to the Afghanistan operation," the NATO spokesman has argued, "[it] is, in many ways, reflecting what the NRF was designed to promote."[8]

Technology and Capability Advancements

Beyond these significant organizational changes, NATO is making advances in other areas associated with the RMA core of military transformation. In order to enhance the deployability of its military forces, in 2003 NATO members reached agreement on a plan to pool military sealift capabilities. Under the terms of the agreement, which was the outcome of the strategic sealift group led by Norway after the Prague summit, the Alliance has assured access to a number of sealift vessels owned by NATO countries. For more rapid deployability, in early 2006 NATO reached agreement on the interim airlift solution that Germany was charged with leading. Under the terms of the contract, a Russian joint venture is to provide NATO with two An-124 Antonov air transporters on full-time charter, with two others on six days notice and two others on nine-days notice—far short of the "up to 20 C-17 or An-124 airlifters" originally foreseen as part of the interim solution.[9] This arrangement is meant to provide NATO with airlift until European countries begin to take delivery of the A400M airlifter early next decade. Yet there are two concerns. First, Russian officials from the joint venture have stated that it will only transport humanitarian cargo, and "If an airlift does not correspond with Russia's interests, it will not take place"[10]—potentially tying the hands of NATO forces for some types of missions. Second, it is arguable as to whether the A400M falls fully into the "strategic" airlift category, which is the NATO shortfall. As noted in Chapter 4, the aircraft is much smaller than the C-17 and indeed is being considered by some countries, like Australia, as a replacement for their C-130 Hercules tactical airlifters. These factors may be behind the decision, at Riga, to launch a Strategic Airlift Capability Initiative under which thirteen NATO members are negotiating the purchase of three or four C-17s to be based in Germany.

Other areas have seen less progress. At Prague, for example, allies agreed to increase their capability in the area of air-to-ground surveillance. The reference was to the Allied Ground Surveillance (AGS) program, which has been under way since the 1990s, and is meant to address the Alliance's capability shortfall in being able to monitor large tracks of land for movement, in any kind of weather, over an extended period of time. To date, NATO has had to rely on U.S. JSTARS aircraft to provide this capability during operations, and more recently on British ASTOR aircraft. Agreement among the lead countries involved—France, Germany, Italy, the Netherlands, Spain, and the United States—on the program has been held up by concerns over funding, what should comprise the AGS capability, and who should build the aircraft's Synthetic Aperture Radar. Originally the United States suggested the Alliance buy JSTARS aircraft but Germany, in particular, sees an unmanned future. As a result, the current program calls for a mixed platform solution, including four modified Airbus 321s, each carrying a multinational crew, and four or five Global Hawk UAVs. At the same time, France prefers a European-built radar, rather than an American one that could be subject to U.S. controls or constraints. In 2006 NATO released the request for proposals for the AGS's design and development phase but longstanding concerns have reemerged, making it unlikely the goal of having an Alliance AGS capability by 2010 will be achieved.

In other areas of C4ISR (command, control, communications, computing, intelligence, surveillance, and reconnaissance) NATO has had, since the late 1980s, a fleet of dedicated Airborne Early Warning and Control System (AWACS) aircraft for air-to-air surveillance. One of NATO's few commonly funded military systems, the AWACS have recently been upgraded through modernization programs. NATO also has common satellite communication capabilities for its forces. Under a program called Satcom Post-2000, in 2005 NATO concluded a fifteen-year agreement with the British, French, and Italian governments under which it will purchase UHF and SHF capacity from two each of British Skynet, French Syracuse, and Italian SICRAL satellites. The Satcom Post-2000 program also foresees NATO purchasing capacity in the EHF band in the future. For network-centric capability and interoperability among NATO military forces, the key system is the Multifunctional Information Distribution System (MIDS). Member countries have been incorporating MIDS, which is based on link-16 technology, into their fighters, bombers, and land, sea, and air command and control centers for several years.[11] In 2004–2005 NATO conducted a study to establish guidelines for a NATO Network Enabled Capability, while at Riga allies agreed they would continue work in this area.

European Initiatives

Since the late 1990s many European countries have been engaged in other efforts aimed at transforming their military forces. At their summit in Helsinki in December 1999, European Union leaders decided to create a European rapid reaction force of about 60,000 troops, deployable within 60 days and sustainable for up to a year. This objective, known as the Helsinki Headline Goal, was to be achieved by 2003. It was to be assisted by the "Berlin Plus" arrangements, agreed at the 1999 NATO Summit, under which the EU was given "assured access" to

NATO planning, and the "presumption of availability" of NATO assets for EU operations. To help move forward the Headline Goal, which within a couple years had lost momentum, in 2002 the EU launched a European Capabilities Action Plan (ECAP) to identify and evaluate capability shortfalls, and find possible solutions. The following year the ECAP moved into its next stage with the creation of ten project groups to recommend specific ways to fill capability gaps. Yet still capabilities did not appreciably increase and the Headline Goal itself was not met within the original time frame.

In late 2003 the EU provided overall strategic context to its military transformation efforts with the release of its first ever European Security Strategy, *A Secure Europe in a Better World.* The strategy calls on EU members "to transform our militaries into more flexible, mobile forces" as part of an overall strategic culture "that fosters early, rapid, and when necessary, robust intervention." The following year the EU agreed on the necessity of setting a new military transformation objective, known as Headline Goal 2010, since "the availability . . . of military assets will often play a crucial role at the beginning of a crisis, during its development and/or in the post conflict phase."[12] This goal adopts a different approach from its predecessor, calling for the creation of 1,500-person battlegroups consisting of a combined arms battalion, combat support and combat service support, and supported by the relevant air and naval assets. They are to be deployable within ten days of an EU decision to launch the operation.

By the end of 2004 national governments had committed to forming thirteen battlegroups, and in 2007 the EU decided to extend the rapid reaction battlegroup concept to Europe's air and naval forces. Meanwhile, work that was originally being done by the ECAP was transferred to the European Defense Agency (EDA), created in 2004 with the aim of determining the new capabilities required by the security strategy and promoting cooperation in the acquisition of defense equipment. Yet it remains unclear the degree to which the battlegroups are more than just paper capabilities. The forces train at the national level but are expected to operate in a multinational mission. In addition, the first call for the deployment of a battlegroup, to the Democratic Republic of the Congo, was marked by indecision as to which country's forces should man the first mission. And as for the Berlin Plus arrangements, this option has remained "virtually inert," with both France and Turkey, for different reasons, objecting to wider consultations between NATO and the EU on defense matters.[13]

Despite this, EU planning capabilities for military operations have moved forward. In 2003, at the height of transatlantic tensions over the Iraq war, a handful of EU countries had proposed the creation of an independent EU military planning capability, but the proposal faced concerns from other EU members about duplication with NATO capabilities. The issue was resolved later in the year with agreement to create an EU defense planning cell based at NATO's Supreme Headquarters Allied Powers Europe. But four years later, with fifteen military or civil security missions under its belt—albeit all modest in scale—the EU formally activated a new operations center in the EU military staff building that is specifically designed to carry out integrated civil-military operations.

The EU and NATO initiatives are similar in that they each seek to create military capabilities that can deploy rapidly to crisis areas outside Europe. But they are implicitly distinct in that by tacit agreement, NATO focuses on high-intensity counterterrorist and combat operations, while the European Union focuses on lower-intensity peacekeeping and post-conflict reconstruction. Although this is probably a useful division of labor, it also creates resource and doctrinal challenges for those countries that are members of both NATO and the European Union since each has only one military force, and that same force is being called upon to contribute to both organizations and both types of missions.

Capability Shortfalls and Strengths

Notwithstanding the changes that have taken place within NATO, and the efforts within the EU over the past several years, there remains a large technology and capability gap between the U.S. military and those of America's allies. The technology gap was illustrated in dramatic fashion during the Kosovo operation, when the vast majority of command and control, ISR, and standoff precision force assets were American. This led to their inclusion in the Prague Capabilities Commitment. Yet, in addition to continuing delays in the AGS (an ISR system), the Alliance continues to have critical shortfalls in both PGMs and sophisticated command and control systems.[14]

At the same time, experts estimate that the vast majority of NATO's European forces—perhaps 95 percent—are still not "expeditionary deployable."[15] This is partly to due to limited strategic lift, but it is also a result of force structure, equipment, and in some cases the continuation of conscription. At the NATO summit in Istanbul in 2004 Alliance defense ministers agreed that 40 percent of their nation's land forces should be structured, prepared, and equipped for deployed operations, and that 8 percent should either be engaged in or earmarked for sustained operations at any one time. This undertaking has been implemented to varying degrees in NATO countries, and an assessment of its success depends in part on whether allied countries count reserves or conscripts in their total usable forces.[16] In addition, the NATO response force will go some way to reducing the capability gap among allies. But the NRF represents, after all, only a very small portion of the close to two million people NATO's European members have under arms.

One RMA-related area where the Alliance excels is in maritime interdiction operations. Since soon after the 9/11 attacks NATO has been carrying out Operation Active Endeavor in the Mediterranean Sea, NATO's only Article V mission. Like the American-led Proliferation Security Initiative, begun by the United States in 2003 and possessing a global mandate, Active Endeavor's primary mission is to counterterrorism and the proliferation of weapons of mass destruction (WMD) by stopping ships suspected of carrying terrorists and/or WMD and their delivery systems. Its original mandate pertained to the eastern Mediterranean and the Strait of Gibraltar, but in 2004 it was widened to include the entire Mediterranean. In future the operation could also be extended to include the Black Sea, seen to be a potential channel for terrorist activity from the Caucasus.

Addressing the Technology and Capability Gap

A number of factors can explain the capability and technology gap between America and its allies. They include: the far larger defense budget on the part of the United States; a U.S. defense budget that has increased over the past decade whereas many European defense budgets have remained the same or declined; the fact that the United States spends a much greater proportion of its defense budget on research and development and on capital acquisitions, as opposed to spending on personnel; a hesitancy on the part of the United States to share technology with its European allies; and, greater economies of scale in the United States for the development and acquisition of military systems. Despite the EDA's creation, many European countries prefer to maintain a national defense industry and therefore are operating on the basis of a smaller population. Perhaps one of the most intractable factors is the aging European population. The resultant need to allocate increasing resources to social welfare programs is likely to have an impact on future defense budgets. "If the defense spending picture is sobering in the present," notes one study on NATO military capabilities, "it is likely to become truly daunting in the future given projected demographic trends in Europe."[17]

Many of the factors behind the technology and capability gap between America and its allies could be ameliorated, if there were the political will. One approach may be for a greater integration in European military research and procurement so as to overcome the economies of scale issue. Or, many have suggested over the years that smaller European countries should develop "niche" capabilities; that is to say, that they should specialize in a particular area of expertise in order to enable them to make a "high value contribution to collective security"[18] This idea, to certain degree, formed the basis of the Prague Capabilities Commitment. Still another approach would be for the United States to promote interoperability through information sharing and technology transfer—things that can be applied to existing European platforms.[19]

A focus on interoperability through compatible technology would best be the number one military transformation priority of NATO members. The connectivity of alliance forces became a major issue in the mid and late 1990s, especially in the war in and around Kosovo, and was a factor in America's decision, in the wake of 9/11, not to request alliance assistance in the 2001–2002 war in Afghanistan even though NATO had invoked Article V. Since then, many NATO countries have integrated or are in the process of integrating compatible technology, notably the link 16 tactical datalink, into their navy, air force, and even land forces (see Chapter 4). As a result the technological gap is likely to narrow during a certain window of time, but this will widen again as the United States invests in and implements link 22. Thus while it is important for alliance members to acquire new and more capable platforms, when allocating competing resources the emphasis may best be placed on ameliorating the technology component of the technology and capability gap.

Changes Associated with "Transforming Transformation"

NATO is adjusting to the "transforming transformation" demands of the "how we fight" component of military transformation. The Alliance has no common counterinsurgency doctrine per se, although new counterinsurgency field manuals developed by countries such as the United States, Britain, and Canada will no doubt be highly compatible. But NATO is attempting to enhance, as an organization, its special operations capacity. At the Riga summit the Alliance launched a special operations forces transformation initiative aimed at increasing joint training, joint doctrine development, and interoperability among the special operations forces of NATO countries.

Driven by its practical experience in Afghanistan, NATO's most significant "transforming transformation" advancement is in the area of stabilization and reconstruction. Following the post-9/11 high-intensity battle in Afghanistan, the UN-authorized and British-led International Security Assistance Force (ISAF) deployed to Kabul in early 2002 to carry out stabilization and reconstruction operations in and around the city. Later that year, as a result of ISAF's relative success, the United States developed the concept of provincial reconstruction teams (PRTs) to spread the "ISAF effect" to other areas of the country, without expanding ISAF itself.[20] In the summer of 2003 NATO took over responsibility for ISAF. Recognizing the utility of the PRTs, it began to take on responsibility for some of the existing teams and also to establish new ones, thereby significantly expanding the mandate and presence of ISAF. From the handful of PRTs deployed in early 2003 under the authority of Operation Enduring Freedom, the PRT presence in Afghanistan has expanded to some twenty-five PRTs under NATO command throughout the north, west, south, and east of the country.

Provincial reconstruction teams average about 250 strong and consist of a mix of military and civilian personnel. Although the operation and focus of each team is unique, generally speaking the military forces within a PRT provide security so that aid workers and non-governmental organizations can undertake reconstruction work. In practice this has meant that PRTs have been engaged in a range of tasks, from election support and building schools, to disarmament and mediating factional conflicts. Moreover, key to providing a secure environment is government institution building and, especially, security sector reform with respect to the police, army, and judiciary; as a result, this has been a major area of emphasis on the part of NATO and coalition military forces. The overall objective of the PRT concept is to gradually extend the reach of the Afghan central government, thereby promoting stability and development across the country. Their success will ultimately be tied to the overall success of the ISAF mission, the outcome of which is far from certain.

Wider Aspects of Transformation

For the first forty years of its existence NATO was a collective defense organization designed, like NORAD, to look outward at threats that might impinge on its members' borders. After 9/11, as noted in Chapter 3, NORAD's mandate was changed so that in addition to looking outward, it also looks inward at airborne threats to the continent. In addition, both Canada and the United States responded to the post-9/11 security environment by developing new military organizations—NORTHCOM and Canada Command—to provide military support to civilian-led homeland security missions. A similar conceptual transformation whereby NATO may play a supporting role to civilian, EU-led operations on European territory has not yet taken place.

The European Union's own security strategy of December 2003 is externally oriented and was criticized, in the wake of the terrorist bombings in Madrid in 2004 and London in 2005, for not taking into account domestic threats to Europe's security.[21] The bombings have prompted the EU to set a number of homeland security goals and undertake several associated initiatives. These center on things like developing new civil emergency networks; protecting critical infrastructure, including ports and harbors; coordinating coastal surveillance procedures; and greater intelligence sharing between national police, judiciaries, customs and immigration officials, and intelligence agencies. However, these have not been brought together into a collective homeland security policy, and the security strategy itself has not yet been modified.

More significantly from a transformation perspective, the military role or contribution is largely absent. NATO's radars monitor Europe's skies for civilian or military intruders and in the past its jets have been scrambled on the orders of local officials. NATO has no authority to shoot down hijacked airliners—this would have to come from the country over whose airspace the aircraft are flying. The Alliance has also supplied AWACS to patrol the skies at numerous high-profile events since 9/11, including the 2004 summer Olympics in Athens. But these activities in the air dimension mark, in essence, the limits of NATO's role in Europe's homeland security. Parliamentarians from both organizations have called for closer EU-NATO consultation on a wide range of homeland security issues—from protection of critical infrastructure, to emergency response planning, to sharing of intelligence.[22]

One area where NATO expertise may be especially useful is in the consequence management of a crisis involving weapons of mass destruction. As part of its military transformation efforts, and in response to a capability gap identified in the Prague Capabilities Commitment, in 2003 NATO created a chemical, biological, radiological, and nuclear defense (CBRN) battalion designed to carry out nuclear, biological and chemical reconnaissance, decontamination, and biological detection and monitoring operations. Capable of reacting within five days to crises around the world and thus presumably within hours to a crisis within Europe, the CBRN battalion is now part of the NATO Response Force. In addition, the alliance has already established a biological and chemical weapons stockpile, a virtual "center of excellence" for NBC weapons defense, and a disease surveillance system.[23]

Beyond this, NATO could take the lead in a future ballistic missile defense system covering the territory of Alliance members. For decades NATO made a distinction between Theater Missile Defenses (TMD) to protect deployed NATO forces against short and medium-range ballistic missiles, and National Missile Defenses to protect the territory of Alliance members against strategic ballistic missiles. National missile defenses were considered destabilizing because strategic stability, it was felt, depended on the mutual vulnerability of Soviet and Alliance territory and populations. This conceptual framework was codified in the Anti-Ballistic Missile (ABM) Treaty of 1972, which limited the United States and the Soviet Union to only one ballistic missile defense site apiece. Theater missile defenses, by contrast, were not considered as something that would upset the strategic balance. As a result, NATO members have readily participated in TMD systems. The United States, Germany, and Italy are developing the Medium Extended Air Defense System (MEADS), a mobile, deployable missile defense system capable of countering tactical ballistic missiles and air-breathing threats like cruise missiles. At the same time, NATO is seeking to deploy, with an initial operating capability by 2010, a "layered" TMD system—meaning that it will target missiles in different phases of flight, including terminal and possibly mid-course—to protect its deployed forces. The system seeks to integrate the various theater missile defenses that alliance members already have or are developing, including MEADS and Patriot missiles held by Greece, Spain, the Netherlands, and Germany.

Europe's stance against national missile defenses, most often referred to simply as ballistic missile defense (BMD), began to change in 2002 after the United States withdrew from the ABM Treaty. Russia seemingly accepted the treaty's demise, lending less weight to the "strategic vulnerability" argument. Moreover, new threats were starting to emerge, particularly from the Middle East, which could place European cities at jeopardy. The 9/11 attacks, too, weighed in since although a missile defense system would not have prevented the attacks, they nonetheless demonstrated the fallibility of deterrence based on threats of retaliation, and the willingness of fanatical adversaries to strike civilian targets such as cities.[24] The combination of all these factors meant that at Prague in 2002 the allies agreed to "initiate a new NATO Missile Defense feasibility study to examine options for protecting Alliance territory, forces and population centers against the full range of missile threats." The study, delivered to Alliance leaders in the spring of 2006, concluded that a BMD system comprised of ground and space based sensors, and ground based interceptors that targeted missiles in their mid-course phase—not unlike the present American system—was technically and financially feasible.

More problematic are the political and military implications of a NATO BMD system. America's decision to seek a missile interceptor site in Poland and a tracking radar site in the Czech Republic as part of its own BMD system (see Chapter 3), has provoked Russian protests that the system is directed not at Middle Eastern rogue states but rather at the former superpower. The United States has sought to assuage Russian concerns, proposing cooperation on missile defense by sharing information and co-locating radar systems, and suggesting that Russia regularly inspect the radar and interceptor base. Nonetheless, with Russia threatening to withdraw from the 1990 Conventional Forces in Europe treaty, it is becoming clear that the demise of the ABM treaty was not as much of a non-issue as was originally believed. At the Riga summit Alliance leaders decided to continue to study the political and military implications of ballistic missile defense, including an update on missile threat developments and an assessment of the implications of America's BMD system for the Alliance, and this work is ongoing.

An aspect of the wider dimension of military transformation where Europe is struggling to move forward is military space policy. In 2004 the European Union and the European Space Agency agreed to define a common space strategy, and to determine how space should fit into the EU's future security policy. Although mainly geared toward commercial purposes, the strategy also has military implications for national governments. The difficulty in finding a common view delayed the release of an EU space strategy until 2007. The strategy itself says relatively little on the subject, stating only that "Space based situation awareness and reaction will play a substantial role" in European security policy, and that "space assets could contribute both to making the EU more capable in the field of crisis management and to fighting other security threats."

Meanwhile, progress in the EU's two most prominent space programs, each with notable military applications, has been slow. The first, Galileo, is a global network of navigation satellites, similar to America's GPS, that is to comprise thirty satellites. The United States has been strongly opposed to the project out of concern that its frequencies could overlap with those of the GPS during a military crisis, but these concerns have essentially been resolved. It has been much more difficult to overcome political differences among the various EU countries over costs and funding, with the result being that while the system was supposed to be fully deployed by 2010, now the most optimistic date is 2014. Questions have been raised as to whether the political consensus exists to complete the system.

The EU's second significant space project is to create an Earth observation capability called Global Monitoring for Environment and Security. In addition to its environmental and commercial applications, the project is intended to provide earth observation capacity for EU military operations, including monitoring civil conflicts, refugee camps, and arms control treaty violations, and other security-related activities. This project, too, has become bogged down in issues of funding and political control; its thirty satellites are also projected to be in place by 2014.

Conclusion

NATO's military transformation is inextricably linked to a broader process of political transformation that began at the end of the Cold War. From an organization founded on collective defense and the view that none of its weapons would ever be used except in self-defense, NATO has undergone a conceptual transformation that sees the Alliance addressing threats as far away from its borders as possible and in the context of missions that are not strictly self-defense. The Alliance's transformation initiatives have reflected this expeditionary mindset, focusing especially on the RMA component of "how we fight." More recently they have also accommodated the new demands of "transforming transformation," and to certain degree the wider military transformation requirements of integrating security abroad with security at home. But with the exception of a few areas, notably those associated with dramatic organizational changes, the initiatives have not been translated into significant advancements in capability. This will begin to change in the coming years as long-planned programs and new initiatives reach the stage where platforms and technologies are deployed. NATO's future challenge will be to fulfill its (well-stated) transformation goals, and to tackle those areas where it has not yet taken even the initial steps.

Notes

1. Final Communiqué of the Ministerial Meeting of the North Atlantic Council, Oslo, June 4, 1992, paragraph 11 and Final Communiqué of the Ministerial Meeting of the North Atlantic Council, Brussels, 17 December 1992, paragraph 4.

2. This is the essence of paragraph 35 of the 1991 Alliance Strategic Concept.

3. Final Communiqué of the Ministerial Meeting of the North Atlantic Council, Reykjavik, May 14, 2002, paragraph 5.

4. Tyce Velde, "ACT Strives to Apply Transformation Through CMF," *The Transformer* 2(3) (October 2006), 3.

5. Rita Boland, "NATO Undergoes Massive Transformation," *Signal* (February 2006), 56.

6. "NATO Response Force Declared Fully Operational," http://www.nato.int, accessed on November 30, 2006.

7. James Jones, "NATO Transformation and Challenges," *RUSI Journal* (April 2005). 16.

8. James Appathurai as quoted in Tom Kington, "As NATO Eyes Cuts to Reaction Force, Doubts Grow About Mission," *Defense News* (October 8, 2007), 20.

9. Nicholas Fiorenza, "NATO to Adopt Capabilities Plan," *Defense News* (November 18–24, 2002), 7.

10. A high-ranking company official as quoted in Nabi Abdullaev, "NATO Inaugurates Long-Range Airlift Charter," *Defense News* (April 3, 2006), 44.

11. Gordon Adams, Guy Ben-Ari, John Logsdon, and Ray Williamson, *Bridging the Gap: European C4ISR Capabilities and Transatlantic Interoperability* (Washington, DC: The George Washington University, 2004), p. 89.

12. Headline Goal 2010, endorsed by the European Council on June 17 and 18, 2004.

13. France because it favors a stronger Europe-only role in European security; Turkey because it is a NATO member that aspires to EU membership, but has not yet been able to obtain it. See Brooks Tigner, "Teaming to Secure Europe," *Defense News* (March 5, 2007), 28.

14. The United States is already moving beyond Link 16 to Link 22.

15. Michele A. Flourney and Julianne Smith, *European Defense Integration: Bridging the Gap Between Strategy and Capabilities* (Washington, DC: Center for Strategic and Budgetary Analysis, October 2005), p. 19.

16. Nicholas Fiorenza, "NATO Members Claim to Meet Troop Deployability Goals," *Defense News* (May 23, 2005), 16.

17. Flourney and Smith, *European Defense Integration: Bridging the Gap Between Strategy and Capabilities*, p. 23.

18. Ibid., p. 9.

19. Jeffrey Bialos and Stuart Koehl, *The NATO Response Force: Facilitating Coalition Warfare Through Technology Transfers* (Washington, DC: Johns Hopkins University, September 2005), vii.

20. Michael J. McNerney, "Stabilization and Reconstruction in Afghanistan: Are PRTs a Model or a Muddle?" *Parameters* (Winter 2005–06), 32.

21. Brooks Tigner, "Policies Diverge: EU, NATO Struggle to Find Common Ground on International Security Roles," *Defense News* (November 20, 2006), 28.

22. Tigner, "Teaming to Secure Europe," 28.

23. Jonathan Stevenson, "How Europe and America Defend Themselves," *Foreign Affairs* 82(2) (March/April 2003).

24. David S. Yost, "The U.S. Nuclear Posture Review and the NATO Allies," *International Affairs* 80(4) (2004), 720.

CHAPTER 6

Military Transformation in China

Military transformation in China is driven by the dual forces of meeting the challenges of the contemporary security environment and responding to the military transformation efforts of the Western world. For the latter China is responding primarily with elements consistent with wider perspectives on transformation, notably the notion of unhindered access to space and new thinking about defense and deterrence. For the former the comparative point—as was the case in discussing Western military transformation—is Cold War versus post–Cold War circumstances and the response (again, in line with the Western experience) has been elements that are consistent with the revolution in military affairs part of transformation. The middle layer of military transformation—the "transforming transformation" parts of "how we fight"—is largely absent in Chinese initiatives, with the exception of an increased emphasis on SOFs. But this could change if China emerges as a responsible player on the international stage.

This chapter examines military transformation in China in all of its Revolution in Military Affairs (RMA), transforming transformation, and wider dimensions. It begins by highlighting China's changed strategic situation today as compared to during the Cold War, which forms the backdrop to military force initiatives—a continuum that, in contrast to the Western experience, is largely unaffected by the 9/11, 2001 terrorist attacks. It then draws out concrete examples, is so far as is possible given China's close guarding of information, of changes that are consistent with the RMA, and also highlights the few developments that are line with transforming transformation. Finally, the chapter examines China's response to military transformation in the West—ideas that can be seen in the context of wider perspectives on military transformation.

The Strategic Context

China's strategic situation has changed significantly in the past fifteen years. During the Cold War its major military threat was a land based, border war against one of the fourteen nations with which it shares a land border. The most notable threat was posed by the Soviet Union, but there were also other potential flashpoints. The requirement was for a large ground force to repel any possible incursions. But in the post–Cold War era China has resolved almost all of its border disputes and its relations with Russia are much better than they have been historically. In the spring of 2001 China and Russia signed a twenty-year treaty of "friendship and cooperation," and shortly thereafter China, Russia, and a handful of Central Asian countries created the Shanghai Cooperation Organization to coordinate antiterrorist measures. In the context of this organization, these countries have conducted combined military exercises, including a joint exercise with Russia in the summer of 2007 that took place in Russia and China and was designed to demonstrate China's ability to project power over land in Asia.

Declining imperatives to maintain a large, in-place, army-dominated military force coincided with incentives to look outward, first to Taiwan and then beyond. Unresolved since 1949, the Taiwan issue took on a new character in the mid-1990s with its leaders' rejection of the "one China" principle and rhetorical emphasis on moving toward separation. Since that time, China has been preparing for military action in order to prevent separation, and Beijing acknowledges that its military modernization is partly driven by the desire to deter Taiwan's independence and promote reunification.

Meanwhile, in the almost two decades since the end of the Cold War China has undergone an economic surge that has both tied its economy to a globalized world, and driven a domestic demand for imported energy. A report by the Chinese Academy of Social Sciences has argued that since much of China's economic growth has been along its coasts, China now has long-range maritime interests and is in the process of transitioning from a continental land power to a sea power.[1] At the same time, the demand for energy and especially oil is generating an outward focus on energy security and a need, for example, to protect the flow of oil from the Arabian Gulf through the Strait of Malacca. The safeguarding of strategic straits in Southeast Asia and the South China Sea has, as a result, become an emerging mission for the PLA Navy (PLAN). "With China increasingly reliant on Africa, the Middle East and South America for the resources to fuel the world's fastest-growing economy," notes one report, "the need for a military that can fight far from its borders is becoming apparent."[2]

Changes Associated with the Revolution in Military Affairs

For the Chinese leadership the wars that the West has fought over the past two decades provide a window on future war. China was profoundly influenced by the nature of the 1991 Gulf War, prompting the PLA leadership to replace its previous guiding doctrine of "people's war under modern conditions," which implied a war of attrition on the heartland, with a new doctrine of "fighting a limited war under high-tech conditions."[3] The 1999 war in Kosovo further illustrated the value of standoff precision strike, while the wars in Afghanistan and Iraq—also studied closely by China—underscored the imperative of small elite forces linked together by advanced C4ISR systems. China's 2006 Defense White Paper, like the previous four released since the mid-1990s, is not transparent by Western standards. Nonetheless, it is illuminating in that it highlights China's overall strategic goal of building a digitized military capable of winning high-tech modern wars by 2050.

Mobile and Deployable Ground Forces

China's new strategic situation, perspective, and goal are having a significant impact on how it structures and equips its military forces. As recently as the early 1990s, the People's Liberation Army (PLA) was a defensive force equipped with largely obsolete platforms. Today, by contrast, the PLA "is pursuing a comprehensive transformation from a mass army designed for protracted wars of attrition on its territory to one capable of fighting and winning short-duration, high-intensity conflicts against high-tech adversaries."[4] Facilitated by sustained and significant defense budget increases, China is in the process of transforming the PLA into the sort of mobile, agile, and flexible military force that is central to the RMA.

The PLA is undertaking many changes that are consistent with RMA organizational trends and central to enabling force deployability. They include reducing overall force size, increasing education levels, professionalizing the force, and developing smaller, more mobile units. Just as France and Germany, with large Cold War conscript armies, reduced their military force sizes in the post–Cold War era, so too is China reducing the size of its army. At the height of the Cold War in the 1950s the PLA, including the army, navy, and air force, numbered some five million soldiers. By the end of the 1990s China had cut this figure in half, and in 2003 it announced further reductions of 200,000 over two years, bringing the PLA's size down to 2.3 million personnel. The majority of the reductions came in the army, historically a much larger force than either the navy or air force. As the PLA has shifted its perspective outward, the navy and air force have necessarily grown larger in proportion to the total force. Even with the reductions, however, the army remains by far the largest component of the PLA.

The idea behind a reduced force size, former Chinese President Jiang Zemin has stressed, is to allow a greater amount of resources to be devoted to acquiring advanced technology and developing a better-educated military force.[5] Advanced technology is central to a process the military leadership calls "informationization", meaning a greater reliance on information and data sharing for operations, and trading mass for quality.[6] The notion of a better-educated military force, too, is key to an advanced military force. Indeed, the Pentagon has emphasized that "Beijing's emphasis on Western-style training, military education and doctrine . . . can strengthen military capability more than equipment alone."[7]

That said China faces many challenges in this area. Experts note that the majority of PLA soldiers come from the countryside where basic education is inadequate, and that if China is to have a high-tech army in the future, it must greatly expand high school and four year college equivalent education.[8] In addition, while some 90 percent of officers have advanced degrees, the vast majority of these are not in the sciences or technology, a fact that hinders the development of a high-tech army. Part of the problem is that military pay is much lower than what those who are trained in technological areas can earn in the booming Chinese economy. Not surprisingly, a significant portion of China's 2007 defense budget is devoted to increasing salaries. But the issue is also wider and institutional. Not only does the PLA lack IT-trained officers and soldiers, but it also lacks IT-based education and training facilities, and IT-based curriculum in its military institutions. The PLA is responding to these challenges by investing heavily in educating those who are to operate sophisticated weapons systems, upgrading the military education system, and tightening recruitment standards to make sure the new generation of PLA leaders is intellectually suited to a career in a high-technology military force. In 2007 Chinese President Hu Jintao announced new measures to attract and retain high-tech talent for the military, including a recruitment drive for technology specialists, increased pay for such recruits, and extra training for them in top Chinese universities.

In line with RMA organizational trends, China is in the process of professionalizing its military forces. The PLA went from more than 80 percent conscript in the early 1990s to less than 65 percent conscript by 2000, and by the middle of the first decade of the twenty-first century had set a goal of instituting force-wide professionalization. As part of this process, the PLA is also developing a corps of volunteer Non-Commissioned Officers, something that the PLA has not had previously.

Finally, China is taking steps to restructure its ground force units into those that are smaller and more mobile and therefore more expeditionary or deployable. Previously the main force units were corps-sized group armies of some 60,000 troops divided into divisions, but since the late 1990s many group armies have been disbanded while those remaining have lost divisions. More importantly in expeditionary terms is that China also began to create brigades as an organizational unit. Intended to make PLA combat units "more rapidly deployable and flexible," Chinese brigades are estimated by experts to be only about one third to one half the size of Chinese divisions.[9] A large number of divisions and regiments have been downgraded to brigades and also to battalions, a still smaller organizational unit.

From about the mid-1980s onward China also began to create what it calls "rapid reaction units," ready to mobilize in twenty-four to forty-eight hours. But these rapid reaction units cannot be compared to North Atlantic Treaty Organization (NATO) or European Union (EU) rapid reaction forces, which are conceived as forces that can deploy anywhere around the world. Rather, according to the Pentagon's 2000 Report to Congress on the Military Power of the People's Republic of China, the approximately fourteen PLA ground force divisions that were designated in the late 1990s as "rapid reaction" units were "combined arms units capable of deploying by road or rail within China without significant train-up or reserve augmentation."[10] More recently, early post-9/11 evidence indicated that the PLA had designated seven group armies, an airborne corps, and two marine brigades as rapid reaction units. When added up, this would be a tremendous figure for numbers of rapid reaction troops—about 370,000 by rough calculation. Yet this is broadly consistent with the Chinese leaderships' statement that 15 percent of its 2.3 million force (or 345,000 personnel) had been selected as an elite force "capable of taking the fight to the enemy."[11] The Pentagon's 2007 report to Congress on China's military states the PLA is improving its ability to carry out expeditionary operations and it includes as PLA expeditionary forces three airborne divisions, two amphibious infantry divisions, two marine brigades, about seven special operations groups, and a regimental size reconnaissance component of the Second Artillery. This would indicate a smaller yet still very substantial rapid reaction force of about 100,000 personnel.

Part of the expeditionary equation is to equip ground forces with more deployable equipment, armed with precision munitions, and therefore requiring less ammunition (and therefore less weight to deploy). China continues to mass-produce upgraded main battle tanks, the new T-99, but it is also producing a family of eight-wheel-drive medium-weight armored vehicles similar to America's Stryker.[12] It is developing self-propelled artillery and howitzers that have been modified for airdrop and rapid deployment missions, and fielding precision-guided artillery, including the A-100 and WS-2 multiple rocket launcher. For battlefield mobility China continues to import Russian-built Mi-17 troop lift helicopters, and it is indigenously producing its first dedicated attack helicopter, the Z-10. The Pentagon's 2007 report to Congress on China's military notes that this helicopter will fire an antitank guided missile and will have a combat performance "equal to the Eurocopter Tiger, but below that of the AH-64 Apache."

But an expeditionary capability depends on much more than smaller, more professional units made up of high quality troops and more deployable equipment. There is also a basic requirement for certain types of platforms, notably strategic air- and sealift. For the former, China has a handful of Ukrainian Antonov An-12 Cub transporters, comparable to the Hercules or A400M in terms of range and capacity, as well as about a dozen heavy transporters, the Russian Ilyushin Il-76, comparable in range and capacity to the C-17 and dating from the 1990s. China is now trying to create an indigenous capability to design and build a fleet of large cargo transporters to enable power projection missions.

For sealift and power projection from the sea onto land China is focusing on amphibious capabilities. The 2007 Military Balance indicates that China has about seventy-five landing ships, with medium landing ships making up about two-thirds of this figure and tank landing ships comprising the rest. China is increasing its amphibious ship production, adding more tank landing ships to its inventory. It is also modernizing its Type 63 amphibious armored personnel carrier and its Type 63A light amphibious tank. Beyond this, China signed a contract in 2007 for six Russian built air-cushion landing craft designed to disembark amphibious forces, including medium battle tanks. It is thought that in a Taiwan scenario the PLA would likely use the hovercraft to transport special forces across the Taiwan Strait as part of initial amphibious operations.[13] But China currently lacks large amphibious ships. Its vessels are relatively small, with only one capable of transporting as many as 500 troops and all having a capacity of ten or fewer tanks. Generally speaking, the PLAN's older amphibious warfare assets are considered ill suited for operations beyond coastal waters.[14] U.S. intelligence estimates that even with the new ship construction, China will still have lift deficiencies.[15]

China's overall ground force vision is to transition from a continental military requiring large ground forces for "in-depth" defense, to that of a "smaller, more flexible, highly trained and well-equipped ground force centered on rapid reaction units,"[16] that is to say, an RMA ground force. But its limited airlift and sealift capabilities make it difficult for China to deploy heavily armed units beyond its borders. As a result, even though rapid reaction force group armies are becoming the elite units of the PLA ground force, experts predict homeland defense rather than force projection is likely to remain their primary mission until at least the middle of the coming decade.[17]

SOFs

Integral to the modernization of PLA ground forces is a focus on enhancing special operations forces. In the 1990s, each of China's seven military regions created a special operations unit comprising about 900 personnel each, and these units are given priority over regular infantry units to train with the helicopters in each military region.[18] The Pentagon's 2003 report to Congress on China's military highlights the emphasis China is placing on special operations forces (SOFs) and identifies a number of possible roles including locating or destroying C4I assets, capturing or destroying airfields and ports, or destroying air defense assets. More recently the emphasis is on the lessons China has learned, by assessing U.S.-led military interventions, about the value of ground force SOFs working jointly with other services.

Jointness

This points to a further area of the RMA component of military transformation—increased jointness. Traditionally, the PLA Army focused on the ability of different units within the army—artillery, armored, infantry, etc.—to work together. There was little interaction with the "specialized" services, meaning the air force, navy, and missile force. Moreover, the overall level of China's military technology prevented anything akin to close air support of ground forces. But coalition operations in the 1991 Gulf War prompted the PLA leadership to broaden its thinking. In the mid-1990s the PLA started to emphasize "mobile joint operations" as being a likely form of engagement.[19] The specialized services were directed to develop the necessary doctrine and technology to enable joint operations with the army, including more precise standoff force. Since that time, combined air-to-ground operations have gained prominence and have been the focus of military training. Over the past several years the PLA has conducted a number of exercises specially designed to enhance China's joint warfare capabilities. Yet although China has shown significant improvements in joint operations, obstacles to organizational cooperation remain. All things being equal, note some China experts, "responses to U.S. military transformation that require less interservice, interagency, and civil-military cooperation would be easier [for China] to adopt."[20]

Standoff Precision Force

China's 2006 defense white paper stresses that the PLA Air Force (PLAAF) "aims at speeding up its transition from territorial air defense to both offensive and defensive operations," and in particular increasing its capabilities in the area of strike operations.[21] Its current and projected standoff precision force capabilities center on advanced fighter aircraft equipped with precision munitions, land attack cruise missiles, what may be described as "precision" short-range ballistic missiles, and possibly unmanned combat aerial vehicles.

With more than 2,000 combat aircraft in the PLAAF and PLAN, including a mix of air-to-air and air-to-ground strike aircraft, China would seem to have a formidable standoff precision force capability. Yet, as one analyst put it, most of these aircraft "are better suited to museum displays than to the front line."[22] Only about 300 are third and fourth generation fighters armed with sophisticated munitions. These include the fourth-generation Russian built Su-27 heavy tactical fighter and Su-30 multi-role strike platform, which the Pentagon's 2006 report to Congress on China's military indicates will be armed with precision strike munitions. In addition, China may buy a naval strike version of the Su-30. China also has a new indigenously developed fighter, the J-10, which is now in operational service with the air force. The 2007 Military Balance indicates China has about sixty J-10s, but the Pentagon expects a final production run of about 1,200 aircraft. To enhance the precision strike capability of its fighter/interceptors China has reportedly developed a strap-on guidance kit for gravity bombs akin to America's Global Positioning System (GPS)-guided JDAM. At the same time, the PLAAF is seeking to increase the long-range power projection capabilities of the Su-30 and J-10 with in-flight refueling tankers. It has acquired eight Il-78 Midas tankers and is developing an indigenous B-6U refueling aircraft. But questions remain as to whether the PLAAF has mastered the complicated in-flight refueling techniques to a degree that this capability can be considered operational.[23]

A further area of focus for China in regards to standoff precision force is land attack cruise missiles (LACM). China has recently begun to deploy its DH-10, a land attack cruise missile with the approximate performance and tactical flexibility of America's Tomahawk cruise missile. The DH-10 has a reported range of about 1,500 kilometers. Already deployed in its ground launched variant, it is expected this LACM will also eventually be fielded in submarine, ship, and air-launched versions. It is likely, for example, the missile will be launched by the PLAN's new Type 093 nuclear powered attack submarine. Some reports also indicate China may be developing a strategic standoff land attack capability using an upgraded version of its H-6 bomber—although even an upgraded H-6 is considered obsolete by Western standards, and China is not manufacturing any new long-range bombers.[24]

China's standoff precision force capability includes what may be considered "precision" ballistic missiles. It already has close to 1,000 short-range ballistic missiles deployed opposite Taiwan, and it has an intercontinental ballistic missile force for deterrence, but recently it has begun fielding the world's first anti-ship ballistic missile. This is a medium range (about 2,500 kilometers) ballistic missile, the Dong Feng 21, which has been deployed for many years but is to be fitted with an infrared guidance system that allows it to strike surface ships at sea, notably aircraft carriers. In addition, China has improved the accuracy of its short-range tactical surface-to-surface missile (SSM), the P12, using satellite-guided technology. With SSMs guided by GPS or by Russia's Global Navigation Satellite System (GLONASS), argues one analyst, "Taiwan now faces precise ballistic missile threats."[25] Generally speaking, China is seeking to integrate GPS and Glonass guidance technology, and also that of its own indigenous Beidou system, into most or all of its new fighters, helicopters, and cruise missiles.

Beyond this, China may be pursuing technologies for unmanned combat aerial vehicles (UCAVs). America's 2005 report to Congress on China's military indicated the PLAAF could convert retired fighter aircraft into UCAVs, but more recent reports are silent on this possibility. China chose a late 2006 airshow to unveil a concept for a supersonic, stealthy unmanned combat aerial vehicle with a primary air-to-air mission. Meanwhile, China continues to deploy its Harpy UAVs which, designed to detect, target, and destroy an enemy's radar sites, are more properly categorized as a UCAV.

C4ISR

To locate targets for precision strike, China is pursuing improved intelligence, surveillance, and reconnaissance capabilities through unmanned aerial vehicles (UAVs), satellites, and more "informationalized" SOFs.[26] For the latter, the Pentagon foresees such forces as providing targeting coordinates for standoff precision strike assets, much as U.S. and allied SOF called in precision force in the war in Afghanistan in 2001–2002. China's UAV assets include tactical drones for battlefield reconnaissance that it has deployed for some years, as well as a long-range air launched reconnaissance drone, the Chang Hong. But the Pentagon's 2003 report to Congress on China's military indicates this UAV does not have capabilities comparable to American long-range drones, like the Predator for example, in that the Chang Hong cannot provide real time information back to the operator (much less to a platform, like a fighter). For the future, China is looking to develop a UAV that will be able to provide continual surveillance beyond the country's coastal waters.

China is placing a major emphasis on space-based surveillance and reconnaissance capabilities. Under the China-Brazil Earth Resources Satellite (CBERS) program China began launching earth-imaging satellites in 1999. CBERS-1 and CBERS-2 can provide satellite imagery with twenty-meter resolution to earth stations. This is far less detailed than the growing Western "standard" of one-meter resolution (for example of Canada's RADARSAT, or Germany's SAR Lupe), but follow-on satellites are expected to have greater resolution. China is also developing an indigenous GPS-like system, the Beidou Satellite Navigation and Positioning System, with the first five satellites of this thirty-five-satellite constellation already deployed. This combination of satellite programs will improve the accuracy of China's ballistic and cruise missiles by providing both terrain mapping and satellite navigation.

Airborne Warning and Control System (AWACS) aircraft figure centrally in the command and control aspect of China's C4ISR capability. China introduced an Airborne Early Warning aircraft, the Y-8, in 1999, it is purchasing up to four AWACS-type Russian A-50 planes, and its developing an AWACS variant, the KJ-2000, which is based on an Il-76 air transporter airframe. At the most strategic level China uses foreign providers like INMARSAT for communications, but it is thought that China's next generation DFH-4 communications satellite is being applied to Chinese military satellite communications needs. And at the tactical level, China is organizing its first experimental digital brigade with the goal of developing the capability—demonstrated by American and Australian forces during the 2003 Iraq War—of providing each soldier with real-time information about the enemy's location.

Littoral Warfare and Power Projection

Throughout the Cold War the United States and the Soviet Union developed naval forces suited to blue-water open ocean warfare against one another. With the change in the security environment after the end of the Cold War America and its Western allies were faced with the need to transform these blue water navies into military forces that could conduct operations in the littorals in support of ground force operations. China is arguably engaged in the opposite process. A traditionally insular nation, its naval forces were designed to protect Chinese coasts or to venture as far as Taiwan, some 125 miles off shore. Its surface combatants and diesel electric submarines, technologically inferior to those of the United States, generally did not operate beyond Chinese territorial waters.

In response to its changed strategic situation, China is now strengthening its ability to conduct naval warfare several hundred miles or more from Chinese coasts. Indeed, Pentagon reports on China's military highlight the country's expressed interest in developing naval capabilities that can "hold at risk" an island chain some 1,000 miles off the Chinese coast, including Guam. Recent acquisitions relevant to this mission include eight stealthy Russian-built Kilo-class diesel electric submarines and two Russian-built Sovremenny II-class guided missile destroyers, while indigenous production includes new Song- and Yuan-class diesel submarines, Type 093 nuclear propelled attack submarines, and four new stealthy frigates, all of which are armed with anti-ship cruise missiles. The frigates will also provide an effective modern capability for littoral operations. Thus while the vast majority of the PLAN's ships and submarines are quite old and possess limited modern capabilities, the Chinese navy has begun to change with the acquisition and development of advanced platforms. Moreover, China is developing a marine corps for maritime and amphibious operations that, instead of being designed to invade Taiwan, appears to have been created for the purposes of expanding China's area of control to the islands surrounding the South China Sea.[27]

An ongoing debate is whether or not China is developing an aircraft carrier for power projection. In its 2006 report to Congress on China's military the Pentagon reversed its 2002 determination that China would not build carriers, citing analysts in and out of government who predict China could have an aircraft carrier as early as 2015 or at latest sometime beyond 2020, and this assessment has remained unchanged. More recently, the government-backed Wen Wei Po newspaper has reported China could have an aircraft carrier as soon as 2010. This development, combined with the PLAN's recent introduction of two domestically designed and built guided missile destroyers that include Aegis-type radars (albeit substantially smaller than even the smallest Arleigh Burke class U.S. Navy Aegis ship), has led to speculation that China is trying to build a blue water navy that could project force into the Pacific and patrol oil-shipping lanes from the Middle East. But even if China were to acquire an aircraft carrier, it would have many challenges to overcome to make it operational, not least the fact that it has little experience with shipborne aviation. China also has no significant replenishment assets, a crucial element for sustaining a naval force at sea. Given that the United States has eleven fully operational carrier battlegroups, it is unlikely China could create a blue-water navy that can challenge U.S. maritime dominance in the near to medium term.

Overall, taking into account the current military capabilities of China's army, navy, and air force, China's ability to project conventional military power beyond its periphery and the Taiwan Strait remains limited. The bulk of its ground forces are still large and unwieldy and its elite units have access to relatively few airlift and sealift assets that can transport them far from Chinese borders. Most of its air force platforms are old and for those that are new, Chinese pilots must still master the art of in-flight refueling. While China's newer ships are suited to a blue water navy, most of its fleet is still more appropriate for coastal, defensive operations and China remains several years away from an aircraft carrier and the ability to actually operate aircraft from a carrier. China's high tech training of officers and enlisted personnel is still considered modest.[28] But the future trends are unmistakable: China is investing heavily in all areas relevant to a deployable, high-tech RMA force, indicating that at some point, whether measured in years or decades, this will eventually be achieved.

Transforming Transformation

Ideas associated with the "transforming transformation" part of military transformation center, in the Western world, on the increased use of SOFs, attention to counterinsurgency capabilities, and ensuring forces can undertake stabilization and reconstruction missions. These ideas do not significantly inform the PLA, except perhaps in the negative. After 9/11 the PLA examined anti-terrorism wars and determined that guerrilla warfare would inflict heavy casualties on a casualty-sensitive invader, prompting one faction of the PLA to argue China should adopt a strategically defensive posture toward power projection beyond China's border.

That said China is, as mentioned, placing significant emphasis on SOFs as a means of modernizing and making mobile and deployable its ground forces. Moreover, it is possible and perhaps even likely that China will develop capabilities for stabilization and reconstruction missions in the future. As a result of its emergence as an economic superpower, note some experts, "China has had global leadership thrust upon it."[29] In addition, the United States has pressured China to become a responsible stakeholder. This combination of factors has forced China to rethink some of its foreign policy priorities and its traditional reluctance to support international peacekeeping operations. As Western powers have withdrawn from UN peacekeeping in favor of stabilization and reconstruction under NATO auspices or in the context of coalitions of the willing China has begun to fill the vacuum. Today, with forces in Africa and in Haiti, China is the world's thirteenth largest provider of UN peacekeeping troops.

Wider Aspects of Transformation

For the United States and its allies, the concept of military transformation has expanded in the post-9/11 era to include, among other things, an integrated approach to security that encompasses measures at home and measures abroad. The 2006 Quadrennial Defense Review outlines a "defense in depth" approach to U.S. territorial security under which the U.S. military defeats threats at a distance from the homeland—its traditional approach—but also focuses more directly on homeland defense and security. Broadly speaking, China has arrived at a similar balance but from the opposite starting point. Recognizing that "in a high-tech war, the enemy can strike from a great distance and that the dividing line between the front and the rear has become academic," PLA war planners have enlarged their previously territorial- and even city-centric view of what is necessary to defend China to include a strategic depth that is not confined to China's borders. Thus the PLA, at one time focused only on China, is being restructured and reequipped to look outward. At the same time, there is an emphasis on military support to civil authority at home. Some fourteen PLA divisions have been transferred to the People's Armed Police (PAP), estimated at about 1.5 million strong. The PAP is tasked with internal or domestic security while the PLA may act in "aid of the civil power," assisting the PAP in maintaining domestic security.

Other elements of a wider view of military transformation include maintaining unhindered access to space, and rethinking the relationship between defense and deterrence. The latter is U.S.-specific and is reflected in America's New Triad (see Chapter 3). But China, too, is thought to be in a process of reexamining its approach to deterrence in the contemporary security environment. The Pentagon's 2007 report to Congress on China's military indicates the country is improving its strategic nuclear forces both "qualitatively and quantitatively." Its primary strategic assets, that is to say those that can hold at risk U.S. territory, have comprised to date about twenty silo-based intercontinental ballistic missiles (ICBMs), the CSS-4. But China has already begun fielding the first of sixty new Dong Feng (DF) series ICBMs. The DF-31 has a range of 4,500 miles, allowing it to reach Hawaii and Alaska, while the more advanced DF-31A road-mobile ICBM has an estimated range of 7,000 miles, making it the first Chinese missile that can hit all of Europe or the continental United States. China is also launching a new class of ballistic missile submarines, the Type 094 or Jin-class, to be armed with a submarine-launched version of the DF-31, called the JL-2, with an estimated range of 6,000 miles—enough for submarines off China's coast to hit targets in the United States. China plans between five and seven of these new ballistic missile submarines, each armed with up to sixteen missiles.

China's move to include mobile and submarine launched ballistic missiles (SLBMs) among its strategic assets is significant. In the first instance, it represents "a quantum leap in Chinese ICBM capability."[30] Because mobile ICBMs and SLBMs are not as vulnerable to a first strike as are fixed land based ICBMs, China's retaliatory force is far more resilient with the DF-31, DF-31A, and JL-2 in the inventory. This in turn leads to a second potentially significant aspect: the impact these missiles could have on, or the relationship they may have to, China's long-standing no-first-use nuclear doctrine. In contrast to the United States and NATO, which have never expressly eliminated the option of being the first to use nuclear weapons in a conflict, China has from the beginning always stated that it would "not be the first to use such weapons at any time and in any circumstances."[31] But, shaken by the Bush administration's doctrine of preemptive strikes on perceived threats, as expressed in the 2002 National Security Strategy of the United States and reiterated in the 2006 version, China may be rethinking its deterrence policy. Chinese scholars with close ties to the PLA have argued "it is inconceivable that China would allow its nuclear weapons to be destroyed by a precision attack with conventional munitions, rather than use them as a true means of deterrence."[32] And doctrinal materials indicate that there may be a new mission for China's nuclear forces—deterrence of conventional attacks against the Chinese mainland.[33] Thus while "no-first-use" remains the officially stated Chinese policy, and was restated in China's 2006 defense white paper, its precise meaning is becoming more and more ambiguous.

The evolution of China's approach to deterrence may be seen in part as a reaction to developments in the West, particularly America's adoption of a new triad and its advanced conventional military capabilities. As noted in chapter 3,

America's deterrence posture now explicitly includes long-range conventional strike capabilities. It is attempting to develop, for example, conventional munitions that can target and destroy underground nuclear sites (with North Korea being the most common scenario in mind). The United States can do this because, notwithstanding the advances China (and other countries) are making in the long-range precision strike aspect of the RMA, the United States has unparalleled capability in this area. Indeed, the lesson America's potential adversaries took from the 1991 Gulf War—reinforced by Kosovo in 1999, Afghanistan in 2001–2002, and Iraq in 2003—is that they can no longer compete with the United States on the conventional battlefield. The response from actors as diverse as international terrorists like al-Qaeda to great powers like China has been to adopt "asymmetric" strategies. The U.S. Joint Chiefs of Staff have described asymmetric approaches as "attempts to circumvent or undermine U.S. strengths while exploiting U.S. weaknesses, using methods that differ significantly from the United States' expected mode of operations."[34] One example may be to confront U.S. aircraft carriers and carrier-borne aircraft not with "like" conventional capabilities but rather with missiles. China experts have underscored the PLA concept that "guided missile forces are the trump card in achieving victory in limited technology war."[35]

The notion of targeting America's vulnerabilities can be seen most clearly in China's approach to a further element of a wider view on military transformation: maintaining unhindered access to space. No country is so dependent on space-based assets for advanced military capability as is the United States. As a result, China is seeking to put at risk America's access to space. "China's military writers stress the need for asymmetric ways to fight the United States," notes one former U.S. government official, "Holding at risk the large number of command, control and communications satellites on which America's military is now deeply dependent is a high priority for the People's Liberation Army."[36] As mentioned in chapter 3, in 2006 China used a laser to blind a U.S. spy satellite, and in 2007 China successfully tested an antisatellite weapon, using a ground-based missile to strike an old Chinese weather satellite in low-earth orbit. These activities demonstrate an antisatellite capability against earth imaging satellites like RADARSAT, SAR Lupe, LaCrosse radar imaging and Keyhole optical imaging satellites, and America's eventual Space Radar. Experts believe that GPS satellites, which operate in medium earth orbit, and communications satellites, which are in geosynchronous (high-earth) orbit, could also eventually be put at risk.[37] Indeed, the PLA has explicitly discussed attacking communications satellites.[38] And questions have been raised about Chinese "mystery satellites" that are in orbits that bring them close to U.S. satellites, but do not appear to be conducting any particular mission.[39]

At the same time, China sees space control as key to future warfare. As noted above, China is increasing its use of navigation, communications, and earth imaging satellites, with their respective military applications of satellite-guided precision force, military communications, and military reconnaissance. China expects space will follow the air power trajectory, becoming the next "strategic vantage point" from which control of the sea, land, and air will be determined.[40] Therefore, it is interested not only in denying America's access to space but also in maintaining its own unhindered access to space. Moreover, again consistent with the air power example, it believes that space power will move from being a reconnaissance asset to being both a reconnaissance and a military strike force. China, experts argue, is convinced that the United States is weaponizing space, and that this poses a threat to China's space assets.[41] Its two-pronged response is to develop like capabilities (e.g. antisatellite weapons) while at the same time pressing for an international space ban with Russia (see Chapter 7).

Conclusion

China is pursuing a military transformation effort that centers primarily in the RMA aspect of military transformation. Driven by the nature of the contemporary security environment, as well as lessons learned by studying conflicts in which the United States has been involved since 1991, China has undertaken a process of developing a smaller, more deployable military force that is expeditionary in so far as it is focusing on power projection well beyond its traditional territorial and coastal area of emphasis. It is also seeking to incorporate advanced technology into all aspects of its military, and it is taking steps in the area of education to develop the skilled military force necessary to operate in a high-tech environment. China's military capability in all areas is inferior to that of the United States, but the trend lines clearly point to a future RMA force.

In the interim, China is focusing on asymmetric measures to counteract America's military superiority, targeting especially America's dependence on space-based assets, and possibly rethinking its nuclear policy. A cursory examination appears to reveal a classic action-reaction cycle as both powers seek to retain their own unhindered access to space and to establish the defense and deterrence stance most appropriate to the global security environment. There are unmistakable signs of the security dilemma at work, and with it the potential for future conflict.

Notes

1. "Coming Over the Horizon: Why China Wants a Bigger Navy," *Economist* (January 6, 2007), 34.

2. David Eimer, "Beijing's Modern War Machine is Closing Rapidly on its 2050 Target," *Sunday Telegraph* (April 2, 2007).

3. You Ji, "Learning and Catching Up: China's Revolution in Military Affairs Initiative," in Emily O. Goldman and Thomas G. Mahnken, *The Information Revolution in Military Affairs* (New York: Palgrave Macmillan, 2004), p. 106.

4. *Annual Report to Congress on the Military Power of the People's Republic of China* (Washington, DC: Department of Defense, 2007), p. I. The Pentagon is mandated by

Congress to produce an annual report on the military power of the People's Republic of China. Hereafter the reports will be referred to as Report to Congress on China's Military, with the appropriate year indicated.

5. Robert Wall, "China to Cut Military Size, Improve Capability," *Aviation Week & Space Technology* (September 8, 2003), 52.

6. Robert Wall, " Coming Out: Beijing Acknowledges J-10 and Issues Defense White Paper Setting New Goals," *Aviation Week & Space Technology* (January 8, 2007), 26.

7. Gopal Ratnam, "China's Officer Training a Top DoD Worry," *Defense News* (August 1, 2005), 1.

8. Ji, "Learning and Catching Up: China's Revolution in Military Affairs Initiative," p. 116; James C., Mulvenon, Murray Scot Tanner, Michael S. Chase, David Frelinger, David C. Gompert, Martin C. Libicki, and Kevin L. Pollpeter, *Chinese Responses to U.S. Military Transformation and Implications for the Department of Defense* (Santa Monica, CA: RAND Corp., 2006), p. 29.

9. Dennis J. Blasko, "PLA Ground Forces: Moving Toward a Smaller, More Rapidly Deployable, Modern Combined Arms Force," in James C. Mulvenon and Andrew N.D. Yang, *The People's Liberation Army as Organization* (Santa Monica, CA: RAND, 2002), p. 116.

10. Report to Congress on China's Military 2000 as quoted in Blasko, p. 322.

11. Richard Spencer, "U.S. Unnerved By Chinese Naval Build-Up," *Telegraph* (March 8, 2007).

12. Wendell Minnick, "China's Think and Move Army," *Defense News* (October 8, 2007), 34.

13. Wendell Minnick, "China To Buy Armed Hovercraft," *Defense News* (September 11, 2006), 48.

14. J. Marshall Beier, "Bear Facts and Dragon Boats: Rethinking the Modernization of Chinese Naval Power," *Contemporary Security Policy* 26(2) (August 2005), 303.

15. Report to Congress on China's Military 2006, p. 30.

16. Keith Crane, Roger Cliff, Evan Medeiros, James Mulvenon, and William Overholt, *Modernizing China's Military: Opportunities and Constraints* (Santa Monica, CA: RAND Corporation, 2005), p. 201.

17. Andrew Nien-Dzu Yang, "China's Revolution in Military Affairs: Rattling Mao's Army," in Goldman and Mahnken, p. 132.

18. Dennis J. Blasko, *The Chinese Army Today* (London: Routledge, 2006), 74.

19. Ji, "Learning and Catching Up: China's Revolution in Military Affairs Initiative," p. 111.

20. Mulvenon et al., *Chinese Responses to U.S. Military Transformation and Implications for the Department of Defense*, p. 37.

21. Robert Wall, "Coming Out: Beijing Acknowledges J-10 and Issues Defense White Paper," *Aviation Week & Space Technology* (January 8, 2007), 26.

22. Douglas Barrie, "Great Leap Forward . . . In Small Steps," *Aviation Week & Space Technology* (November 8, 2004), 51.

23. Paul H.B. Godwin, "China as a Major Asian Power: The Implications of its Military Modernization," in Andrew Scobell and Larry M. Wortzel, eds., *Shaping China's Security Environment: The Role of the People's Liberati on Army* (Carlisle, PA: U.S. Army War College Strategic Studies Institute, October 2006), p. 119.

24. Douglas Barrie, "China Looks to Equip its H-6 With Long-Range Cruise Missile," *Aviation Week & Space Technology* (January 22, 2007), 26.

25. Taiwanese analyst as quoted in Wendell Minnick, "Satellite Guidance Improves Accuracy of China's P12 Missile," *Defense News* (February 2007), 14.

26. Report to Congress on China's Military, p. 16.

27. James C. Bissett, "China Builds Modern Marine Corps Force," *Signal* (April 2006), 49.

28. Robert Marquand, "US More Cautious Than Wary as China's Reach Grows," *Christian Science Monitor* (November 18, 2005).

29. Elizabeth Economy, Council on Foreign Relations, as quoted in Colum Lynch, "China Filling Void Left by West in U.N. Peacekeeping," *Washington Post* (November 24, 2006), A12.

30. Larry Wortzel, chairman of the U.S.-China Economic and Security Review Commission as quoted in Wendell Minnick, "China Speeds ICBM Plans," *Defense News* (July 10, 2006), 1.

31. Report to Congress on China's Military 2006, p. 28.

32. Ibid.

33. Report to Congress on China's Military 2007, pp. 19–20.

34. As quoted in Elinor C. Sloan, *The Revolution in Military Affairs* (Montreal: McGill-Queen's University Press, 2002), p. 108.

35. Wortzel as quoted in Wendell Minnick, "China's Threatening Policy," *Defense News* (May 21, 2007), 20.

36. James Hackett, "Ramifications of China's ASAT Test," *Defense News* February 5, 2007), 29.

37. See Michael Pillsbury, *An Assessment of China's Anti-Satellite and Space Warfare Programs, Policies and Doctrines* (Washington, DC: U.S.-China Economic and Security Review Commission, January 2007), pp. 29, 46.

38. Mulvenon et al., *Chinese Responses to U.S. Military Transformation and Implications for the Department of Defense*, p. 71.

39. Vago Muradian, "China's Mystery Satellites," *Defense News* (February 5, 2007), p. 1.

40. Mulvenon et al, *Chinese Responses to U.S. Military Transformation and Implications for the Department of Defense*, p. 68.

41. Michael Pillsbury, as quoted in Vago Muradian, "China's Mystery Satellites," *Defense News* (February 5, 2007), 1.

Russia and Military Transformation

It is ironic that although the Soviet military was the first to recognize the beginnings of a Military Technical Revolution (MTR), in the late 1970s and early 1980s, the Russian military remains today the least "transformed" of those that are examined here. The "Russian Image of Future War," argued Russia scholar Mary FitzGerald in 1994, involves "smart conventional weapons destroying precisely located targets and limiting casualties...As the newest precision weapons...enter the inventory, there will also be changes in the structure of armed forces and the forms and methods of their employment."[1] The image, in other words, was one of advanced military technologies leading to and facilitating organizational and doctrinal changes to bring about, in combination, a Revolution in Military Affairs (RMA).

And yet, perhaps reflecting the MTR origins of its thinking, to the extent that the Russian military is engaged in the RMA component of military transformation it has remained focused on the technological aspect. "Like its Soviet predecessor," notes FitzGerald, "the Russian military views the MTR as the nucleus of future warfare."[2] Since the end of the Cold War doctrinal and, most notably, organizational change have been largely absent in the Russian military, and even in the area of advanced technology Russia remains well behind its Western counterparts. Changes associated with the "transforming transformation" part of military transformation have also been minimal, despite more than a decade of combating nonstate actors in Chechnya. But, as is the case with China, Russia is paying close attention to wider aspects of military transformation, placing perhaps even greater emphasis on this third transformation basket than the Middle Kingdom.

The Strategic Context

Russia's perspective on its strategic context has remained largely unchanged since the end of the Cold War and even in the wake of 9/11, 2001, although the terrorist attacks did prompt a temporary shift in outlook. In October 2003 former Russian Defense Minister Sergey Ivanov released a defense "white paper," *Urgent Tasks for the Development of the Armed Forces of the Russian Federation.* This was the first such Russian document since a military doctrine and a national security concept, produced in the waning days of the Yeltsin administration, were ratified by Russian President Vladimir Putin when he came to power in 2000. The white paper marked a departure from the earlier documents that, ten years after the fall of the Berlin Wall, had continued to focus to a significant degree on the Western/NATO threat to the territorial security of Russia. By contrast, *Urgent Tasks* identified the most pressing threats to Russia as being things like instability along its southern border; radical religious, separatist or nationalist movements; illegal arms trafficking; and transnational crime and other activities associated with international terrorism. "The Russian armed forces," stated Ivanov soon after the document's release, will be prepared for "anti-guerrilla warfare, the struggle against different types of terrorism, and peacekeeping operations."[3] At the time, analysts interpreted the policy as indicating, at long last, a shift away from identifying North Atlantic Treaty Organization (NATO) and the United States as probable attackers, and toward the view that the main direct threat to Russia came from the south along an extended "arc of instability."[4]

Despite this apparent change in emphasis, Ivanov continued to interpret "today's global realities" as necessitating, for Russian military policy, "traditional tasks like maintaining Russia's territorial boundaries, preventing attacks on our country, and maintaining strategic stability"—echoes of the Cold War perspective.[5] Two years later Putin moved away from the nonstate focus of *Urgent Tasks,* stressing during a speech that Russia's armed forces should be ready to counter attempts by other states to put political and military pressure on Russia. Finally, in January 2007 the chief of the general staff presented elements of a new draft military doctrine. Unofficial accounts indicate that while terrorism and the proliferation of weapons of mass destruction are identified as posing threats to Russia, the greatest threats are seen to emanate from the United States and its desire to establish bases around the Russian periphery, and from NATO as a whole as it enlarges further eastward.

Russia's strategic perspective may be explained in part by the activities of the West and especially NATO expansion—although Russia had the same viewpoint before NATO began expanding in 1999. More convincing are two other important and interrelated factors. The first is a deeply rooted mentality in the Russian officer corps, as well as among much of the political community and even the public at large, that Russia must maintain an enormous mobilization capacity. Some scholars date this mentality to "the institutional and ideational legacies of military power" that began during the reign of Peter the Great in the early eighteenth century.[6] A second factor is the vested interests of Russian generals who need Russia to have a large military force if they are to retain their position. "Only a large threat can justify [a million-man army] and a mobilization reserve of millions more," points out one scholar. "Thus, since 1991 the Russian defense ministry has concentrated great effort on identifying potential adversaries against whom such capabilities would be appropriate. Separatist groups and nonstate terrorist organizations do not fit this profile."[7] Russia's threat assessment reinforces the need for, or justifies, the retention of a large Soviet-style conscription army. The combined result is the persistence in Russian military planning of major war with the West. "It would not be an exaggeration," notes another analyst, "to say that Russia's armed forces...are 70–80 percent oriented toward a war with the West."[8]

Changes Associated with the Revolution in Military Affairs

Organization and Doctrine

The longstanding and essentially unchanged strategic perspective held by many of Russia's political leaders, and perhaps most of its military leaders, has influenced Russia's approach to military transformation. Most notably, it has resulted in only limited progress in the organizational and doctrinal changes associated with the revolution in military affairs. The key development here is the move toward a force structure comprised of smaller, more rapidly deployable units made up of high quality, well educated, professional (volunteer) troops.

With a population of about 141 million people, Russia has an active military force of around 1.1 million members. This is a large ratio of military members to overall population size in comparison to other great powers. The United States has 300 million people and a 1.4 million-member military while China, with a population nine times that of Russia, has an armed force only twice the size. Although the Russian military remains very large, it is not nearly as large as it once was. The armed forces that Russia inherited from the USSR in the spring of 1992 stood at some 3.7 million members. By the time Putin came to power this had been reduced to 1.3 million, and his government in turn instituted further force reductions. *Urgent Tasks* called for a Russian armed force of about one million people, but Russian Defense Minister Anatoly Serdyukov has settled on a slightly higher figure, arguing that 1.1 million "is the most optimal size to effectively tackle all tasks set [sic] to our country's Army and fleet."[9] This suggests that there will be no further cuts. But experts have suggested that Russia would be better served with a still smaller force of between 500,000 and 750,000, with more money being spent per military member.[10] "If you've got 1.2m men who've got the wrong kit and can't be deployed," noted one Western liaison officer, "the situation is not much better than when the Germans came."[11]

The evidence indicates that military structural changes that are central to the organizational component of military transformation have been largely absent in Russia. One expert has argued that from the limited information that is made available, it is impossible to make even a broad determination about the structure of the Russian armed forces and their deployment.[12] Others have stated more definitely that Russia—influenced by a strategic perspective that calls for a large-scale war against a formidable Cold War-like enemy rather than a capacity to manage smaller regional conflicts and threats from nonstate actors—has chosen to preserve Soviet-era force structures.[13] For his part, Ivanov noted in his October 2003 *Urgent Tasks* document that "On the whole we can assert that the large-scale changes in the armed forces associated with their radical restructuring…have been completed."[14] With few details on exactly what this radical restructuring comprised, one may infer that the reference was to the significant force reductions of the previous decade.

The Russian military also remains a largely conscript force, despite several efforts to professionalize the force since the end of the Cold War. During his 1996 election campaign, former Russian president Boris Yeltsin proposed eliminating conscription by 2000. But, facing strong opposition from the army generals who would lose their positions in a pared down military, Yeltsin eventually abandoned the plan. Similarly, when Putin came to power in 2000 he proposed eliminating conscription by the end of the decade yet at first was unable to take action in this area. America's 2003 military campaign in Iraq, which clearly illustrated the obsolete structure of Russia's armed forces, strengthened Putin's position and enabled him to push a military reform plan through parliament.

According to the 2003 Military Balance, the July 2003 Special Federal Program to Transform the Staffing of the Armed Forces Primarily to Contract Servicemen called for the Russian military to convert 72 MoD high-readiness units, or about 130,000 servicemen, from conscript to contract service over a four year period. Other sources placed the levels at 148,000 servicemen and 36,000 officers.[15] Putin, citing the high cost of transitioning from a conscript to a professional force, set the professionalization goal at 17 percent of the total force by the end of 2007. But a lack of volunteers, due primarily to low wages, poor and often dangerous living conditions in the Russian army, and also the overall population decline in Russia, has meant that even this goal has been difficult to meet. It is possible that significant defense budget increases in more recent years as a result of high oil and gas revenues will facilitate a greater transition rate. Professionalization is moving forward, but slowly, and primarily only in those units designated for deployment abroad. Moreover, there are no foreseeable plans to eliminate conscription altogether.

Apart from its position on increased professionalization, the 2003 military reform plan was significant in that it introduced the idea of contract (volunteer) non-commissioned officers (NCOs), with the goal of creating a pool of contract sergeants and petty officers of the sort that are so central to Western military operations. Volunteer and conscript units alike are to have a "layer" of professional NCOs between the average marine, soldier, and airman, and the officer level.

A well-educated force is a central organizational component of the RMA and here the Russian armed forces lags far behind that of its Western and perhaps also Chinese counterparts. Statistics indicate that close to 40 percent of the force does not have the equivalent of a high school education, with many of these not having gone past the primary level. Moreover, once entering conscript service—which has been reduced as of 2008 from two years to one year—draftees are given only elementary military training. More significantly, when the program to convert some units from conscript to professional manning was first introduced, the volunteer soldiers were given the same—extremely limited—training as the conscript soldiers, a clear hindrance to creating a high quality military force. This problem is slowly being addressed, with a new combat training program for contract service personnel having been established in 2007. Still, experts indicate there are too many military schools in Russia and these do not have the training facilities and educational staffs to institute wide spread high quality education and training.[16]

Technology

Advances in the technological sophistication of Russia's armed forces has been limited by the severe financial constraints faced by Russia in the years following the Cold War, culminating in the financial crisis of 1998, and by the related limited Russian defense budgets. Unable to field a high-tech conventional force, Russia's leaders chose to direct most of the country's military resources toward its nuclear forces as the guarantor of Russian security (see later). Meanwhile, those elements of the country's defense industry that survived the 1990s and early 2000's did so by reorienting themselves away from the domestic market and the highly integrated military-industrial complex of Soviet times and toward the export market. Thus a further irony in Russian military transformation efforts is that although the Russian armed forces has only recently begun to receive advanced military platforms, the country's defense industry has been producing and exporting such equipment (although not of the American caliber) to countries like China and India for several years. As of mid-decade Russia held a 10 to 15 percent share of the world weapons market. While most exports in the 1990s comprised upgraded Soviet era weapons, Putin-era sales have involved sophisticated fighter aircraft, precision-guided munitions, and air-defense systems. Experts say that Russia is increasingly capable of turning out cutting-edge weaponry.[17]

The rising price of oil and gas has had a significant impact on the financial situation of Russia, which is a major oil and gas producer. This, in turn has meant higher defense budgets and more money for domestic sales of advanced military equipment. "In 2005 we passed a kind of psychological barrier," Putin has noted, "now Russia is spending more money on weapons than it is earning in exports."[18] The following year the Russian government approved the State Weapons Program 2015 (GPV 2015), a comprehensive plan for reequipping the Russian armed forces. The classified document lists the weapons and technologies the Russian military is to receive between 2007 and 2015, including both type and quantity, and encompassing both nuclear and conventional weaponry. It also set some ambitious acquisition goals for 2010. But more recent evidence suggests that the reform program has slowed somewhat, and that Russian military exports continue to overshadow domestic sales.

One area of conventional weaponry focus is long-range standoff precision strike capabilities. In 2007 Ivanov stated that the development of state-of-the-art precision weapons was the number one conventional weapons priority of the Russian defense industry over the next several years. In the wake of America's decision to base interceptors in Poland as part of its ballistic missile defense system, which Moscow believes is aimed at Russia, Ivanov, now promoted to First Deputy Prime Minister, argued "in a situation like this we shall have to equip our armed forces with up-to-date, high-accuracy weapons."[19] Nonetheless, generally speaking Russia is developing its precision strike capabilities with a view to targeting terrorist organizations, not combating state adversaries. "Precision weapons' properties make for their (*sic*) ability [to strike] the enemy's military infrastructure and troops and, what is most important to us, at terrorist bases," Ivanov has stressed.[20] Kremlin strategists believe Chechen rebels are part of the international terrorist movement and that equipping the Russian armed forces with conventionally armed standoff precision weapon systems is both strategically important and a key condition for the survival of the Russian federation intact. But operational planners are also considering using Russia's bomber fleet in antiterrorist operations to strike terrorist bases anywhere in the world.

The Russian air force has about 1,650 combat capable aircraft, yet the vast majority of these aircraft date to Soviet times. Russian parliamentary hearings in 2006 indicated that only 20 aircraft in the line units had been built since 9/11, and more than half the fleet dated to the end of the Cold War. New fighter procurement is limited to Sukhoi Su-34 Fullback attack fighters, which can be broadly compared to America's ground attack F-15E strike eagle that first deployed at the end of the Cold War. In 2006 Ivanov announced plans to buy 24 aircraft over four years with the first fully operational Su-34 unit expected in 2010, and a total of 60 aircraft to be in the inventory by 2015. Russia also hopes to field a new "fifth-generation" fighter in the coming decade. Designers say the Sukhoi T-50, also known as the Prospective Aviation Complex for Frontal Aviation or PAK FA, is already under development and could be flying as early as 2009, with acceptance trials beginning in 2012. Media reports indicate that the stealthy T-50 will have the same weight and size as America's Joint Strike Fighter.[21] In the future MiG could also produce a fifth-generation fighter, the Light Multifunction Frontal Aircraft, which would be a successor to the MiG Fulcrum.

Beyond this, Russia is upgrading older fighters—like the MiG-29 Fulcrum, MiG-31 Foxhound, and Su-27 Flanker—to give them a ground strike capability, and upgrading older ground attack aircraft—like the Su-24 Fencer and Su-25 Frogfoot—to give them next generation air to surface precision strike technology and weapons. The Frogfoot, for example, is now configured to carry both laser-guided and satellite-guided bombs and missiles. The upgraded versions have been designated, respectively, as MiG-29OVT, MiG-31BM, Su-27SM, Su-24M2, and Su-25SM. Meanwhile, "redundant aircraft" such as the MiG-27 are being considered for conversion into unmanned combat aerial vehicles.[22] A doubling of the air force's procurement budget enabled it to begin taking delivery of upgraded aircraft in 2006, but experts assess that the upgrade programs are modest both in terms of numbers and technical ambition, given that the air force has received only a handful of new aircraft since the end of the Cold War.[23]

Russia is also developing a standoff precision strike capability by equipping its long-range bombers with precision-guided cruise missiles. The Tu-160 Blackjack and Tu-95MS Bear bombers are being upgraded with the ability to deliver conventionally armed precision-guided air-to-surface missiles (the Raduga Kh-555). "These cruise missiles have a range of 3,000 kilometers and can miss targets by no more than a few meters," Russia's air force chief of staff stated in 2004.[24] Russia has about fifty long-range bombers and these are slowly being upgraded. In 2007 Putin ordered the Russian military to resume regular long-range flights of its strategic bombers over the Atlantic, Pacific, and Arctic oceans—patrols that had previously not taken place since the end of the Cold War. Precision weapons are only as accurate as their targeting information and so Russia is also emphasizing, at least rhetorically, intelligence, surveillance, and reconnaissance (ISR) systems and the ability to rapidly transmit information. In concrete terms, progress in this area has been relatively limited. Russia has twenty A-50 Mainstay AWACS, but it has no equivalent of America's JSTARS or Britain's ASTOR aircraft, and its development of unmanned aerial vehicle (UAVs) has been "fragmented and limited."[25] The conflict in Chechnya should have prompted an increased focus on UAVs, much as it did for the United States in Iraq and for many countries in Afghanistan, but this was not the case. Only in 2007 did the Russian military begin testing a new reconnaissance UAV, the Klest. It is also fielding an upgraded tactical aerial reconnaissance system, the Stroi-PD, which uses upgraded tactical UAVs, the Pchela-1K. An older version of the system, the Stroi-P, was first developed in the early 1990s but its value was questionable given that the system could not transfer data to other aircraft. Soviet era platforms like the heavy and tactically inflexible Tu-143 and Tu-243 UAVs, designed for use over a large battlefield against advancing enemy soldiers, are also being upgraded. Russia's defense industries are looking at new UAV concepts, but the air force has not yet formulated requirements for a next generation UAV.

At the most strategic ISR level Russia has begun launching new earth-imaging satellites, with resolutions of between eight and twenty meters, for civilian and military applications. But Russia's greatest area of space-based emphasis is with respect to the communications component of C4ISR. Russia is seeking to develop its Global Navigation Satellite System, or Glonass, to the same technical performance as America's GPS system. Glonass was launched in the 1980s but severe budget cuts meant that even when Putin came to power the system comprised only between six and eight satellites. By mid-decade there was about a dozen satellites in the system, but in 2007 the Russian Space Agency announced that Glonass would be developed to a total of twenty-four satellites by the end of 2009, all of them the contemporary Glonass-M design. Russia already has full coverage of its own territory (an 18-satellite requirement) and once fully deployed Glonass will provide coverage of the whole world. After 2009 the individual satellites are to be replaced with the next generation Glonass-K, increasing the precision of the system from ten meters (the Glonass-M target) to one meter.

Glonass will sell high-precision navigation services to commercial users, but it also has a large military component. The systems' upgrade is expected to go some way toward addressing concern in the ground forces over the slow pace of C4ISR modernization. Some analysts have characterized the Russian military, and perhaps especially the army, as being "stuck in the pre-digital age."[26] The army's land systems include main battle tanks (T-90s), infantry fighting vehicles (BMP-3Ms), armored personnel carriers (BTR-80s), and artillery howitzers (MSTAs), all of which are improved variants of Soviet-era systems. By 2010 the ground troops will get a new tank support combat vehicle for use at the company level. In addition, the Army's Iskander theater missile system, which may be broadly compared to the Scud, has been armed with a new long-range high-precision missile that "will boost, by an order of magnitude, the combat capability of [Russia's land forces] in terms of precise striking of targets."[27] And for battlefield mobility the Mi-28N (night attack) helicopter, comparable to America's Apache, has been earmarked as Russia's next-generation attack helicopter, with a total of fifty to be delivered by 2010. But despite these advances, experts assess that "much work remains before Russia's forces are mobile, sophisticated and integrated enough for modern military operations."[28] Although the Russian army has access to substantial airlift (An-12 Cub, An-124 Condor, and Il-76MF Candid air transporters), the state of its technology and equipment, and its limited structural reform, is such that it cannot be characterized as an expeditionary force.

There are, however, signs that the Russian navy is at the early stages of pursuing an expeditionary capability. Design work is being completed on a next-generation destroyer, a follow on from the Sovremenny-class destroyers that have been sold to China (see Chapter 6), and naval procurement plans for the medium term also include about twenty new frigates, armed with anti-ship cruise missiles and designed to be the main platform for long- and short-range maritime operations until the mid-2020s. But the most significant development in expeditionary terms is the possibility that Russia will build one or more new aircraft carriers. The Russian navy's current and sole carrier, the Admiral Kuznetsov, is seaworthy and has a fighter fleet of twenty aircraft, naval variants of the air force Flanker. In 2005 the commander in chief of the Russian navy stated that the force would receive at least two next-generation aircraft carriers by 2017, one for each of the Northern and Pacific fleets, and that these would accommodate next-generation carrier-borne aircraft. GV 2015 contained no stipulation for building aircraft carriers, but the more recent spending plan unveiled by Ivanov in 2007 explicitly included provisions for a carrier.

The Russian navy is also developing its littoral warfare capabilities. The service plans to buy new corvettes, which (as noted in Chapter 4) are similar in function to America's Littoral Combat Ship and would serve to strengthen Russia's ability to patrol its adjacent waters. In addition, it has introduced new artillery cutters in the Caspian Sea for antitrafficking, counterterrorism and littoral patrolling. The Navy may be "forced" to modernize somewhat more rapidly than the other services by virtue of the fact that it has started to operate with Western navies in counterterrorism operations. In December 2004 Russia concluded a political agreement with NATO for Russian ships to participate in Operation Active

Endeavor, NATO's post-9/11 maritime surveillance and monitoring operation in the Mediterranean. The navy worked to meet the very challenging predeployment and interoperability standards that are applied to all participating nations, finally joining the operation approximately two years later.

The overall picture of the Russian military with respect to the RMA component of military transformation is one of a force that is moving only slowly forward organizationally and doctrinally, and that is at the early stages of acquiring or developing advanced military technologies. The limited organizational change is largely the product of a particular strategic mindset, although the cost of professionalization is also often mentioned (and disputed by some analysts), while the technological lag is the result of dramatically reduced defense budgets in the 1990s and the concurrent emphasis on nuclear over conventional forces. "The Russian Federation Land Forces, Air Force, and Navy," notes one analyst, reflecting on the strategic nuclear focus, "are predominantly equipped with Soviet-era weapons... [and] receive whatever funds remain."[29] Increased defense budgets, especially in Putin's second term, have enabled Russia to focus more on conventional forces; in testimony before Congress in 2007 Secretary of Defense Robert Gates described Russia as pursuing "a sophisticated military modernization program." But it will be some years before advanced conventional technologies and platforms associated with the RMA can be in place.

Transforming Transformation

The Russian armed forces have also undertaken relatively limited measures in those areas associated with "transforming transformation"—the increased use of special operations forces combined with skills in carrying out counterinsurgency and stabilization and reconstruction missions. Reports indicate that Russia is building up its special operations forces,[30] however few details are available. At the same time, while two wars in Chechnya have changed the traditional tactics used by Russian special forces, these changes and requirements have not been captured in current published doctrine. For example, the most recent manual for the Spetnaz GRU, the special forces of Russia's military intelligence units, was released in 1991 and describes their primary task as destroying mobile nuclear missile systems behind enemy lines.[31] Moreover, "there is nothing in the document about counterguerrilla warfare and about how to train servicemen to handle it."[32]

More is known about Russia's response to stabilization and reconstruction operations, which Russia refers to as peacekeeping missions. In an editorial written around the same time his *Urgent Tasks* white paper was released Ivanov stressed "Conducting armed operations during peacetime, including... participating in peacekeeping operations," was one of the Russian military's tasks, and to this end it would study the creation of a separate peacekeeping brigade within the land forces.[33] Russia's first fully contract special peacekeeping brigade became operational in 2005 and although it is trained for missions along Russia's borders, like South Ossetia, in future it could be deployed to multinational peacekeeping operations. The brigade itself is representative of the modernization and military reform that is slowly taking hold in elite and specialist units of Russia's army. A former head of the NATO military liaison mission to Moscow has described the peacekeeping brigade as being comprised of "lightly-equipped and highly-deployable battalion groups"[34] —a glimmer of an RMA force. In 2006 Russia sent part of its peacekeeping force to Lebanon following the conflict between Israel and Hizbullah, and in 2007 the brigade conducted joint peacekeeping exercises with France.

Wider Aspects of Transformation

A notable feature of Russia's 2007 draft military doctrine is its emphasis on an integrated approach to security. With this new doctrine, assesses one analyst, Russia recognizes "that a distinction can no longer be made between internal and external security and military and nonmilitary threats . . . security is comprehensive and comprises all dimensions."[35] Russia is thus attempting to coordinate an interdepartmental response to internal and external threats. This involves, for example, the creation of a National Counter Terrorism Committee under the directorship of the Federal Security Forces, which have reportedly been increased in size as a means of enhancing counterterrorist measures. Beyond this, Russia's internal security troops and border guards, which number close to 400,000, are starting to be professionalized and to receive new equipment, although progress here is slow. And Russia is enhancing its homeland defense with more efficient radar stations than those constructed during the Soviet era, to reduce its dependence on former Soviet republics and fill holes in the military's warning capabilities.

Maintaining unhindered access to space is also important to Russia. In 2002 Russia and China jointly proposed a multilateral treaty that would ban the deployment of conventional weapons in outer space (the 1967 Outer Space Treaty already bans the deployment of weapons of mass destruction). Two years later Russia unilaterally declared that it would not be the first country to deploy weapons in space, and it called on other countries to follow suit with a similar pledge.

The wider aspect of military transformation that stands out most predominantly in Russia's transformation approach is its focus on nuclear weapons. "In 1982," Mary FitzGerald has pointed out, "General Secretary Leonid Brezhnev announced the Soviet pledge to never use nuclear weapons first. This pledge reflected above all the Soviet Union's confidence that it had achieved conventional superiority over the West."[36] Yet as discussions about the MTR increased in tempo in the 1980s this confidence began to wane, and it was ultimately shattered by the display of U.S. conventional superiority during the 1991 Gulf War. In 1993 Russia replaced its decade-old "no-first-use" doctrine with a statement virtually identical to that maintained by the United States—which (as mentioned previously) has never renounced the first use of nuclear weapons.

Russia's difficult financial situation in the 1990s, the ongoing war in Chechnya, and its inability to afford both a robust nuclear force and a modern conventional force, sparked a debate within the Russian defense community as to the proper balance between conventional and nuclear forces. When Putin came to power, he initially placed his emphasis on strengthening Russia's conventional armed forces for regional conflicts such as the war in Chechnya. In August and September 2000 he took decisions to greatly reduce the size of Russia's strategic nuclear forces and shift resources from strategic to conventional forces. These reductions were codified in the May 2002 Strategic Offensive Reduction Treaty (SORT) with the United States, under which Russia will have reduced its nuclear forces from about 5,000 to between 1,700 and 2,200 strategic weapons by 2012. At that time almost all of Russia's Soviet-era systems will have been dismantled.

But the conventional forces emphasis was short lived. In his *Urgent Tasks* document of 2003, Ivanov did not take a clear stance on the conventional/nuclear debate, however in spending programs since that time army, navy, and air force procurement have consistently taken second place to the nuclear forces, with conventional programs often delayed to accommodate ballistic missile programs. The majority of the military spending in GV 2015 is geared toward maintaining Russia's nuclear deterrent, with the top priority being "to provide the country with a compact and modern nuclear deterrent force by 2015–20, which will guarantee 'unsustainable damage' to any potential first strike aggressor."[37] The primary explanatory factor for this approach appears, once again, to be strategic perspective. Experts have argued that Moscow's military and political leaders are missing the dangers posed by Islamist extremism, and that "For them, it is all about deterring the main adversary, the United States and NATO."[38]

Neither China nor Russia has attempted to move to a New Triad for nuclear deterrence in the manner that has the United States. In fact, Russia is opposed to missile defense systems (beyond the one it established around Moscow during the Cold War) and it has voiced its strong opposition to America's decision to include, in its ballistic missile defense plan, a missile tracking radar in the Czech Republic and missile interceptors in Poland to address the threat from Iran. Russia is of the view that "no such threat exists for Europe or the U.S. today, or in the foreseeable future."[39] Nonetheless, it has proposed, in place of the radar and interceptors, sharing data from the Gabala radar that Russia leases from Azerbaijan, and placing interceptors farther south, in Turkey or at sea. This, Putin has argued, would offer better protection against Iranian missiles, and it would mean that "Russia would no longer have to aim its warheads at Europe" as Putin had threatened.[40] The United States, however, has determined that the Soviet-era early warning system does not have the necessary technological capability for tracking and targeting individual missiles coming from the Middle East.

Like China, Russia has a traditional triad of nuclear forces made up of ground based, air launched, and submarine launched missiles. The ground-based Nuclear Strategic Missile Troops are the principal component of Russia's triad. They are being reequipped with Topol-M (SS-27) new-generation intercontinental ballistic missiles (ICBM) which are being fielded in both a silo and mobile version. The Russian military plans sixty-nine new missiles by 2016, half of which will be mobile. Many of these are already in place and the first mobile regiment has already been declared fully operational. As is the case with China, Russia's focus on mobile systems is significant in that it is meant to ensure higher survivability from a first strike. Moreover, the commander of the Strategic Missile Forces expects the Topol-M missile systems will have a "MIRVed" or Multiple Independently Targetable Reentry Vehicle capability by about 2010. In this context, Russia has stressed that the Topol-M is designed to penetrate multi-layered missile defense systems. A naval version of the Topol-M, the Bulava SS-N-30, is planned for eight new Borei-class nuclear submarines that the navy is to receive by 2017, at the latest. But while the first submarine has already been launched, the missile itself is "nowhere near ready for production."[41] Once completed, however, this will be a significant nuclear deterrent capability: each Borei submarine will carry twelve Bulava missiles, and each missile will have up to ten warheads.

As early as 1993 the Russian general staff had decided that because of Russia's lag in new technologies, MIRVed ballistic missiles were "the sole means of ensuring retaliation against strikes by advanced non-nuclear systems."[42] Both the United States and the Soviet Union had developed MIRVed missiles in the 1970s in response to the missile limit restrictions of the 1972 Strategic Arms Limitation Treaty. But the 1993 Strategic Arms Reduction Treaty (START II) banned the use of MIRVs on ICBMs. Although the agreement was never ratified Russia abided by its provisions, however when the United States announced its intention to withdraw from the 1972 anti-ballistic missile (ABM) treaty in late 2001 Russia stated it would no longer abide by START II. "Russian experts used to cite the ABM treaty as an unvarnished success," notes one analyst, "Once it disappeared from the scene, however, they did not lose too much time regretting it ... they used its demise as a convenient excuse to rid themselves of START II."[43] The subsequent SORT agreement made no mention of MIRVed weapons. Since that time, Russia has focused its attention on developing next-generation MIRV-equipped missiles, which in essence offer a more cost-effective means of maintaining a robust nuclear deterrent. Thus whereas China is focusing on information warfare as its asymmetric counter to American conventional superiority, Russia, it may be argued, is focusing on multiple-warhead nuclear weapons.

Conclusion

Military transformation as conceived by the Western world is largely a conventional forces phenomenon. Its genesis is in the advanced military technologies and resultant changes in military doctrine and organization that have characterized the RMA, and it has expanded to encompass conventional responses to non-state actors. These "how we fight" components of military transformation have been the central focus of much of the Western world, and China, too, is placing significant emphasis on transformation's RMA core. Russia's approach, by contrast, is centered predominantly in the nuclear aspect of transformation's wider dimension. It is making limited advances in the technological aspect of the RMA, and is also taking some steps with regard to things associated with "transforming transformation." But considering it was the first country to notice the MTR, and considering it has substantial post–Cold War experience in conflict against non-state actors, its progress in the "how we fight" dimension of military transformation has been remarkably limited. Russia's approach to military transformation is such that it is likely to have relatively little to contribute to the management of regional crises in the near to medium term, and it is inevitably reminiscent of the nuclear standoff between the superpowers during the Cold War.

Notes

1. Mary C. FitzGerald, "The Russian Image of Future War," *Comparative Strategy* 13 (1994), 168.

2. Ibid., 167.

3. Sergey Ivanov, "Russia Rethinks Security," *Defense News* (December 1, 2003), 44.

4. Matthew Bouldin, "The Ivanov Doctrine and Military Reform: Reasserting Stability in Russia," *Journal of Slavic Military Studies* 17(4) (2004), 629; Alexei G. Arbatov, "Military Reform: From Crisis to Stagnation," in Steven E. Miller and Dmitri V. Trenin, eds., *The Russian Military: Power and Policy* (Cambridge, MA: American Academy of Arts and Sciences, 2004), p. 107.

5. Ivanov, "Russia Rethinks Security," 44.

6. See Alexander M. Golts and Tonya L. Putnam, "State Militarism and Its Legacies," *International Security* 29(2) (Fall 2004), 123.

7. Ibid., 128.

8. Arbatov, "Military Reform: From Crisis to Stagnation," p. 106.

9. "Russian Army To Be Downsized To 1.1 Million Troops By 2011—Serdyukov," *Interfax* (May 30, 2007).

10. Bouldin, "The Ivanov Doctrine and Military Reform: Reasserting Stability in Russia," 626.

11. As quoted in "How Are The Mighty Fallen: The Russian Army," *Economist* (July 2, 2005).

12. Arbatov, "Military Reform: From Crisis to Stagnation," p. 97.

13. Golts and Putnam, "State Militarism and Its Legacies," 121.

14. Bouldin, "The Ivanov Doctrine and Military Reform: Reasserting Stability in Russia," 621–622.

15. Lyubov Pronina, "Russia to Shift Toward Pro Army," *Defense News* (July 14, 2003), 6.

16. "Military Education, Training In Russia Still Ineffective," *Interfax* (May 3, 2007).

17. Fred Weir, "Russia Intensifies Efforts to Rebuild Its Military Machine," *Christian Science Monitor* (February 12, 2007).

18. Henry Ivanov, "Country Briefing: Russia—Austere Deterrence," *Jane's Defence Weekly* (May 3, 2006).

19. "Deputy PM Ivanov Says Russia Forced to Create New High Accuracy Weapons," *Itar-Tass* (May 29, 2007).

20. "Russia: Precision Weapons Available for Targeted Strikes on Terrorist Bases," *Itar-Tass* (November 8, 2006).

21. Nabi Abdullaev, "Russian Industry Awaits New Fighter," *Defense News* (June 18, 2007), 32.

22. *The Military Balance 2003* (London: International Institute for Strategic Studies), p. 99.

23. Alexey Komarov, "Russian Renewal: Modest Air Force Ambition Provides Route to Key Inventory Improvements," *Aviation Week & Space Technology* (January 29, 2007).

24. As quoted in Lyubov Pronina, "Russian Military's Combat Potential Unrealized," *Defense News* (December 13, 2004).

25. Alon Ben David, Robert Hewson, Damian Kemp, and Stephen Trimble, "Special Report: UAVs—Frontline Flyers," *Jane's Defence Weekly* (May 10, 2006).

26. Mark Kramer, "The Perils of Counterinsurgency: Russia's War in Chechnya," *International Security* 29(3) (Winter 2004/05), 23.

27. "State Trials of Russia's New Cruise Missile to Begin in 2008," *Itar-Tass* (June 1, 2007).

28. "Right Reforms for Moscow," *Defense News* (September 6, 2004).

29. Ivanov, "Country Briefing," 25.

30. Bill Gertz, "Russian Military Seen in Decline," *Washington Times* (May 12, 2006).

31. Nabi Abdullaev, "Field Experience: Chechen Battles Reshape Russian Tactics," *Defense News* (June 5, 2006), 9.

32. Retired Russian special forces officer as quoted in ibid.

33. Ivanov, "Russia Rethinks," 44.

34. Peter Williams, "NATO-Russia Military Cooperation: From Dialogue to Interoperability?" *RUSI Journal* (October 2005), 45.

35. "Russia's Upcoming Revised Military Doctrine," *Power and Interest News Report* (February 26, 2007), www.pinr.com

36. FitzGerald, "The Russian Image of Future War," 178.

37. Ivanov, "Country Briefing." 25.

38. Heritage Foundation specialist Ariel Cohen as quoted in Gertz, (May 12, 2006).

39. Russian Foreign Minister Sergei Lavrov, "A Crucial Debate on Europe's Anti-Missile Defenses," *Financial Times* (April 11, 2007), 15.

40. "Strategic Surprise," *Economist* (June 16, 2007), 60.

41. Nabi Abdullaev, "Russia Launches First of 8 New Nuclear Subs," *Defense News* (April 23, 2007), 6.

42. FitzGerald, "The Russian Image of Future War," 178.

43. Rose Gottemoeller, "Nuclear Weapons in Current Russian Policy," in Steven E. Miller and Dmitri V. Trenin, eds., *The Russian Military: Power and Policy* (Cambridge, MA: American Academy of Arts and Sciences, 2004), p. 197.

How Relevant? Military Transformation and Modern Conflict

Dramatic change in the conduct of war from the 1991 Gulf War onward has been accompanied almost from the beginning, and especially since 9/11, by debates about how relevant these changes are to addressing the threats and risks faced by America and its allies. One aspect of the debate involves the reliance on advanced technologies and new doctrines in the conduct of the conventional wars for which the Revolution in Military Affairs (RMA) was arguably designed. A second, much more prevalent area of concern since 9/11 centers on the applicability of transformation's RMA origins to nonconventional, irregular warfare.

Generally speaking, the war against the Taliban in late 2001 and 2002, and the Iraq War of 2003 served to validate the technological and doctrinal trends that were under way as a result of the RMA in the late 1990s. Both Afghanistan and Iraq demonstrated the effectiveness with which it is possible to bring together a combination of advanced command, control, communications, computing, intelligence, surveillance, and reconnaissance (C4ISR) technologies, precision munitions, and platforms in a joint environment to achieve rapid and decisive victory over enemy forces. In Afghanistan specially equipped Central Intelligence Agency (CIA) teams and special operations forces, some operating on horseback, pinpointed targets for precision strike, while unmanned aerial vehicles, imaging satellites and Joint Surveillance and Target Attack Radar System (JSTARS) helped maintain near-continuous reconnaissance of enemy forces. Advances in battlefield communications dramatically reduced the time between detecting and destroying a target. The conflict also featured the debut of unmanned combat as Predator unmanned aerial vehicles (UAVs) equipped with Hellfire precision missiles carried out several missions. In Iraq, U.S. Army, Navy, and Air Force personnel worked together in an unprecedented display of jointness as army platforms moved rapidly over terrain, utilizing information, and calling in support, from air force and navy intelligence, surveillance and reconnaissance (ISR) and precision strike platforms. The performance of the ground forces, supported by naval and air assets, supported the doctrinal trend toward lighter, more deployable and mobile forces made up of smaller units operating swiftly on the battlefield. "The integration of air power, special forces and mobile ground formations," noted one commentator, "[enabled] the American military to be more effective with less mass."[1]

The overall effect of the Afghanistan and Iraq conflicts was to give a boost to most, if not all, of the technological, doctrinal, and organizational elements that are considered part of the RMA. "I think this war is going to give you the revolution in military affairs,"[2] stated an expert in military strategy ten days into the Afghanistan conflict. "This war has been a manifestation of the ongoing Revolution in Military Affairs,"[3] argued another analyst shortly after the end of the Iraq war in April 2003.

Yet even during these conflicts, caveats were emerging. In Afghanistan the major issue was the failure to commit sufficient U.S. ground forces to ensure the capture of Osama bin Laden in the mountain caves of Tora Bora in December 2001—an early indication that technology could not fully substitute for mass. In Iraq there were cases where technology did not live up to its promises, for example the failure to detect enemy forces around an important bridge south of Baghdad in early April 2003. The issue, more generally, is that while concepts of military transformation had promised to dramatically reduce the "fog of war" with near-perfect intelligence about the disposition of enemy forces, and the ability to communicate that data in near real time, real life events demonstrated that challenges remain and that the fog is still very much with us.

Far greater questions have been raised about the RMA's applicability to conflicts that do not approximate conventional force on force. Even before protracted low-level conflict became apparent in Afghanistan and Iraq, critics argued the RMA addressed only a small portion of U.S. military activities—medium-intensity conflict against weak opponents.[4] The notion of moving rapidly over the battlefield and calling in standoff precision force was not considered very helpful against guerrilla adversaries because they are often hard to find and identify. In addition, the poor success rate of airpower in destroying targets in the 1999 war in and around Kosovo had demonstrated the limitations of standoff precision strike.

In the period since 2003 a growing number of people have argued that high-tech, information aged warfare is inappropriate to combating insurgencies. In Iraq, speed and technology could win the war but mass was required to seal the victory. "Pinpoint attacks can effectively take out tanks and missile silos," noted RAND Corporation's James Dobbins in a 2006 assessment, "But lightning strikes don't work in house-to-house raids or when rooting out guerrillas in caves. Those scenarios require manpower."[5] In Iraq, it quickly became apparent that military technology was "less decisive against an opponent that faded away into Iraqi cities only to fight another day"[6] —a general lesson that was reinforced by Israel's experience in Lebanon in the summer of 2006 when it attempted, unsuccessfully, to use high-tech standoff precision strike to combat a Hezbollah guerrilla force that used civilian infrastructure as cover for its activities. Concepts of network centric warfare, it is argued, are more suited for attacking fixed nodes than small, shadowy cells of loosely organized terrorists.[7] And even as militaries continued to invest in lighter, more advanced versions of contemporary army platforms, 70-ton Abrams tanks and Bradley fighting vehicles were being lost in Iraq to low-tech roadside bombs, calling into question whether future lighter vehicles would be able to survive anti-armor threats. It is these sorts of concerns that have driven the move to broaden the "how we fight" component of military transformation to include its "transforming transformation" elements.

Yet there are also caveats to the caveats. First, the two aspects of the "how we fight" component of military transformation are not mutually exclusive. Some technological aspects of the RMA can be applicable to the sorts of foes the United States is facing in Iraq and in the southern part of Afghanistan. Because insurgents often work in small groups, and often in urban environments, the ability to transmit information quickly, to generate shared situational awareness, and to precisely, discriminately, pinpoint targets is important. In this regard, advanced C4ISR can be just as important in counterinsurgency and stabilization and reconstruction missions as in conventional warfighting. Unmanned aerial vehicles are especially useful for ISR in the whole range of conflicts; North Atlantic Treaty Organization (NATO), for example, is calling for more UAVs in Afghanistan to provide ISR capabilities.[8] In addition, things like high-resolution satellite imagery can provide crucial information to peacekeepers attempting to address humanitarian crises.

Various platforms associated with the RMA are also cross-suited to roles beyond conventional warfare. Tanks, it was noted in Chapter 2, have been reintroduced into the counterinsurgency environment of southern Afghanistan. In addition, they can provide an important presence in urban warfare, indicating a future requirement for the Future Combat System. Artillery howitzers with precision-guided shells have been specifically deployed to meet the threat environment of Afghanistan. Army officials have argued such munitions "are suited for asymmetrical warfare, which often challenges soldiers to hit small, mobile targets in urban environments."[9] Land-based fighter aircraft have carried out numerous missions in Afghanistan, providing close air support with precision munitions. The Littoral Combat Ship is designed to operate in coastal areas where terrorist bombings are a growing threat, but other navy platforms that are normally conceived of in conventional terms also have nonconventional applications. America's amphibious assault ships, for example, can be used to carry marines ashore in a warfighting operation, or to support humanitarian operations. "This is not a fleet that's being oriented to the Chinese threat," notes defense analyst Loren Thompson, "It's being oriented around irregular warfare, stability operations, and dealing with rogue states."[10]

Third, the future low-intensity threat environment will not only comprise Iraq and Afghanistan. There will be other scenarios and these may prove more in line with earlier ideas about military transformation. A key concern, for example, is that terrorists, squeezed out of sanctuaries in Afghanistan and Iraq, will be looking to ungoverned areas of Africa as training and staging areas for terrorism. In addition to the joint task force it established in Djibouti after 9/11, the United States has launched a Trans-Saharan Counter-Terrorism Initiative under which it is helping nine West African states deal with lawless areas where militant Muslim groups could find a haven for their activities. The nature of these U.S. activities is such that they may be amenable to RMA doctrinal changes. "The areas (in Africa) are large," a high-ranking U.S. officer has noted, "you have to be able to respond fast as intelligence becomes actionable . . . and that forces us to think of more mobile, smaller, lighter, nimble forces."[11]

Requirements for carrying out the wider homeland security and defense dimension of military transformation will also need to be accommodated. The F-22, for example, may be of little use in seeking out the perpetrators of roadside bombs in overseas urban environments. But they are necessary for combat air patrols over U.S. cities, and they may also be useful for intercepting cruise missiles or unmanned aerial vehicles fired from ships off U.S. shores.

Military forces will also need to be able to contribute to wider missions that demand a civilian lead but nonetheless are central to United States and allied security and therefore may involve a military role. A good example of this is energy security. The growing dependence of America and its allies (as well as China) on imported oil and liquid natural gas has drawn attention to the security of pipelines in volatile places like the Caucasus and Africa, and of tankers traveling through a handful of narrow choke points around the world. Already NATO is examining what it could do to contribute to security in both of these areas; vessels for littoral operations, mobile and deployable ground forces, and special operations forces could be especially useful in this context.

Finally, more conventional types of warfare cannot be ruled out in the future, however unlikely that may seem at the present time. "If China were to attack Taiwan, the United States would probably be drawn in—and the resulting conflict would look very little like an insurgency campaign," notes one scholar, "Very quickly, Pentagon planners would be rushing to long-neglected bookshelves for writings on escalation and crisis bargaining."[12] Indeed, an analysis of American, NATO, Chinese, and Russian forces through the prism of three overlapping and sometimes competing "layers" of military transformation—(1) the conventional-force dominated revolution in military affairs, (2) the low-level counterinsurgency emphasis of "transforming transformation," and (3) the wider dimensions of transformation comprising primarily homeland defense, nuclear policy, and unhindered access to space, reveals an interesting dynamic. Driven by the Iraq and Afghanistan experiences, the Western world is focusing its attention on transformation's middle layer. China, by contrast is pursing the revolution in military affairs and the space dimension of military transformation, while Russia is centering its efforts on transformation's wider nuclear aspect.

Contemporary experience has revealed a clear requirement to reorient military forces toward greater capability in special operations, counterinsurgency, and stabilization and reconstruction missions. But as the United States and its allies struggle to address terrorism and counterinsurgency, the rest of the world will not stand still. Although it may be true that Western militaries are currently structured and (especially) equipped more for potential future conflicts than actual real life conflicts, it may equally be true that the security landscape of the future could look very different from that of today.

Notes

1. Michael R. Gordon, "New War, New Strategy, New Foes, New Questions," *International Herald Tribune* (April 5, 2003).

2. Eliot Cohen of Johns Hopkins University, as quoted in Thomas E. Ricks, "U.S. Arms Unmanned Aircraft," *Washington Post* (October 18, 2001), A01.

3. Michael Vickers as quoted in Edward Epstein, "Jury Still Out On Rumsfeld War Strategy: Reliance on High-Tech Stirs Debate," *San Francisco Chronicle* (April 11, 2003).

4. John A. Gentry, "Doomed To Fail: America's Blind Faith in Military Technology," *Parameters* (Winter 2002–2003), 89–90.

5. As quoted in Keith S. Collins, "Will Rumsfeld's Reforms Last?" *Christian Science Monitor* (November 13, 2006).

6. Michael R. Gordon and Bernard E. Trainor, *COBRA II: The Inside Story of the Invasion and Occupation of Iraq* (New York: Pantheon Books, 2006), p. 500.

7. Richard D. Hooker, Jr., H.R. McMaster, and Dave Grey, "Getting Transformation Right," *Joint Force Quarterly* 38 (July 2005), 23.

8. David Pugliese, "NATO Seeks More ISR For Afghan Combat," *Defense News* (June 4, 2007).

9. Kris Osborn, "Precision Shells Reshape U.S. Army Tactics," *Defense News* (May 7, 2007), 1.

10. As quoted in David S. Cloud, "Navy To Expand Fleet With New Enemies in Mind," *New York Times* (December 5, 2005).

11. Air Force General Charles Wald, deputy head of U.S. forces in Europe as quoted in Todd Pitman, "U.S. General Says Al-Qaida Eyeing Africa," *The Guardian* (March 6, 2004).

12. Michael J. Mazarr, "Extremism, Terror, and the Future of Conflict," *Policy Review* (March 2006).

Postscript

The essence of transformation is a marked change in character or form—usually for the better. The core of contemporary military transformation is a move away from the legacy systems of the Cold War and toward an alternate vision. For those who focus on the Revolution in Military Affairs (RMA) component of military transformation the vision includes things like unmanned aerial vehicles, long range precision strike, advanced command, control, communications, computing, intelligence, surveillance, and reconnaissance (C4ISR), and lighter, speedier, and more dispersed ground forces. For those that advocate a more recent "transforming transformation" perspective, the vision involves enhanced capabilities for counterinsurgency and stabilization and reconstruction missions. Special Operations Forces (SOFs) are relevant to both of the "how we fight" components of military transformation, although RMA advocates place greater emphasis on direct action SOF operations, while transforming transformation advocates stress the counterinsurgency work of SOFs.

The RMA and transforming transformation visions are very different, but they are united in the view that new and better ships, tanks, and fighters form costly obstacles to obtaining the necessary capabilities for addressing the future security environment. The most visible advocate of the RMA was former Secretary of Defense Rumsfeld, who sought to operationalize the theoretical ideas that had emerged in the 1990s and been included in Bush's 1999 speech to The Citadel. In some cases he succeeded. With his departure the momentum in this direction has inevitably declined, but it is unlikely to disappear entirely. Ideas inherent in the RMA well preceded the Bush administration and are likely to continue to be a factor in the next presidency, particularly if China's military capabilities continue apace.

Advocates of a transforming transformation perspective have come from many quarters but notably include high-ranking U.S. military officers. This is a positive factor from the perspective of those who note that the United States became experienced in counterinsurgency tactics in Vietnam and then lost these skills, and who therefore raise the question of whether the current focus on counterinsurgency will last beyond the missions in Iraq and Afghanistan. Implicit in the development of the new counterinsurgency manual by an Army General and a Marine Corps General is a recognition that low-intensity wars are here to stay. "If American commanders' response to Vietnam was to foreswear nasty small wars," notes an *Economist* assessment when the manual was released, "their reaction to the fiasco in Iraq seems so far to be quite different: to learn to fight them better."

These latter changes are still at an early stage. Nonetheless, the overall picture is one of a better balance in defense thinking and allocations. The Pentagon is devoting continued resources to RMA systems and additional funds to transforming transformation, notably the increased force size. But it is also spending a significant amount on what may be considered legacy systems. The new balance has been bought with the luxury of increased defense budgets, and only when this comes to an end will the future course of military transformation become more apparent.

Biographies

Thomas P.M. Barnett

When Arthur Cebrowski took on the task of leading the office of force transformation in the fall of 2001, one of the first things he did was establish five study areas. Although one focused specifically on the military transformation efforts of the U.S. services, others were much broader. Thomas Barnett, a Harvard educated expert on Russia and the Warsaw Pact who was a strategy professor at the U.S. Naval War College while Cebrowski was its president, was brought to Washington and asked to conduct a wide reaching study on "how the U.S. military should look at the world." At the office of force transformation he developed a power point presentation that catapulted him to prominence in the years immediately following 9/11. He eventually delivered the presentation over 500 times to audiences of government officials, military officers, and think tanks in and outside America.

The central idea of Barnett's presentation, and the 2004 book for which he is best known, *The Pentagon's New Map*, is that the world can best be understood through the lens of globalization. He divides the world into two: a "functioning core" of nations, fully plugged into the world economy, including the old core of North America, Western Europe, Japan, Australia, and New Zealand, and also the emerging core of Eastern Europe, Russia, China, South Africa, India, Brazil, Chile, and Argentina; and a "non-integrating gap" of nations comprising theocracies, dictatorships, and failed states that are unwilling or unable to participate in a globalized world economy. Barnett argues that if we want to know where future conflicts will take place we need to look at where globalization has taken root and where it has not. Where globalization has spread we find stable governments that do not require military interventions and do not warrant consideration as threats, but where globalization has not spread we find "failed states that command our attention and rogue states that demand our vigilance." Not only has the vast majority of the crises since the end of the Cold War taken place within the nonintegrating gap, he points out, but in his view "this gap is the expeditionary theater for U.S. military forces in the 21st century."

Barnett's contribution to the conceptual thinking surrounding military transformation lies in his particular view on the sorts of forces that will be necessary to operate in this nonintegrating gap. He argues the United States needs two militaries: one to fight wars, a Leviathan force, and one to wage peace, a System Administrator force—and it is on the latter where he places his greatest emphasis. While the leviathan force may occasionally be necessary, he argues, the focus should be on funding a system administrator force that can "shrink the gap" by helping failed and conquered join the functioning core of nations. In his view war with China is highly unlikely, given that it is part of the functioning core, and resources expended to meet this potential peer competitor would be better spent on capabilities for peacekeeping and nation building. These would comprise primarily ground troops and especially the marine corps—which he feels is better suited to a system administrator role—while the Leviathan force, which would grow progressively smaller as nations integrated into the global economy, would draw primarily from the air force and the navy, as well as heavy armor. Barnett's focus on peacekeeping was consistent with ideas that emerged more generally in the office of force transformation in 2003 about stability and reconstruction divisions.

It is unclear how much influence Barnett, who expanded his ideas in a 2005 book *Blueprint For Action* and is now a private consultant, had on the current course of military transformation in the United States. Nonetheless, his ideas sparked a valuable debate on the appropriate prism through which to view the world, and on the types of forces necessary to address contemporary threats.

Arthur Cebrowski

The starting point for Arthur Cebrowksi's contribution to thinking surrounding military transformation lies in Alvin and Heidi Toffler's observation, in their 1993 book *War and Anti-War*, that the way society makes war reflects the way they make wealth. Cebrowski, a former Vice-Admiral in the U.S. Navy who commanded an aircraft carrier during the 1991 Gulf War and subsequently became president of the Naval War College, co-authored an influential 1998 article in the *United States Naval Institute Proceedings* on network centric warfare. In it, Cebrowksi argued three key themes had changed the nature of American business—the shift in focus from the platform to the network, the shift from viewing actors as independent to viewing them as part of a continuously adapting ecosystem, and the importance of adaptation in order to survive in such an ecosystem—and that these themes "have changed and will continue to change the way we conduct the sometimes violent business of the military." Warfare would move from being platform-centric to network-centric in that ships, aircraft, ground forces, and satellites would be linked together to create a shared picture of the battlefield. This was significant, he felt, because it would enable greater situational awareness and with it an improved ability to deter conflict, or prevail if conflict became unavoidable.

Cebrowski's 1998 article, which helped make network centric warfare a well-known term, revealed just that sort of "outside the box" approach to military operations that attracted Donald Rumsfeld. Thus when he became Secretary of Defense in 2001 and was looking to transform the U.S. military, Rumsfeld turned to Cebrowski, who had recently retired from the Navy, to head up the Office of Force Transformation. Created a month after 9/11, the office was charged with advising Rumsfeld on how to prod the U.S. military, a traditionally conservative organization, into carrying out the revolutions Andrew Marshall and protégés like Andrew Krepinevich had been theorizing about for over a decade. The office undertook five studies, one of which centered on evaluating the individual Army, Navy, and Air Force transformation programs. In 2003 it released the *Transformation Planning Guidance*, designed to help the services develop transformation road maps to meet the critical operational goals for transformation that had been outlined in the 2001 Quadrennial Defense Review. Later that year the office further elaborated its ideas in *Military Transformation: A Strategic Approach*.

There is some debate as to how effective the office of force transformation was in achieving its objectives. In practical terms transformation called, among other things, for abandoning some legacy systems, investing in C4ISR technologies, and fostering a "cultural" change toward risk taking and innovation. Critics note that the office had relatively little effect on programming and cutting legacy systems. But new technologies were adopted and integrated, and a 2004 *Defense News* account indicates that at least some operations during the Iraq War amounted to an "extensive demonstration...of how network-centric capabilities can improve an army's ability to fight by sharing information and situational awareness." Cebroswki himself, who left the office of force transformation in early 2005 for health reasons and died later that year of cancer, felt that the main successes had been in the cultural area—creating an openness to new ways of doing business and organizational changes to make them possible. He cited, in particular, the Army's decision to break its longstanding division structure in favor of smaller, more easily deployable brigade combat teams.

Cebrowski's conceptual contribution to military transformation went beyond network-centric warfare. He put forward a view of jointness that echoed that of William Owens in which jointness did not simply mean that the services could talk to one another, but that they came to rely on one another for providing some aspect of military capability. While President of the Naval War College he was a strong proponent of the Streetfighter, a small, fast ship that could operate close to coasts and be networked together to respond quickly to threats. These ideas led to the Littoral Combat Ship, now being built. And in 2003, admitting that he was among those who had thought a lot about rapid battlefield victory but failed to foresee the difficulty in reconfiguring U.S. forces for long-term political victory, Cebrowksi and his office developed a whole new area of research that centered on the creation of stabilization and reconstruction divisions. But in 1998 network-centric warfare was a relatively unknown concept. Articulating this vision, and seeing it come to reality in the 2003 Iraq War, was perhaps Cebrowski's most lasting contribution to military transformation.

Andrew Krepinevich

The career of Dr. Andrew Krepinevich, notes a 2002 *Washington Post* account, stands as a classic example of how intellectuals inside the military can come to have far more sway over defense policy from the outside than they ever had from inside. A retired lieutenant colonel in the U.S. Army, Krepinevich worked for Andrew Marshall in the Office of Net Assessment in the early 1990s. Marshall, who had been studying Soviet writings on the Military Technical Revolution (MTR) for some years, assigned Krepinevich to write an assessment of whether the Soviets were correct in their belief that an MTR was underway that would lead to major changes in the nature of warfare. The outcome was a July 1992 report, *The Military Technical Revolution*, classified at the time but released in 2002 by the Center for Strategic and Budgetary Assessments, the think tank of which Krepinevich has been President since leaving the Pentagon in 1993.

The Military Technological Revolution became the intellectual basis for the Pentagon's pursuit of the revolution in military affairs (RMA) in the 1990s, and the Bush administration's emphasis on military transformation during its first term. In it, Krepinevich stated that an MTR occurs when technological change combines with innovative operational concepts (i.e. doctrinal change) and organizational adaptation to change the nature of warfare so dramatically that former forms of warfare are invalidated (rendered obsolete). This formulation has become the working conceptual framework for most RMA theorists since that time. Krepinevich's ideas on the nature of RMAs have marked a significant contribution to the intellectual thinking surrounding military transformation. They are elaborated both in the 1992 report, where he argues there were probably two RMAs in the twentieth century and two in the nineteenth century, and also in a 1994 *National Interest* article where he discusses the pattern of military revolutions since the fourteenth century.

Krepinevich was perhaps the first to outline the technological and doctrinal elements that have come to be associated with the RMA. His ideas in this regard are captured in his 1992 assessment and also in the 1997 *Report of the National Defense Panel* (NDP) of which he was an influential member. Krepinevich argued that effective military operations in future conflicts would require information dominance through advanced C4ISR technologies, as well as technologies for long-range precision strike. He questioned the value of heavy tanks, because future war would likely center around formations of highly-mobile, dispersed forces with a smaller "footprint"; of manned short-range aircraft because future war would require operating at extended stand-off ranges since there was unlikely to be allied bases near by; and of large naval platforms like aircraft carriers because they were increasingly vulnerable to detection and destruction.

In *Transforming Defense*, the National Defense Panel (NDP) was particularly critical of the Pentagon's continued adherence to a "two major regional conflict" (2 MRC) construct that held that the United States needed to be able to fight and win two major regional conflicts in overlapping timeframes. In its view, because the construct served to justify the existing force structure it was "fast becoming an inhibitor to reaching the capabilities we will need in the 2010–2020 timeframe." These included the need to focus more on asymmetric adversaries, urban warfare, special operations forces, unmanned aerial vehicles, and long-range power projection. Krepinevich was an advocate of developing the Arsenal ship, a stealthy barge armed with hundreds of cruise missiles that was cancelled by the navy in 1997; of converting stealthy Trident nuclear missile subs into those that can carry non-nuclear cruise missiles; and of canceling the mammoth Crusader artillery piece. In his view there was little need for two separate programs for new short-range fighter aircraft—the Joint Strike Fighter and the F-22; new generation carriers should be deferred; and tanks should be scaled back, as should be proposed acquisitions of the Future Combat System (FCS).

As a disciple of Marshall, who was chosen by Donald Rumsfeld to lead the Pentagon's strategic review of early 2001, Krepinevich's ideas can be seen in the policy documents written, and decisions taken, during the Bush administration's first term. The 2001 Quadrennial Defense Review moves away from the 2 MRC construct, and its six operational goals for transformation mirror ideas in *Transforming Defense*. In addition, Rumsfeld cancelled the Crusader program in 2002, and he approved the conversion of four Trident submarines into what are essentially cruise missile Arsenal ships. Nonetheless, overall progress in military transformation has, in Krepinevich's view, been relatively limited. Although significantly more money is being spent on special operations forces and unmanned aerial vehicles, almost all the military's "legacy" systems—destroyers, carriers, fighter aircraft, submarines, tanks, and the FCS—continue relatively unscathed.

For Krepinevich, the state-on-state conflicts for which large ships, tanks, and fighters prepare the United States are a thing of the past. In his 1986 book, *The Army and Vietnam*, Krepinevich argued "low-intensity warfare represents the most likely arena of future conflict for the Army, and counterinsurgency the most demanding contingency." He echoed this perspective in *The Military-Technical Revolution* and in a 2002 *Joint Force Quarterly* article about transforming land warfare. In the latter he provides a caveat to a core element of the RMA, noting that air strikes and precision munitions are of limited use in urban environments where enemies are mixed in with civilians, or near hospitals and religious sites, and that tactical human intelligence is key to providing the information needed to operate on the urban battlefield. He argues, in a 2005 *Foreign Affairs* article on "How to Win in Iraq," for a "real strategy built around the principles of counterinsurgency warfare" in which the U.S. military provides security and opportunity to certain key areas, enabling stability to expand as would an oil spot. These ideas have already begun to figure in America's approach to "transforming transformation."

Andrew Marshall

Intellectual thinking about the military technical revolution and the revolution in military affairs began with the musings of the highly influential yet little known Andrew Marshall. Now in his late 80s, Marshall, who had been working as a RAND corporation nuclear expert since 1949, was appointed by Secretary of Defense James Schlesinger to head the Office of Net Assessment in 1973, and has been reappointed by every President since. In the late 1970s his office began to pick up on Soviet writings that suggested they believed a major change in warfare was beginning and that this would constitute an MTR. Marshall's office followed these developments and over the subsequent decade became convinced that Soviet writings in this regard were motivated by anxiety about U.S. capabilities, not belief in their own capabilities. The Soviet Union was far weaker than most people realized, he felt, and the Soviet military was in decline. Marshall's views, closely guarded in the Pentagon in the late 1980s, were confirmed by the demise of the Soviet Union.

In the early 1990s Marshall began to argue that the world had entered a period of military history that resembled the interwar period of the 1920s and 1930s when major shifts occurred in land, sea, and air warfare. The most remarkable aspect of that period, Marshall argued in a 1995 *Joint Force Quarterly* commentary—one of his very few published works—was not technological advancement, since this had already been underway for some time, but rather the emergence of innovative operational concepts and organizations to exploit commonly available systems. The origin of Blitzkrieg, aircraft carrier strike forces, amphibious warfare, and long-range airpower theory, he argued, could all be traced back to the years immediately following World War I. Marshall assigned analysts within his office to examine the nature of military revolutions and the elements of the contemporary MTR. By 1993 he and his staff were convinced that new technologies that had been developed over the previous decade and a half could be married with new doctrines and organizations to produce something much broader than an MTR—it would be an RMA. An eight-page memo written for incoming Secretary of Defense William Perry in 1993, "Some Thoughts on Military Revolutions," earned Marshall his reputation as the founding visionary behind the RMA school of thought.

When Donald Rumsfeld became Secretary of Defense in early 2001 he hand-picked Marshall to guide a strategic review of how the U.S. military might be transformed, thereby ensuring that Marshall had a strong influence on subsequent decisions in this area. But his impact has been far broader than on issues associated with the MTR, RMA, and military transformation—a term he reportedly dislikes because it sounds too extensive and indiscriminant. (In his view, it is possible for an RMA to take place if only a small portion, perhaps 10 to 15 percent, of the force transforms). Reports indicate that Marshall was behind some of the key strategic decisions of the Reagan years, including an early version of the Strategic Defense Initiative, thought to have contributed to the demise of the Soviet Union by out-spending the Soviet war machine.

From the mid-1990s onward Marshall's primary focus has been not the RMA but rather China, which he sees as a looming threat on the horizon. Even in the post-9/11 period, accounts indicate, the rise of China remained his central concern. "The Marshallites aren't indifferent to terrorism or regional conflict," noted an early 2002 *New York Times* commentary, "but over the years their main worry has been . . . China, a country with the size, infrastructure and ambition to challenge America." It is probably no coincidence that even as the Pentagon struggles with the transforming transformation demands of responding to terrorism and counterinsurgency, it is equally expending significant effort assessing and determining a response to the military power of the People's Republic of China.

William Owens

Admiral (retired) William A. Owens is a submariner who served some thirty-four years in the U.S. Navy, retiring in 1996 after two years as the Vice Chairman of the Joint Chiefs of Staff. He is one of three people who are considered the architects of the early American revolution in military affairs—the others being the "technologically minded" Secretary of Defense, William Perry, who was appointed by President Clinton in 1994 and had earlier worked for Harold Brown when he developed the offset strategy, and the Pentagon's longstanding Director of Net Assessment, Andrew Marshall, who had studied the military technical revolution extensively in the 1980s and early 1990s and whose office coined the term "revolution in military affairs". While Perry provided the political and strategic support to pursue revolutionary change, Marshall and his team brought with them a broader historical sense of previous RMAs and how they occur. What was missing at that time, notes James Blaker in his 1997 monograph, *Understanding the Revolution in Military Affairs*, was a military advocate of the RMA. When Owens arrived in the Pentagon in 1994, after tours as Deputy Chief of Naval Operations and commander of the Sixth Fleet in Europe, he became the uniformed champion of rapid military change. Owens' contribution centered on two distinct but interrelated areas: putting forward the idea of a "system of systems," and discerning the meaning of, and repeatedly stressing, jointness and the need for the services to move in this direction.

It is the notion of a system of systems for which Owens is probably most remembered. When he became Vice-Chief Owens identified three types of advanced systems in the U.S. military's inventory. Those that provided for "battlespace awareness" were sensing technologies and platforms involved in intelligence gathering, surveillance, and reconnaissance; those that provided for "battlespace control" were technologies that could process the vast amounts of data that was gathered by sensing systems, change it from information to knowledge, and enable commanders to act on the information in near real time; and those that enabled the precise use of military force involved precision guided weaponry and also things like information warfare (and, one may add today, special operations forces). Examples in each of these three areas included, respectively, JSTARS, link 16, and hellfire missiles. Owens famously drew up three lists of systems, one each for sensors, C4I, and PGMs. As he notes in his 1995 *Military Review* article, "The Emerging System of Systems," he determined that most people within the Pentagon tended to see the lists as separate, compartmentalized, or "stovepiped" and unable to interact with one another. JSTARS, for example, could not directly transfer information to platforms that fired hellfire missiles.

What was needed, Owens argued, was to integrate the disparate columns of systems into one "system of systems." This was important, he stated in a 1996 *Foreign Affairs* article, because it was the "information edge" that would make the difference in future warfare. To create a synergy among the traditional military functions of "to see," "to tell," and "to act," he further argued in his 1999 book *Lifting the Fog of War*, was to create the conditions for combat victory. In a 2002 *Joint Force Quarterly* article, where he published many of his ideas, Owens elaborated that war is "a deadly contest in which the side that best understands the battlespace and can best transfer that knowledge among its own elements to apply force faster, more precisely, and over greater distance wins." Yet even as early as 1995, also in *Joint Force Quarterly*, he was careful to qualify that the architects of the American RMA have never claimed to be able to completely dissipate the fog of war or eliminate friction, two terms associated with Carl von Clausewitz. Rather, they have only introduced the idea that a disparity in the degree to which fog or friction applies to one or the other side can give one side "unprecedented dominance."

The notion of a system of systems is linked to that of jointness. Just as technologies were stovepiped into separate services or program offices, so too was each entire service (army, navy, and air force) operating in what were essentially separate spheres, even as there existed an impression of jointness. Owens elaborates, in two further *Joint Force Quarterly* articles from the 1990s, that even though the 1986 DoD Reorganization Act had created unified commands comprising land, sea, and air forces, and even though the 1991 Gulf War was touted as the advent of joint operations, in fact planning and operations remained more joint in name than in conduct. Joint commanders took individual service submissions from each of the subordinate commanders, packaged them together, and sent them to the Pentagon as "joint", while operations in the Gulf War still reflected the view that a service had to have the range of capabilities so as to avoid reliance on another service for some aspect of a military operation. "A joint perspective," Owens stated succinctly, "comes down to cross-service trust and the belief that another component can reliably provide a military function." Because joint operations increase the efficiency with which military power is utilized, it was imperative to keep pushing to make them "second nature" to the Armed Forces.

Owens, who has gone on to become CEO of a number of large high-tech companies, has equated military transformation with the RMA. Writing in 2002— before the drawn out insurgency in Afghanistan became apparent—Owens argued that asymmetric adversaries like Serb forces in Kosovo and al-Qaeda fighters in Afghanistan "could best be deterred and defeated by consolidating the revolution in military affairs." His vision with respect to both a system of systems and jointness was arguably achieved in the 2003 war in Iraq. According to an April 2003 *Defense News* account the Chairman of the Joint Chiefs of Staff, General Richard Myers, attributed the efficient progress of the war to a vastly improved picture of the battlefield—and a new willingness on the part of commanders to use the most appropriate capabilities, regardless of which service provided them.

Donald Rumsfeld

Military transformation began its emergence as a well-known phrase with a 1999 speech by then-presidential candidate George W. Bush. In his speech to The Citadel, Bush stated that if elected he would begin creating the "military of the next century," a force comprising all the (now familiar) elements of the RMA plus a focus on special operations forces. He promised to "skip a generation of technology" in order to effect a transformation of the U.S. military. To this end, his Secretary of Defense would launch an immediate, comprehensive review of the U.S. military and, when complete, endeavor to ensure the military's budget priorities matched the strategic vision.

When Bush was elected President he chose Donald Rumsfeld as the person who would carry out this task. Arriving in the Pentagon in January 2001, Rumsfeld was no stranger to defense issues. He had already been Secretary of Defense once before, from 1975 to 1977 in the Gerald Ford administration, and in the intervening years in the business world he had maintained his interest in defense issues, having chaired a commission to assess the threat of ballistic missiles in 1998, and a commission to assess U.S. national security interests in space in 2000. Rumsfeld's particular futuristic specialties thus centered on ballistic missiles and the military use of space, not conventional force transformation, but he quickly became committed to military transformation.

Launching the strategic review Bush had called for, Rumsfeld assigned a key guiding role to Andrew Marshall, the director of the Office of Net Assessment. His team produced a "blueprint for transformation," delivered to the services in spring 2001, who were then asked how they would carry it out. But the service chiefs, who were not involved in the secretive exercise, gave the blueprint a lukewarm reception, and members of Congress were also alarmed by the approach to transformation. In the months before 9/11 Rumsfeld and his deputy, Paul Wolfowitz, had become so isolated that conventional wisdom had Rumsfeld losing his job. The September 11th attacks, and the 2001–2002 war in Afghanistan that followed, completely changed this by supporting the transformational developments for which Rumsfeld had been arguing. It was the combination of special operations forces, long-range precision strike and unmanned aerial vehicles working with indigenous forces, Rumsfeld argued in a 2002 *Foreign Affairs* article on "Transforming the Military," that brought about the swift defeat of the Taliban. The U.S. success in Iraq a year and half later further confirmed that the integration of precision air power, special forces, and smaller, more mobile ground forces could enable the U.S. military to be more effective with less mass. This became the core of Rumsfeld's thinking and was given the term "Rapid Decisive Operations," or simply the Rumsfeld Doctrine, with the central focus being fewer troops and speed of action.

The validation of theoretical concepts on the practical battlefields of Afghanistan in 2001–2002 and Iraq in 2003 gave Rumsfeld the political leverage to cancel or reduce some of the U.S. military's legacy systems in order to finance "transformational technologies." The Crusader artillery system and the Comanche helicopter were cancelled outright, while the number of F-22 purchases were reduced to a fraction of the Cold War number. Funding was increased in areas such as unmanned aerial vehicles, tomahawk precision-guided missiles, and AC-130 special operations transport aircraft. Rumsfeld aimed his funding requests at what he considered six "key transformational goals," first detailed in the September 2001 Quadrennial Defense Review (QDR): protecting the U.S. homeland and forces abroad against weapons of mass destruction, conducting effective information operations, projecting forces into hostile areas, denying enemies sanctuary through persistent surveillance, enhancing the capability and survival of space systems, and developing joint C4ISR capabilities.

But generally speaking Rumsfeld's second tenure as Defense Secretary was not marked by transformational budgets. Most of America's large armaments programs—of which there are forty-eight according to the *Economist*—were only trimmed, and it was substantial increases in the defense budget, not a significant move away from legacy systems, which has allowed for greater investments in new technologies and platforms. The 2006 QDR presented a new picture of America fighting a "Long War" against international terrorism, but this view was not matched by a similarly dramatic change in budget priorities. (The QDR also called for a reduction in troops, a decision that has since been reversed). Rumsfeld's last budget, submitted at roughly the same time as the QDR was released, supported spending programs that were almost exactly the same as his first, in 2001. "Four years into what the 2006 Quadrennial Defense Review calls a 'long war' against terrorist networks," noted one analyst at the time, "Rumsfeld has abandoned attempts to . . . fundamentally transform the U.S. military."

What cost Rumsfeld his job in late 2006 was not his inability to fully effect the transformation Bush had laid out in his Citadel speech; some progress was made in this direction. Rather, it was his failure to adapt this vision, in concrete terms, to changing circumstances on the ground. The requirements for winning wars, it is now well known and accepted, were far different from those for ensuring long-term stability. Critics contend that Rumsfeld had an unrealistic confidence in technology to replace manpower, and that his efforts at transforming the military were largely irrelevant to the counterinsurgencies under way in Afghanistan and Iraq. Despite strong evidence that the Army had too few soldiers to fight wars in Afghanistan and Iraq, and despite growing calls from retired generals for him to resign over this point, Rumsfeld resisted any permanent increase in the "end strength" of the U.S. military.

Whether future Secretaries of Defense will continue the reforms started by Rumsfeld is an open question. It seems clear that his replacement, Robert Gates, was given the task of addressing Iraq, not military transformation, and the next Secretary may also be assigned different Presidential priorities. Ultimately, Rumsfeld's lasting legacy is likely to be in the organizational dimensions of transformation. The former Secretary of Defense created Northern Command to defend the U.S homeland, elevated the status of Special Operations Command, and, under the Global Defense Posture Review, set in train the most dramatic restructuring of America's overseas force posture in half a century. It is these organizational changes that are likely to contribute most significantly to long-term military transformation.

Key Documents

Author's Note:

In the late 1970s and 1980s Andrew Marshall, director of the Pentagon's in-house think tank, the Office of Net Assessment, began to pick up on Soviet military writings about how a Military Technical Revolution (MTR) would change the nature of future war. After Andrew Krepinevich joined the Office in 1990, Marshall asked him to conduct an assessment of the MTR to determine if the Soviets were correct in their beliefs. The outcome was *The Military-Technical Revolution: A Preliminary Assessment*, which was the first official U.S. document to comprehensively state many of the technological, doctrinal, and organizational elements of what later became known as the Revolution in Military Affairs (RMA). The document's more than fifty pages cover a whole range of issues, including: technological change, such as the growing ability to collect information, major improvements in the range and accuracy of conventional munitions, and network integration; military systems, such as space platforms, unmanned air-breathing aircraft, and extended range fire systems—as well as the declining utility of tanks, manned aircraft, and large surface combatants; operational innovation, such as information dominance, strategic mobility, and space, air, and sea control; and organizational innovation, such as creating a flatter, less hierarchical organizational structure. The document also includes a useful discussion of the nature of military revolutions, putting them in historical perspective. It is this part of *The Military-Technical Revolution* that is reproduced here.

Excerpt from
The Military-Technical Revolution: A Preliminary Assessment
Andrew Krepinevich
Office of Net Assessment
July 1992

... MILITARY-TECHNICAL REVOLUTIONS, PAST AND PRESENT

A Military-Technical Revolution occurs when the application of new technologies into military systems combines with innovative operational concepts and organizational adaptation to alter fundamentally the character and conduct of military operations.

... These elements combine to produce a dramatic improvement in military effectiveness and combat potential. The rate of transition into a new military-technical regime will also be influenced by the geopolitical environment, and the nature of the military-technical competition.

... *What is revolutionary is not the speed with which the change takes place, but rather the magnitude of the change* itself (emphasis in original). At some point the cumulative effects of technological advances and military innovation will invalidate former conceptual frameworks by bringing about a fundamental change in the nature of warfare and, thus, in our definitions and measurement of military effectiveness.

... MILITARY-TECHNICAL REVOLUTIONS: AN HISTORICAL OVERVIEW

There appear to have been at least two previous MTRs in this century, and probably two in the 19th century. Between the Napoleonic Wars and the American Civil War, railroads, telegraphs, ironclads, and rifled muskets and artillery dramatically transformed the nature of warfare; i.e. the way in which military forces are organized, equipped, and employed to obtain maximum military effectiveness. Union and confederate generals who were retained the tactics and operations of the Napoleonic era exposed their men to fearful slaughter, as at Fredericksburg, Spotsylvania, and Gettysburg. Both sides did adapt, eventually. The campaigns of 1864 and 1865 were marked by a dramatic increase in entrenchments and field fortifications over what had been the practice only a few years before. Arguably, many of the major battles toward the war's end bore a greater resemblance to operations on the western front in the middle period of World War I than they did to early Civil War battles like Shiloh or First Manassas.

The machine gun, airplane, submarine, and the *Dreadnought* class of ships dramatically altered conflict again between the mid-19th century and the early 20th century. Again, military leaders who ignored technological changes and failed to adapt risked their men and their cause. One recalls here the mutiny of the French army after the futile and bloody Nivelle Offensive, and the destruction wreaked on British shipping by German submarine warfare operations. Toward the war's end, however, new operational concepts were developed to exploit new technologies and military systems. On land, massed frontal assaults preceded by long artillery preparations gave way to infiltration of troops and brief artillery preparation fires. At sea, elaborate convoy operations were established to counter the U-boat threat.

Between 1917 and 1939, internal combustion engines, improved aircraft design, and the exploitation of radio and radar made possible the *blitzkreig*, carrier aviation, and strategic aerial bombardment. After a scant 20 years, the nature of conflict had changed dramatically, and those—like the French—who failed to adapt suffered grievously.

The early years of World War II—in some respects like the Napoleonic revolution—demonstrate what can happen when only one power makes the "correct" choice concerning how advances in technology will change the nature of warfare. In this instance, Germany proved far more adept than France, Britain, and Soviet Russia at operational and organizational innovation on land. At sea, both the United States and Japan saw the potential of carrier aviation forces, and acted upon it. Thus, although the nature of war at sea shifted dramatically, as it did on land, neither the Americans nor the Japanese realized the kind of dominance Germany enjoyed in land warfare from 1939 to 1942. In the air, Germany's failure to exploit emerging technologies thoroughly left it at a significant disadvantage in strategic aerial bombardment, as, for example, during the Battle of Britain.

Finally, in mid-century, nuclear weapons, especially after their mating with ballistic missiles, brought the prospect of near-instantaneous destruction of a state's economic and political fabric into the strategic equation. Here was a shift in technology so radical it convinced nearly all observers that a fundamental change in the nature of warfare was at hand.

Author's Note:

In 1996 Congress mandated the creation of a bipartisan National Defense Panel to conduct an independent, nonpartisan review of future challenges to the United States and the U.S. military force structure necessary to meet those challenges. Meeting in a timeframe that partially overlapped the deliberations that led to the May 1997 Quadrennial Defense Review (QDR), the National Defense Panel released its report, *Transforming Defense: National Security in the 21st Century*, in December of that year. The panel's report was prolific in that in this pre-9/11 era it was the first U.S. defense-related document to place homeland defense first on its list of future security challenges. At the time, it recommended the creation of an America's Command, which may be considered the precursor to today's Northern Command. The panel focused significantly on the asymmetric threat to the United States, arguing America should take risks now (in 1997) in order to better prepare for future threats. This meant reducing the force structure designed to fight Cold War threats and allocating these resources to the development of new technologies and capabilities. The force that the panel envisioned was one that was very much in line with the ideas of the revolution in military affairs (RMA), but the panel was also careful to stress the need for the U.S. military to be able to operate in urban environments and to carry out stability operations. This mix of capabilities, as well as the panel's evident concern with the prevailing force sizing construct (which had been reiterated in the 1997 QDR) is captured in the following excerpt.

Excerpt from
Transforming Defense: National Security in the 21st Century
Report of the National Defense Panel
December 1997

. . . Current defense strategy states that U.S. forces should be capable of fighting two regional wars at almost the same time. Potential threats in North Korea and

Southwest Asia define the type of threat we may confront. This two-theater war concept is predicated on the belief that the ability to fight more than one major war at a time deters an enemy from seeking to take advantage of the opportunity to strike while the United States is preoccupied in another theater.

… The Panel views the two-military-theater-of-war construct as a force-sizing function and not a strategy. We are concerned that this construct may have become a force-protection mechanism—a means of justifying the current force structure—especially for those searching for the certainties of the Cold War era.

… The two-theater construct has been a useful mechanism for determining what forces to retain as the Cold War came to a close. To some degree, it remains a useful mechanism today. But, it is fast becoming an inhibitor to reaching the capabilities we will need in the 2010–2020 time frame.

… Therefore, the Panel concludes … that the Defense Department must move beyond its current focus to pursue a transformation strategy that safeguards our qualitative edge now and in the future.

… Protecting the territory of the United States and its citizens from "all enemies both foreign and domestic" is the principal task of government. The primary reason for the increased emphasis on homeland defense is the change, both in type and degree, in the threats to the United States. Besides the enduring need to deter a strategic nuclear attack, the United States must defend against terrorism, information warfare, weapons of mass destruction, ballistic and cruise missiles, and other transnational threats to the sovereign territory of the nation. In many of these mission areas, the military will necessarily play the leading role; however, many other threats exist which will require Defense to support local law enforcement agencies, as well as a host of other federal, state, and local entities.

… The challenge confronting U.S. military planners is that the forces, training, and equipment used to maintain ready power projection capabilities do not necessarily lend themselves to the requirements of stability operations. The unpredictable and unique challenges generated by regional crises often require forces tailored to fit specific requirements. This will likely entail restructuring of some forces now focused on regional conflicts to conduct these less demanding but more likely contingencies.

… To meet future requirements to project military power and conduct combat operations, the United States must transform the present force, taking advantage of new technology, operational concepts, and force structures. Major combat operations in the future may well require forces and systems that are legacies (e.g., mechanized forces, naval surface combatant, short-range fixed and rotary-wing aircraft) of those currently in use. However, the cutting-edge ability to accomplish U.S. national security objectives will come from new approaches and new thinking about power projection and asymmetric warfare capabilities.

. . . We must be able to project military power much more rapidly into areas where we may not have stationed forces. The ability to project lethal forces—in the air, on the sea, or on the land—will be essential. Toward that end, our ability to project combat power anywhere in the world will require new technologies, operational concepts, and capabilities to meet the new challenges. First among these new challenges is the need for a much smaller force "footprint" characterized by fewer but more capable attacking troops and platforms supported by an even smaller logistics element.

. . . there is a high premium on forces that can deploy rapidly, seize the initiative, and achieve our objectives with minimal risk of heavy casualties.

. . . Forward-deployed land forces would have to operate dispersed. They would not operate from a few fixed bases characterized by "iron mountains" of supplies, but would rather rely on a combination of numerous small, dispersed supply points. Along with dispersion, ground units would emphasize speed to facilitate the ability to concentrate rapidly for close combat as required. They also may operate in smaller units that place great emphasis on seeing deep (through Special Operations Forces and deep-reconnaissance teams, along with reconnaissance helicopters and unmanned aerial vehicles).

. . . Maritime forces would rely more heavily on a "distributed" and networked battle fleet that would comprise, along with carriers, extended-range precision strike forces based on surface and submerged combatants, including submarines, arsenal ships, land-attack destroyers and integrated amphibious forces.

. . . Air forces would place greater emphasis on operating at extended ranges, relying heavily on long-range aircraft and extended-range unmanned systems, employing advanced precision and brilliant munitions and based outside the theater of operations. Aircraft, unmanned aerial vehicles, and unmanned combat aerial vehicles operating in theater could stage at peripheral bases outside enemy missile range, or on Mobile Offshore Bases or carriers.

. . . Such a force would be fully joint and increasingly combined, engaging in multidimensional (i. e., integrated ground, sea, and aerospace) and, where possible, multinational operations at close and extended ranges. It would be fully integrated through a global, distributed reconnaissance and intelligence architecture composed of satellites, unmanned aerial vehicles, sensors, and infiltration forces. Unmanned systems would likely provide a growing proportion of airborne reconnaissance and strike forces.

. . . Although we might prefer to avoid urban situations, mission requirements in peace and war may not allow this preference.

Author's Note:
The speech President George W. Bush delivered to The Citadel as presidential candidate in the fall of 1999 represented the point at which theoretical discussions surrounding

the military technical revolution (MTR), the revolution in military affairs (RMA), and military transformation made the leap to the highest political level in the U.S. government. Prior to this, the Chairman of the Joint Chiefs of Staff had released a document, Joint Vision 2010, which discussed revolutionary changes in warfare, the 1997 Quadrennial Defense Review (QDR) had discussed the "so-called revolution in military affairs" in a section on "Transforming U.S. Forces for the Future," and the National Defense Panel had released its report on military transformation which contained numerous RMA components. But without political support, these ideas would languish on the shelf. It was thus significant that the Presidential candidate and future president specifically endorsed many aspects of the RMA, as is indicated in the excerpt below. The President's choice for Secretary of Defense, Donald Rumsfeld, attempted to implement this vision, with a mixed rate of success. Most would argue, almost a decade after the speech, that the most remembered promise of the speech, to "skip a generation of technology," has not been achieved. Perhaps more remarkable is its prolific statement about the increased importance of homeland defense, and its points about open ended deployments and peacekeeping that were overturned by subsequent events.

Excerpt from
A Period of Consequences
Speech by Presidential candidate George W. Bush
The Citadel, South Carolina
Thursday, September 23, 1999

... I want to begin with the foundation of our peace—a strong, capable and modern military.

... if elected, I will set three goals: I will renew the bond of trust between the American president and the American military. I will defend the American people against missiles and terror. And I will begin creating the military of the next century.

...our military requires more than good treatment. It needs the rallying point of a defining mission. And that mission is to deter wars—and win wars when deterrence fails. Sending our military on vague, aimless and endless deployments is the swift solvent of morale.

As president, I will order an immediate review of our overseas deployments—in dozens of countries. The longstanding commitments we have made to our allies are the strong foundation of our current peace. I will keep these pledges to defend friends from aggression. The problem comes with open-ended deployments and unclear military missions...We will not be hasty. But we will not be permanent peacekeepers...

...My second goal is to build America's defenses on the troubled frontiers of technology and terror. The protection of America itself will assume a high priority in a new century. Once a strategic afterthought, homeland defense has become an urgent duty.

For most of our history, America felt safe behind two great oceans. But with the spread of technology, distance no longer means security. North Korea is proving that even a poor and backward country, in the hands of a tyrant, can reach across oceans to threaten us. It has developed missiles capable of hitting Hawaii and Alaska. Iran has made rapid strides in its missile program, and . . . [in 1996] a Chinese general reminded America that China possesses the means to incinerate Los Angeles with nuclear missiles.

Add to this the threat of biological, chemical and nuclear terrorism . . . These weapons can be delivered, not just by ballistic missiles, but by everything from airplanes to cruise missiles, from shipping containers to suitcases.

And consider the prospect of information warfare, in which hacker terrorists may try to disrupt finance, communication, transportation and public health.

. . . At the earliest possible date, my administration will deploy anti-ballistic missile systems, both theater and national, to guard against attack and blackmail.

. . . We will defend the American homeland by strengthening our intelligence community—focusing on human intelligence and the early detection of terrorist operations both here and abroad. And when direct threats to America are discovered, I know that the best defense can be a strong and swift offense—including the use of Special Operations Forces and long-range strike capabilities . . . I will put a high priority on detecting and responding to terrorism on our soil . . .

But defending our nation is just the beginning of our challenge. My third goal is to take advantage of a tremendous opportunity—given few nations in history— to extend the current peace into the far realm of the future. A chance to project America's peaceful influence, not just across the world, but across the years.

This opportunity is created by a revolution in the technology of war. Power is increasingly defined, not by mass or size, but by mobility and swiftness. Influence is measured in information, safety is gained in stealth, and force is projected on the long arc of precision-guided weapons. This revolution perfectly matches the strengths of our country—the skill of our people and the superiority of our technology. The best way to keep the peace is to redefine war on our terms.

Yet today our military is still organized more for Cold War threats than for the challenges of a new century—for industrial age operations, rather than for information age battles. There is almost no relationship between our budget priorities and a strategic vision.

. . . As president, I will begin an immediate, comprehensive review of our military—the structure of its forces, the state of its strategy, the priorities of its procurement—conducted by a leadership team under the Secretary of Defense. I will give the Secretary a broad mandate—to challenge the status quo and envision a new architecture of American defense for decades to come. We will modernize some existing weapons and equipment, necessary for current tasks. But our relative peace allows us to do this selectively. The real goal is to move beyond marginal improvements—to replace existing programs with new technologies and strategies. To use this window of opportunity to skip a generation of technology.

… Our forces in the next century must be agile, lethal, readily deployable, and require a minimum of logistical support. We must be able to project our power over long distances, in days or weeks rather than months. Our military must be able to identify targets by a variety of means—from a Marine patrol to a satellite. Then be able to destroy those targets almost instantly, with an array of weapons, from a submarine-launched cruise missile, to mobile long-range artillery.

On land, our heavy forces must be lighter. Our light forces must be more lethal. All must be easier to deploy. And these forces must be organized in smaller, more agile formations, rather than cumbersome divisions.

On the seas, we need to pursue promising ideas like the arsenal shipa stealthy ship packed with long-range missiles to destroy targets from great distances.

In the air, we must be able to strike from across the world with pinpoint accuracy—with long-range aircraft and perhaps with unmanned systems.

In space, we must be able to protect our network of satellites, essential to the flow of our commerce and the defense of our country.

… Even if I am elected, I will not command the new military we create. That will be left to a president who comes after me. The results of our effort will not be seen for many years…

Author's Note:
The Office of Force Transformation was established a month after 9/11, under the leadership of retired Vice Admiral Arthur Cebrowski, with the mission of assisting Secretary of Defense Rumsfeld in pushing forward the military transformation envisioned in President Bush's 1999 speech to The Citadel, and further elaborated in the 2001 Quadrennial Defense Review (QDR). Part of the challenge was to clarify just exactly what was expected of each of the services. According, as an appendix to its 2004 Defense Planning Guidance the Pentagon included a Transformation Planning Guidance that contained guidelines on what should be included in each of the service's transformation roadmaps, to be submitted in time for the 2004 budget deliberations. The blueprints were, for example, to include timelines, organizational plans, and specifics on when certain capabilities would be fielded, and were to identify initiatives undertaken to improve interoperability with the other services. The Transformation Planning Guidance was very much a working document, assigning roles and responsibilities for promoting transformation and for assessing the degree to which transformation had been implemented. It also took a step back to touch on broader issues like the scope and rational behind transformation. But these were much more fully elaborated in a follow-on document, Military Transformation: A Strategic Approach, released about a half a year later. Its executive summary, reproduced here almost in its entirety, provides a useful overview of what the Secretary of Defense, his

office, and perhaps also the President and Vice-President, as supporters of Rumsfeld and Cebrowski, felt was the essence of military transformation.

Excerpt from
Military Transformation: A Strategic Approach
Office of Force Transformation
Fall 2003

The strategy for defense transformation is a vital component of the United States' defense strategy. At the outset of his administration, President George W. Bush elevated transformation to the level of defense strategy, and he has repeatedly emphasized its importance to the future defense of the United States... [Transformation] is about how a competitive space is selected within which U.S. forces can gain an important advantage. The strategy identifies the attributes within that space that will ultimately lead to an advantage for U.S. forces, not only during combat operations, but also in the conduct of all missions across the full range of operations.

The Department describes transformation as "a process that shapes the changing nature of military competition and cooperation through new combinations of concepts, capabilities, people, and organizations that exploit our nation's advantages and protect against our asymmetric vulnerabilities to sustain our strategic position, which helps underpin peace and stability in the world." Overall, the Department's transformation must address three major areas: how we do business inside the Department, how we work with our interagency and multinational partners, and how we fight. The transformation process must develop forces capable of defending the U.S. population, homeland, and interests, as well as swiftly defeating an adversary from a posture of forward deterrence with minimal reinforcements.

...The compelling need for military transformation may be examined in terms of four imperatives: strategy, technology, threat, and risk mitigation. U.S. defense strategy requires agile, network-centric forces capable of taking action from a forward position, rapidly reinforced from other areas, and defeating adversaries swiftly and decisively while conducting an active defense of U.S. territory.

...Technology in the military sphere is developing as rapidly as the changes reshaping the civilian sector. The combination of scientific advancement and the globalization of commerce and communications has contributed to several trends that significantly affect U.S. defense strategy and planning. Falling barriers to competition caused by ubiquitous, low cost information technology contribute significantly to the compelling need for military transformation.

Although U.S. military forces today enjoy significant advantages in many aspects of armed conflict, the United States will be challenged by threats...the trends that will provide adversaries with capabilities and opportunities to do harm to the

United States include: diminishing protection afforded by geographic distance, the emergence of regional threats, growing asymmetric threats, and increasing threats from weakened states and ungoverned areas.

...Six critical operational goals identified by Secretary of Defense Donald H. Rumsfeld provide the focus for the Department's transformation efforts: (1) Protecting critical bases and defeating chemical, biological, radiological, and nuclear weapons; (2) Projecting and sustaining forces in anti-access environments; (3) Denying enemy sanctuary; (4) Leveraging information technology; (5) Assuring information systems and conducting information operations; and (6) Enhancing space capabilities.

...The four military transformation pillars identified by the Secretary—strengthening joint operations, exploiting U.S. intelligence advantages, concept development and experimentation, and developing transformational capabilities—constitute the essential elements of the Department's force transformation strategy. The first pillar focuses on strengthening joint operations through the development of joint concepts and architectures and the pursuit of other important jointness initiatives and interoperability goals...The second pillar involves exploiting U.S. intelligence advantages through multiple intelligence collection assets, global surveillance and reconnaissance, and enhanced exploitation and dissemination...The third pillar, concept development and experimentation, involves experimentation with new approaches to warfare, operational concepts and capabilities, and organizational constructs through war gaming, simulations, and field exercises focused on emerging challenges and opportunities.

...Although the transformation of the U.S. Armed Forces is a continuing process, the recent performance of U.S. forces in the successful conduct of Operations Enduring Freedom and Iraqi Freedom has provided a glimpse of the future potential of the emerging way of war. Constructed around the fundamental tenets of network-centric warfare and emphasizing high-quality shared awareness, dispersed forces, speed of command, and flexibility in planning and execution, the emerging way of war will result in U.S. forces conducting powerful effects-based operations to achieve strategic, operational, and tactical objectives across the full range of military operations...

Author's Note:

The years immediately following the 2003 war in Iraq were marked by growing and widespread criticism that the Pentagon neglected to plan sufficiently for securing stability after the end of major combat operations. This lack of planning was in line with America's traditional hesitancy to become involved in what have been generally referred to as peacekeeping or stability operations. In his 1999 speech to The Citadel, written with the experience of the Balkans in mind, presidential candidate George W. Bush had stated that if elected he would ensure U.S. forces did not become permanent peacekeepers. The sentiment reflected that of Condoleezza Rice, the future National Security Advisor and Secretary of State. As foreign policy advisor to candidate Bush, Rice had published an article in *Foreign Affairs* in early 2000 that stressed America's military instrument should not be used to build civilian society, and that U.S. soldiers should not become bogged down in peacekeeping roles. Against the backdrop of Iraq and Afghanistan, the Pentagon began to rethink this position. A 2004 study by the Defense Science Board concluded that while the United States was adept at winning wars, it did not pay sufficient attention to managing the aftermath. It recommended the U.S. military treat stability missions with the same degree of seriousness as it did combat operations. The outcome was the directive on Military Support for Stability, Security, Transition, and Reconstruction Operations, a portion of which is reproduced below.

Excerpt from
Military Support for Stability, Security, Transition and Reconstruction (SSTR)
Operations
U.S. Department of Defense Directive 3000
November 28, 2005

1. PURPOSE

This Directive:

1.1. Provides guidance on stability operations that will evolve over time as joint operating concepts, mission sets, and lessons learned develop. Future DoD policy will address these areas and provide guidance on the security, transition, and reconstruction operations components of SSTR operations and DoD's role in each...

3. DEFINITIONS

3.1. Stability Operations. Military and civilian activities conducted across the spectrum from peace to conflict to establish or maintain order in States and regions.

3.2. Military support to Stability, Security, Transition and Reconstruction (SSTR). Department of Defense activities that support U.S. Government plans for stabilization, security, reconstruction and transition operations, which lead to sustainable peace while advancing U.S. interests.

4. POLICY

It is DoD policy that:

4.1. Stability operations are a core U.S. military mission that the Department of Defense shall be prepared to conduct and support. They shall be given priority comparable to combat operations and be explicitly addressed and integrated across all DoD activities including doctrine, organizations, training, education, exercises, materiel, leadership, personnel, facilities, and planning.

4.2. Stability operations are conducted to help establish order that advances U.S. interests and values. The immediate goal often is to provide the local populace with security, restore essential services, and meet humanitarian needs. The long-term goal is to help develop indigenous capacity for securing essential services, a viable market economy, rule of law, democratic institutions, and a robust civil society.

4.3. Many stability operations tasks are best performed by indigenous, foreign, or U.S. civilian professionals. Nonetheless, U.S. military forces shall be prepared to perform all tasks necessary to establish or maintain order when civilians cannot do so. Successfully performing such tasks can help secure a lasting peace and facilitate the timely withdrawal of U.S. and foreign forces. Stability operations tasks include helping:

> 4.3.1. Rebuild indigenous institutions including various types of security forces, correctional facilities, and judicial systems necessary to secure and stabilize the environment;
>
> 4.3.2. Revive or build the private sector, including encouraging citizen-driven, bottom-up economic activity and constructing necessary infrastructure; and
>
> 4.3.3. Develop representative governmental institutions.

4.4. Integrated civilian and military efforts are key to successful stability operations. Whether conducting or supporting stability operations, the Department of Defense shall be prepared to work closely with relevant U.S. Departments and Agencies, foreign governments and security forces, global and regional international organizations (hereafter referred to as "International Organizations"), U.S. and foreign nongovernmental organizations (hereafter referred to as "NGOs"), and private sector individuals and for-profit companies (hereafter referred to as "Private Sector").

4.5. Military-civilian teams are a critical U.S. Government stability operations tool. The Department of Defense shall continue to lead and support the development of military-civilian teams...

Author's Note:

The Pentagon first officially signaled its recognition of the requirement to address irregular warfare in its 2005 National Defense Strategy. The strategy, notes the 2006 Quadrennial Defense Review, "acknowledges that although the U.S. military maintains considerable advantages in traditional forms of warfare, this realm is not the only, or even the most likely, one in which adversaries will challenge the United States during the period immediately ahead." Specifically, the U.S. military needed to be able to address conflicts in which enemy combatants are not regular military forces of nations-states—including terrorism, insurgency and guerrilla warfare. To assist in this regard, Generals David Petraeus of the U.S. Army and James Mattis of the U.S. Marine Corps, oversaw the production of a new manual to guide future military action in the area of counterinsurgency. Its some 280 pages cover a range of issues, from intelligence gathering and civil-military integration, to pre-deployment planning and developing host nation security forces. The manual has a significant historical emphasis, and it includes a useful section on "Paradoxes of Counterinsurgency" which is reproduced here.

Excerpt from
Counterinsurgency
United States Army FM 3-24
December 2006

The More You Protect Your Force, The Less Secure You Are
Ultimate success in COIN is gained by protecting the populace, not the COIN force. If military forces stay locked up in compounds, they lose touch with the people, appear to be running scared, and cede the initiative to the insurgents. Patrols must be conducted, risk must be shared, and contact maintained. This ensures access to the intelligence needed to drive operations and reinforces the connections with the people that establish real legitimacy.

The More Force Used, The Less Effective It Is
Any use of force produces many effects, not all of which can be foreseen. The more force applied, the greater the chance of collateral damage and mistakes. It also increases the opportunity for insurgent propaganda to portray lethal military activities as brutal. The precise and discriminate use of force also strengthens the rule of law that needs to be established.

The More Successful COIN Is, The Less Force That Can Be Used and the More Risk That Must Be Accepted
This is really a corollary to the previous paradox. As the level of insurgent violence drops, the requirements of international law and the expectations of the populace allow less use of military actions by the counterinsurgent. More reliance is placed on police work. Rules of engagement get stricter, and troops have to exercise increased restraint. Soldiers and Marines may also have to accept more risk to maintain involvement with the people.

Sometimes Doing Nothing Is the Best Reaction
Often an insurgent carries out a terrorist act or guerrilla raid with the primary purpose of enticing the counterinsurgent to overreact, or at least to react in a way that can then be exploited. If a careful assessment of the effects of a course of action concludes that more negative than positive effects may result, an alternative should be considered—potentially including a decision not to act.

The Best Weapons for COIN Do Not Shoot
Counterinsurgents achieve the most meaningful success by gaining popular support and legitimacy for the host government, not by killing insurgents. Security plays an important role in setting the stage for other progress, but lasting victory comes from a vibrant economy, political participation, and restored hope. Often

dollars and ballots have a more important impact than bombs and bullets. Soldiers and Marines prepare to engage in a host of nonmilitary missions to support COIN. Everyone has a role in nation building, not just the State Department or civil affairs soldiers.

The Host Nation Doing Something Tolerably Is Sometimes Better Than Us Doing It Well

It is just as important to consider who performs an operation as to assess how well it is done. In cases where the United States is supporting a host nation, long-term success requires the establishment of viable indigenous leaders and institutions that can carry on without significant American support. The longer that process takes, the more popular support in the United States will wane, and the more the local populace will question the legitimacy of their own forces and government...

If a Tactic Works This Week, It Might Not Work Next Week; If It Works in This Province, It Might Not Work in the Next

Competent insurgents are adaptive and today are often part of a widespread network that constantly and instantly communicates. Insurgents quickly disseminate information about successful COIN practices throughout the insurgency and adapt to them. Indeed, the more effective a COIN tactic is, the faster it becomes out of date because the insurgents have a greater need to counter it. Effective leaders at all levels avoid complacency and are at least as adaptive as their enemies. There is no "silver bullet" set of procedures for COIN. Constantly developing new practices is essential.

Tactical Success Guarantees Nothing

...Military actions by themselves cannot achieve success in COIN. Tactical actions must not only be linked to operational and strategic military objectives, but also to the essential political goals of COIN. Without those connections, lives and resources may be wasted for no real gain.

Most of the Important Decisions Are Not Made by Generals

Successful COIN relies on the competence and judgment of Soldiers and Marines at all levels. Senior leaders set the proper tone for actions by their organizations with thorough training and clear guidance, and then trust their subordinates to do the right thing. Preparation for tactical-level leaders requires more than Service doctrine; they must also be trained and educated to adapt to their local situations, understand the legal and ethical implications of their actions, and exercise subordinates' initiative and sound judgment to meet their senior commanders' intent.

Chronology of Events

Late 1970s	Soviet military writers begin to write about a Military Technical Revolution
Mid-1980s	Nicolai Ogarkov, Chief of the Soviet General Staff, voices concerns that the United States is ahead in the MTR
Late 1970s/1980s	Andrew Marshall, Director of the Office of Net Assessment, begins to take note of Soviet writings
Early 1991	Gulf War
Fall 1991	In a *Foreign Affairs* article William Perry writes about the revolutionary technologies that had been used in the Gulf War
Nov 1991	NATO adopts a new Alliance Strategic Concept
1992	NATO creates Allied Command Europe Rapid Reaction Corps
Jul 1992	Office of Net Assessment completes an influential report on *The Military Technical Revolution*
1993	Office of Net Assessment coins the phrase "Revolution in Military Affairs"
Jan 1994	NATO adopts Combined Joint Task Force concept
Feb 1994	William Perry becomes Secretary of Defense
Mar 1994	William Owens becomes Vice Chairman of the Joint Chiefs of Staff
Feb 1996	France releases Model 2015, including plans to professionalize the French armed forces
Jun 1996	Chairman of the Joint Chiefs of Staff releases *Joint Vision 2010*

May 1997	Quadrennial Defense Review released
Dec 1997	Australia's Strategic Policy released
	Report of the National Defense Panel, *Transforming Defense*, released
Jul 1998	Britain releases Strategic Defence Review
1999	Joint Forces Command created
Apr 1999	NATO adopts new Alliance Strategic Concept
	NATO adopts Defense Capabilities Initiative
Sep 1999	George W. Bush delivers speech at The Citadel in which he promises to pursue military transformation if elected
Dec 1999	EU adopts Helsinki Headline Goal
May 2000	The Chairman of the Joint Chiefs of Staff releases *Joint Vision 2020*
Dec 2000	Australia releases Defense White Paper
Jan 2001	Donald Rumsfeld becomes Secretary of Defense
Spring 2001	China and Russia sign treaty of friendship and cooperation
May 2001	Office of the Secretary of Defense completes a strategic review of U.S. military forces, calling on the services to transform
Summer 2001	China and Russia and other countries create Shanghai Cooperation Organization
Sep 2001	Terrorist attacks on New York and Washington
	Quadrennial Defense Review released
Oct 2001	Office of Force Transformation created
	War in Afghanistan begins
Nov 2001	French armed forces become fully professional
Dec 2001	International Security Assistance Force established in Afghanistan
	U.S. Nuclear Posture Review released
	President Bush announces U.S. intention to withdraw from the 1972 Anti-Ballistic Missile Treaty
May 2002	The United States and Russia sign the Strategic Offensive Reductions Treaty
Jun 2002	U.S. withdrawal from ABM Treaty comes into effect

Jul 2002	Britain releases Strategic Defence Review New Chapter
Sep 2002	National Security Strategy of the United States released
Oct 2002	United States Northern Command established
Nov 2002	NATO adopts Prague Capabilities Commitment
	NATO announces response force initiative
	NATO announces plans to create Allied Command Transformation and Allied Command Operations
	NATO announces BMD feasibility study
Fall 2002	The United States creates Combined Joint Task Force—Horn of Africa
2003	Australia creates Special Operations Command
Feb 2003	Australia releases Defence Update
Mar 2003	U.S. Department of Homeland Security established
	War in Iraq begins
May 2003	Germany releases new Defense Policy Guidelines
Jul 2003	Russia releases military reform plan
Aug 2003	NATO takes over command of ISAF
Oct 2003	Russia releases Defense White Paper
Dec 2003	EU approves European Security Strategy
	Britain releases Defense White Paper
	Canada creates Department of Public Safety, comparable to DHS
Jun 2004	EU adopts Headline Goal 2010
Aug 2004	Pentagon releases Global Defense Posture Review
Mar 2005	Pentagon releases National Defense Strategy of the United States
Apr 2005	Canada releases Defence Policy Statement
Dec 2005	Australia releases Defence Update
Feb 2006	Canada creates Canada Command, Expeditionary Forces Command, and Special Operations Command
	Quadrennial Defense Review released

Mar 2006	National Security Strategy of the United States released
May 2006	NATO completes BMD feasibility study
Sep 2006	Office of Force Transformation dissolved
Fall 2006	Chinese military illuminates U.S. satellite with a laser beam
Oct 2006	The United States releases a new National Space Policy
	Germany releases Defense White Paper
Nov 2006	Donald Rumsfeld dismissed as Secretary of Defense
	Robert Gates becomes Secretary of Defense
	NATO adopts Comprehensive Political Guidance
	NATO Response Force declared fully operational
Dec 2006	China releases Defense White Paper
Jan 2007	Chinese military conducts successful antisatellite test
	Russia releases new draft military doctrine
Feb 2007	Bush approves plans to create United States Africa Command by the end of 2008
Jun 2007	The Pentagon reconsiders force reductions under the Global Defense Posture Review
Jun 2007	Russia offers to share radar data with United States for BMD system
Jul 2007	Russia suspends participation in Conventional Forces in Europe treaty
Aug 2007	Russia resumes long-range bomber patrols
Sept 2007	United States finds Russian radar inadequate for BMD system
Oct. 2007	NATO Defense Ministers discuss scaling back NATO Response Force concept
Oct 2007	United States Africa Command achieves initial operating capability

Glossary

4GW Fourth Generation Warfare

ABM Anti-Ballistic Missile

ACT Allied Command Transformation

ADF Australian Defence Force

AEHF Advanced Extremely High Frequency

AFRICOM Africa Command

AGS Air Ground Surveillance

ARRC Allied Command Europe Rapid Reaction Corps

ASTOR Airborne Standoff Radar

AWACS Airborne Warning and Control System

C4I Command, Control, Communications, Computing, and Intelligence

C4ISR Command, Control, Communications, Computing, Intelligence, Surveillance, and Reconnaissance

CBERS China-Brazil Earth Resources Satellite

CBRN Chemical, Biological, Radiological, and Nuclear defense

CCRF Civil Contingency Reaction Force

CF Canadian Forces

CJTF Combined Joint Task Force

COIN Counterinsurgency

CSOR Canadian Special Operations Regiment

DCI Defense Capabilities Initiative

DHS Department of Homeland Security

DPS Defense Policy Statement

DSP Defense Support Program

EBO Effects Based Operations

ECAP European Capabilities Action Plan

EDA European Defence Agency

EHF Extremely High Frequency

FCS Future Combat System

FELIN French future soldier system

FIST Future Infantry Soldier Technology

FOAS Future Offensive Air System

FRES Future Rapid Effects System

GLONASS Global Navigation Satellite System

GMTI Ground Moving Target Indicator

GPS Global Positioning System

HF High Frequency

ICBM Intercontinental Ballistic Missiles

IED Improvised Explosive Device

IFOR Implementation Force

ISAF International Security Assistance Force

ISR Intelligence, Surveillance, and Reconnaissance

ISTAR Intelligence, Surveillance, Target Acquisition, and Reconnaissance

JASSM Joint Air-to-Surface Standoff Missile

JDAMS Joint Direct Attack Munitions

JSTARS Joint Surveillance and Target Attack Radar System

J-UCAS Joint Unmanned Combat Air System

LACM Land Attack Cruise Missile

LAV Light Armored Vehicle

LCS Littoral Combat Ship

LDH Amphibious landing ships

MEADS Medium Extended Air Defense System

MIDS Multifunctional Information Distribution System

MIRV Multiple Independently Targetable Reentry Vehicle

MRAP Mine Resistant Ambush Protected

MTR Military Technical Revolution

NCO Non-Commissioned Officer

NDP National Defense Panel

NEC Network Enhanced Capability

NORAD North America Aerospace Defense Command

NORTHCOM Northern Command

NRF NATO Response Force

OODA Observe-Orient-Decide-Act

OOTW Operations Other Than War

PAP People's Armed Police

PCC Prague Capabilities Commitment

PGM Precision-Guided Munition

PLA People's Liberation Army

PLAAF People's Liberation Army Air Force

PLAN People's Liberation Army Navy

PRT Provincial Reconstruction Team

PSC Public Safety Canada

QDR Quadrennial Defense Review

RAR Royal Australian Regiment

RMA Revolution in Military Affairs

SACEUR Supreme Allied Commander Europe

SAR Synthetic Aperture Radar

SBIRS Space-Based Infrared System

SBR Space-Based Radar

SDR Strategic Defence Review

SFOR Stabilization Force

SHF Super High Frequency

SLBM Submarine Launched Ballistic Missile

SOCOM Special Operations Command

SOF Special Operations Forces

SORT Strategic Offensive Reductions Treaty

SPADATS Space Detection and Tracking System

SPASUR Space Surveillance System

SPIRALE Preparatory System for Early Warning

SSC Smaller Scale Contingencies

SSM Surface-to-Surface Missile

SSN Space Surveillance Network

START Strategic Arms Reduction Treaty

TMD Theater Missile Defense

TSAT Transformational Satellite System

TUAV Tactical Unmanned Aerial Vehicles

UAV Unmanned Aerial Vehicles

UCAV Unmanned Combat Aerial Vehicle

UHF Ultra High Frequency

UNPROFOR United Nations Protection Force

VBCI Véhicule Blindé de Combat d'Infanterie

VHF Very High Frequency

WMD Weapons of Mass Destruction

Annotated Bibliography

Blasko, Dennis J. *The Chinese Army Today* (London: Routledge, 2006).
The author of this book, a former U.S. Army military intelligence officer who served as a military attaché in China and Hong Kong in the mid-1990s, provides perhaps the most comprehensive examination available of how the Chinese Army is organized and equipped to fight. It is particularly useful for explaining the distinction between the PLA and the various other security forces in China. The extensive detail reads much like a textbook, but it is not overwhelming and is necessary material for any student seeking to understand the largest and still predominant component of the PLA.

Boot, Max. "The Struggle to Transform the Military." *Foreign Affairs* 84(2) (March/April 2005).
In this article the author, a senior fellow at the Council on Foreign Relations, argues the U.S. military must move to the "next stage of transformation," that is to say, focus less on technology and more on methods for addressing irregular war. He discusses America's traditional reluctance to become involved in nation building, the need to increase the size of the U.S. military for such operations, the desirability of offsetting the cost of these increases with reductions in "legacy" systems, and the utility of training foreign forces to carry out operations in their own countries. Written in an engaging style, the article covers a range of transformation issues that have become increasingly evident the further we move away from the 2003 war in Iraq.

Cohen, Eliot A. "A Revolution in Warfare." *Foreign Affairs* 75(2) (March/April 1996).
This article by a well-known professor of strategic studies at Johns Hopkins University discusses various elements of the RMA, including precision weapons, jointness, the system of systems and, significantly, organizational change. It also gives a framework for assessing what the future RMA will look like. As with the Krepinevich article noted below, Cohen brings a historian's perspective to military revolutions, providing the reader with significant context, including the Russian role in the RMA. However the Cohen article is distinct in that it focuses more on current events. The article is somewhat disorganized, switching back and forth between the historical and contemporary periods, but read in its entirety it offers the most succinct and readable account available of what were considered, in the mid-1990s, to be the components of, and underlying forces behind, the RMA.

Coonen, Stephen J. "The Widening Military Capabilities Gap Between the United States and Europe: Does It Matter?" *Parameters* (Autumn 2006).
The author, a Lieutenant Colonel in the U.S. Army, briefly discusses the military capability gap between the two sides of the Atlantic and then moves to the central question of his article. He makes the case that while Europe is weak in comparison to the United States it is not weak in objective terms. Moreover, a useful division of labor has emerged between the United States and Europe based on their differing strengths. This article, which is best read in conjunction with the Yost article below because of its greater detail, may not be entirely convincing to some. Nonetheless, it is useful for its counter perspective to the prevailing view—as reflected, for example, in NATO's numerous capability initiatives— that the growing gap matters and must be addressed.

Gentry, John A. "Doomed to Fail: America's Blind Faith in Military Technology." *Parameters* (Winter 2002–2003).
In this article the author, a retired Lieutenant Colonel in the U.S. military with a Special Operations Force background, likens advanced military technologies to the Maginot line of the twenty-first century. He discusses two military concept statements produced by the Joint Chiefs of Staff, *Joint Vision 2010* in 1996 and *Joint Vision 2020* in 2000, briefly describing the four basic capabilities that, according to these documents, technology is supposed to engender, and then drawing out four fundamental flaws in this approach. These include its narrow applicability, DoD's weak technological infrastructure, the likelihood of adversary countermeasures, and the bureaucratic challenges of implementing the vision. The article's shortcoming lies in its overly abstract approach—the reader searches without success for concrete examples where technology did not live up to its billing in a conflict, such as the 1999 war in and around Kosovo. It also dwells a bit too much on the inner workings of DoD. Nonetheless, written at a time when advanced technologies appeared vindicated by the 2001–2002 war in Afghanistan, the article is valuable and even somewhat prolific in that it was one of the first to argue that the virtues of technology may not be what at first they might seem.

Goldman, Emily O., and Thomas G. Mahnken, eds. *The Information Revolution in Military Affairs in Asia* (New York: Palgrave Macmillan, 2004).
This book fills a significant gap in the literature because it is one of the few, if not the only, book that discusses Asian approaches to the RMA. An edited volume, it contains articles on Australia, China, Japan, Singapore, and Taiwan. Its two articles on China, one each by You Li of the University of New South Wales, and Andrew Nien-Dzu Yang of the National Sun Yat-sen University in Taipei, cover the range of military transformation issues in China, including historical and differing views on the RMA, drivers behind its current pursuit of advanced technologies, ground force modernization, the acquisition of new long-range ballistic missiles and satellite technologies, ideas about information and asymmetric warfare, and obstacles, including educational and bureaucratic, to achieving an RMA-like force. Read together the two articles provide an excellent overview and analysis of the Chinese perspective on, and approach to, the revolution in military affairs.

Golts, Alexander M., and Tonya L. Putnam. "State Militarism and Its Legacies: Why Military Reform Has Failed in Russia." *International Security* 29(2) (Fall 2004).
In this article the authors, a longstanding military correspondent for a Moscow weekly who was a visiting scholar at Stanford University, and a PhD candidate at Stanford, respectively, examine why it is that while the Russian economic and political system have undergone

significant change since the end of the Cold War, major changes in military structure have yet to occur. They assess and discount four standard explanations for why reform efforts have failed in the past, and argue that a better explanation lies in institutional legacies that can be traced back to the early eighteenth century. In light of this, they discuss the long-term prospects for current reform efforts. A somewhat lengthy article, it is nonetheless well written, clearly organized, and convincing. It provides the reader with a very useful overall context within which to understand Russian military reform.

Hammes, Thomas X. "Insurgency: Modern Warfare Evolves Into a Fourth Generation." *Strategic Forum* No. 214 (January 2005).

In this paper, the author, a Colonel in the United States Marine Corps, carries forward and elaborates ideas that originated with William S. Lind and his colleagues in the 1989 article noted below. An instructor at the National Defense University in Washington, DC, Hammes discusses the origins and history of Fourth Generation Warfare (4GW), which for him is an evolved form of counterinsurgency, and then talks about the strategic aspects, political aspects, operational techniques, and tactical considerations of 4GW. Hammes' assessment—which is presented in more comprehensive form in a 2004 book, *The Sling and the Stone: On War in the 21st Century*, and in a 2005 article in *Contemporary Security Policy*—has been criticized for exaggerating the novelty of 4GW, and for seemingly neglecting the rise of other, more conventional threats. Nonetheless, his viewpoint provides a thought provoking and useful counter to the technology driven agenda of the MTR, the RMA and some conceptualizations of transformation, and is necessary reading for students seeking a holistic perspective on military transformation.

Krepinevich, Andrew F. "Calvary to Computer: The Pattern of Military Revolutions." *National Interest* (Fall 1994).

This article is written by one of the preeminent thinkers about the RMA in the early 1990s (see biography), yet its primary emphasis is historical. Krepinevich defines what is a military revolution and then identifies and briefly discusses ten military revolutions since the fourteenth century, drawing out the technological, doctrinal, and organizational changes in warfare with regard to each revolution. The author also assesses the revolutions as a whole, identifying seven general observations about the character of military revolutions, and makes some points as to what the history of military revolutions may indicate for the United States in the future. This article is an excellent starting point for students looking to study the whole area of RMAs, military revolutions and military transformation. It brings understanding as to what is meant by the term RMA, and puts the current changes in warfare into historical context.

Lind, William, Keith M. Nightengale, John Schmitt, Joseph W. Sutton, and G.I. Wilson. "The Changing Face of War: Into the Fourth Generation." *Military Review* (October 1989).

This article, written by a civilian whose coauthors included four military officers, provided the genesis of the idea of Fourth Generation Warfare (4GW), a concept now extensively discussed in military and defense policy circles. Some conceptions of military transformation, especially those that focus on its RMA origins, are seen as having little relevance or applicability to 4GW. This article is therefore necessary reading for any student wishing to have a complete picture of military transformation, including its strengths and weaknesses. Concisely written and including a prolific discussion of terrorism as a future example of 4GW, the article is also useful for the broad historical picture it presents.

Miller Steven E., and Dmitri V. Trenin, eds. *The Russian Military: Power and Policy* (Cambridge, MA: The MIT Press, 2004).
Two chapters in this edited volume are pertinent to the issue of military transformation: one by Alexei G. Arbatov, a scholar at the Russian Academy of Science Center for International Security, on military reform in Russia; and another by Rose Gottemoeller, the Director of the Carnegie Moscow Center, on nuclear Weapons in Russian defense policy. Arbatov's article supports the assessment by Golts and Putnam (noted above), reaffirming the essential orientation of Russia's armed forces as being against the West, and thus unlikely to be transformed. It is slightly out date in that a major concern he identifies is low levels of defense spending; this has changed in recent years. But most of his analysis remains relevant. Gottemoeller's chapter discusses the debates behind the tradeoff between nuclear weapons and conventional forces, and then provides an illuminating discussion of Russian interests with regard to nuclear weapons and arms control efforts. In doing so, it gives the reader a clear picture of the primary place of nuclear over conventional forces in Russian military reform efforts.

Murray, Williamson, and Robert H. Scales, Jr. *The Iraq War: A Military History* (Cambridge, MA: Harvard University Press, 2003).
This book, the first to be published on the Iraq war after the end of major combat operations in 2003, is written, respectively, by a preeminent U.S. military historian, and a Major General in the U.S. army who has commented extensively on military issues since his retirement. Chapter 7 of the book, "Military and Political Implications," provides an excellent and concise analysis of what the Iraq War can tell us about the future of war. The authors include not only factors such as speed, knowledge, and precision, which align well with the RMA component of transformation, but also—at this early stage—identified the need to focus on what they call combined military and stability operations.

Nye, Joseph S., and William A. Owens. "America's Information Edge." *Foreign Affairs* 75(2) (March/April 1996).
The student who reads the first half of this article in conjunction with the Cohen article noted above will get a fairly complete picture of what was considered, in the 1990s, to comprise the RMA. The aspects this article contributes are largely technological, notably advanced ISR and C4I for battlespace awareness and control, however it also touches on doctrinal (e.g. precision force) and organizational (e.g. the importance of education) changes. The article itself reflects the expertise of the two authors, with that of Owens coming first, followed by that of Nye. While Owens is one of the original thinkers behind the RMA (see biography), Nye's ideas are only tangential to military transformation. It is for this reason that only the first half of the article is recommended for the student of transformation.

O'Hanlon, Michael. "A Flawed Masterpiece." *Foreign Affairs* 81(3) (May/June 2002).
In this article the author, a senior fellow at the Brookings Institution who has published extensively on defense issues, provides an overview of the 2001–2002 war in Afghanistan and assesses its conduct. Easy to read and concisely written, the article discusses numerous aspects of the war which supported the RMA component of military transformation. Yet he also draws attention to the "flaw" of not deploying U.S. forces to close off escape routes along the Afghan-Pakistan border, and thus gives an early indication of the shortfalls in the Rumsfeld Doctrine that would become more readily apparent in Iraq.

Pudas, Terry J. "Disruptive Challenges and Accelerating Force Transformation." *Joint Force Quarterly* 42(3) (July 2006).
The author was the acting director of the now disbanded Office of Force Transformation, who took over after the original director, Arthur Cebrowski (see biography), had to leave for health reasons. The article discusses the four security challenges that are identified in the 2005 National Defense Strategy, and further operationalized in the 2006 Quadrennial Defense Review. The challenges reflect an evolution in what is taken to comprise military transformation; most notably, irregular and asymmetric threats are considered alongside traditional threats. Written for a military audience, or for civilians who follow U.S. military issue on a regular basis, the article is not an easy read. It is included here because it neatly captures the thinking behind the 2006 Quadrennial Defense Review, and indeed the most recent official DoD perspective on military transformation.

Rumsfeld, Donald H. "Transforming the Military," *Foreign Affairs* 81(3) (May/June 2002).
In this article the former Secretary of Defense touches on the new way of warfare demonstrated in Afghanistan, comparing it to past examples of RMAs, and then moves on to a number of ideas that are part of military transformation. They range from elements of the RMA component of transformation, like unmanned aerial vehicles and jointness, to aspects of transformation's wider dimension, like a new triad for deterrence. Rumsfeld reiterates and briefly discusses the transformation goals that are identified in the 2001 Quadrennial Defense Review. A somewhat disorganized article, it is nonetheless useful because it gives readers an overall picture of what was conceived to comprise military transformation in the first Bush administration and thus the sorts of ideas that informed a military that was about to embark on a major war in Iraq.

Scobell, Andrew, and Larry M. Wortzel, eds. *Shaping China's Security Environment: The Role of the People's Liberation Army* (Carlisle, PA: U.S. Army War College Strategic Studies Institute, October 2006).
This volume, edited by an Associate Research Professor at the U.S. Army War College and a Commissioner on the U.S.-China Economic and Security Review Commission (a Congressionally appointed body), respectively, contains a range of chapters on the People's Liberation Army, many of them largely political in nature. However three chapters address more specifically military reform efforts on the part of China. Ellis Joffe of the Hebrew University of Jerusalem examines the long-term objectives of China's military modernization, which go well beyond the Taiwan issue; Susan M. Puska, a retired U.S. Army Colonel with expertise on Asia and Pacific Affairs discusses how China's assessment of America's wars has impacted its approach to military transformation; and Paul Godwin, a former professor and China expert at the National War College provides a useful overview of the capabilities China is seeking. The combined result is a comprehensive picture of the drivers behind, and current trends and areas of emphasis with regard to, PLA modernization.

Sloan, Elinor. *The Revolution in Military Affairs* (Montreal: McGill-Queen's University Press, 2002).
This book contains chapters that elaborate on ideas that are only briefly discussed in the present book. The most useful are a chapter on the history of RMAs, which highlights a number of thinkers and gives general points about military revolutions, and a chapter on U.S. efforts with respect to the RMA, which details changes in U.S. service doctrines in the 1990s.

———. *Security and Defence in the Terrorist Era* (Montreal: McGill-Queen's University Press, 2005).
This book contains chapters that elaborate on elements that are considered part of the wider dimension of military transformation. Relevant areas that are covered include space and ballistic missile defense, U.S. homeland security, and U.S. homeland defense.

Yost, David S. "The NATO Capabilities Gap and the European Union." *Survival* 42(4) (Winter 2000–2001).
In this article the author, a professor at the Naval Postgraduate School in Monterey, California, examines the technology and capability gap between American and European military forces. Whereas many articles speak in generalities, this article is filled with concrete, specific points about military systems and forces. Yet it also gives a broader analysis, providing explanations as to the origins of the gap, and exploring the idea of whether the gap matters. The article, which draws on the 1999 war in and around Kosovo as its case study, is inevitably dated—but not overly so. Almost a decade after it was written, it remains the starting point in understanding some of the key military transformation issues between the United States and its European allies.

Index

About the Author

ELINOR SLOAN is Associate Professor of International Relations at Carleton University in Ottawa, Canada, where she teaches international security studies. A former Captain in the Canadian Armed Forces, she is a graduate of the Royal Military College of Canada and received her PhD from the Fletcher School of Law and Diplomacy, Tufts University, in 1997. From 1996 to 2002 she was a defense analyst in Canada's Department of National Defense where she focused on U.S. defense policy. She is the author of *Bosnia and the New Collective Security* (1998), *The Revolution in Military Affairs* (2002), and *Security and Defence in the Terrorist Era* (2005).